The Higher-Education Advisers' Handbook

Practical steps for one-to-one guidance

Second Edition

Andy Gardner

Published by
JFS School
The Mall, Kenton
Harrow, HA3 9TE

Editor: Lesley Hussell
www.editingedge.co.uk

Cover designer: Sarah Pearson

Cover photograph: Laurent Shinar

The named author and contributors are responsible for the views expressed in this publication.

British Library Cataloguing-in-Publication Data
A catalogue record for this book is available from the British Library

ISBN 978-0-9568463-0-3

Printed and bound by MPG Biddles Ltd

Acknowledgements

Many thanks to the following people who have in some way contributed to this book:

At JFS School: Tim Miller; Deb Mellor; Simon Appleman; Pat Maxted; Jackie Silverstone; Mary Nithiy; Sharron Krieger, Helen Furman and the sixth-form team.

At La Sainte Union Catholic Secondary School: Lynne Franklin; Rebecca Field; Brian McGowan; Emma Jones and the sixth-form team.

I would also like to thank: John Beckett; Peter Boursnell; Alan Bullock; Trisha Greenhalgh; Sue Holden; Helen Kempster; Moji Muse; Mike Nicholson; Richard Partington; Martin Ransley; Ruth Richards.

Finally, I would like to thank Anne Canning, Barbara Hamnett and Suzanne Meaden for taking me on as an independent careers adviser when I left the careers service in 1999. Without you this book would never have happened.

Contents

Introduction

Welcome to the second edition of this book. For those of you who have the first edition, I have tried to build on and improve the content, and have also brought in some outside expertise for areas such as interview structure, the unique HE Advisers' qualification at London South Bank University, managing higher-education advice, references, the International Baccalaureate and the BTEC National.

The first edition was written in the Aimhigher climate with widespread encouragement of young people to go to university. Then, a workforce was lacking to provide the guidance to help students choose the right course for them. Now there is much more of an acceptance that HE advice needs to be improved. This is expressed in words, such as the reports of Harris, Milburn and Browne, or in action: the 300 or so workers who have undertaken the Applying to HE: Advisers' Certificate. They include in their ranks Connexions personal advisers, teachers, careers advisers, HE advisers, Aimhigher and university schools liaison staff.

At grassroots level there have been some genuine concerted attempts to improve HE advice and guidance, through the actions of schools and colleges, the Specialist Schools and Academies Trust, Connexions services, Aimhigher and the universities themselves. At the time of writing in March 2011, we are still unsure what might be a national policy in England to improve HE advice, although the current government do say they want to do so. We wait to hear plans for the all-age career guidance service and other developments in this field.

With the rise in student fees and a structural change in the higher-education system where we now have a private higher-education system funded through a state loan package, this clearly could affect the behaviour of those applying to higher education, making it even more important that students applying for or thinking about higher-education receive informed, impartial guidance and advice.

This book is not just for designated HE advisers – on the contrary, I want it to be just as relevant to sixth-form and college management staff, tutors, careers teachers, careers advisers and personal advisers, all of whom will regularly give one-to-one guidance on higher education. It is most decidedly *not* an academic work. Rather, it is a set of practical suggestions by me (and colleagues) – a "jobbing" careers officer with 25 years' experience in 26 different secondary schools!

The single most important – and perhaps the most difficult – part of an HE adviser's role is to conduct one-to-one guidance interviews with students. This is a complex subject and I have aimed for a middle point between writing for those with guidance training, and offering advice to those with none. I accept I will never please everyone, but I have deliberately adopted a practical approach that I hope will be useful to most people. Subsequent chapters of the book take you through the decision-making and application process, giving general information with details on how to find out more. *Appendix A* contains detailed reference material relating to specific university subjects.

Finally, an apology. I realise I am writing this book from my worldview as a careers adviser working in two state comprehensive school sixth forms in England, where most of my students do A levels. I hope, however, that the general principles will be of use if you are in other parts of the UK, or dealing with other qualifications, age groups or institutions.

Part One: Getting started

1. Managing higher-education information, advice and guidance

By Tim Miller, Deputy Headteacher, JFS School, north London
millert@jfs.brent.sch.uk

In an ever more fragmented education system with "Free" schools now joining Academy, Comprehensive, Grammar and Independent in the thesaurus of school nomenclature, it is no surprise that higher-education (HE) guidance is similarly disjointed and uneven across the country. The Sutton Trust discovered, in a 2009 Report into Careers Education, that meetings with a careers adviser had fallen dramatically over the previous ten years: only 25% of year 10 and 11 students had had a formal consultation as opposed to 46% a decade earlier. Young people themselves do not have positive attitudes to the guidance they may have received. Some 82%, according to a Department for Children, Schools and Families survey in 2009, viewed formal IAG services as "only a little bit" or "not at all" helpful.

While at sixth-form level most schools and colleges undoubtedly put more resources into HE guidance, it is still patchy, with many schools – and their students – heavily reliant on a few stalwart members of interested staff. Some have even argued that for young people nurtured now on internet research, you only need to provide some starter website addresses to set them off and then the tutor will write their reference and send it to UCAS.

This chapter sets out an approach that rejects such minimalism and aims to show how a headteacher, perhaps new in post, a college principal or relevant senior leader with HE Information, Advice and Guidance (IAG) or careers responsibility in his or her portfolio, can create and manage a high-quality system of guidance.

When launching the annual cycle of HE preparation to year 12 students over many years, I have sought to reduce the decisions each student faces to six questions: Why apply? What should I study? Where should I study? When should I apply (the deferred entry or post-A level application question)? How do I apply? Who will help/advise me?

A similar set of questions can provide the framework for the ideas in this chapter:
1. **Why** is higher-education Information, Advice and Guidance relevant to the wellbeing and success of your school/college?
2. **What** does effective HE guidance look like in a school or college context and **who** is best equipped to provide high-quality guidance?
3. **When** is guidance required: what is the annual pattern for such guidance in relation to the UCAS and applications cycle?
4. **Where** should guidance take place?
5. **How** does a school or college go about improving existing guidance processes and practices and monitor the quality of the service offered to its students?

Why is HE guidance relevant to the wellbeing and success of your school/college?
Schools have become very good at measuring success in public examinations and rightly use the achievements of their students and teachers in this area to publicise themselves to prospective parents. It seems to me that, for many schools, the destinations of their leavers is often not presented as clearly or as publically yet, with good guidance and support leading to well-informed and realistic applications, this area is likely to be one which would, in many cases, be a significant PR success.

Schools also take on so many responsibilities beyond core teaching and learning: from SEAL and PSHE to citizenship and careers. Ensuring your students make a successful transition to the next phase of education is undeniably a core responsibility for headteachers and principals. Schools and colleges themselves should be doing more to reduce the university drop-out rate that approaches one in five.

Supporting your students into the appropriate HE course and keeping in regular touch through asking them to assist in the guidance process with younger students is also a key strategy for maintaining a good reputation among families and boosting your pupil recruitment in the future. Prioritising this is even more important for those schools that do not send many students to university. For them, the trendsetter who gets into Oxbridge or a Russell Group institution can act as a powerful catalyst for further applications.

There is also a close inter-relationship between good teaching and good guidance. If both are of high quality they will be mutually supportive strategies to raise attainment and boost aspirations. Well-taught students will perform better, realistically aim for better universities and be better prepared for independent learning and success once there. Guidance can act as the "glue" here, helping provide students with high ambitions, showing them what is feasible and realistic, motivating them to perform in an even more committed way in sixth-form lessons.

Good guidance can also serve to help pick up the pieces when a student has underperformed. After poor AS results, for example, the ability to consult a well-informed guidance expert can help the sixth-form team refocus and remotivate a student who may have wanted to just give up. It's all about improving life chances – and top-quality IAG certainly does that!

What does effective HE guidance look like in the school or college context and who is best equipped to provide it?
Firstly, you need the people with expertise to offer impartial advice. Over-reliance on teachers who are out of touch with current HE issues and application strategies is dangerous, so invest in the training of your advisers. A school that values the role played by effective IAG for its post-16 students in raising achievement can tap into various means of training teachers: UCAS courses, visits to university open days and teachers' conferences, and links with other schools that have proven expertise and are willing to share.

Connexions advisers often have a much wider remit than just post-16 IAG and not all their advisers have gained experience of or focused on the post-16 field. Sadly, too, the future of the service is also imperilled by cutbacks so my advice is to see a good Connexions adviser as a considerable bonus, but to establish a core of trained school-based staff to be the leaders of your guidance programmes, ideally supported by impartial, external careers guidance professionals.

The theme of this whole publication is to provide a template for guidance. Effective HE guidance must embrace the following elements:
* Planned programmes aimed at each year group from year 9 onwards to help young people plan and manage education, training and career choices.
* A wide range of written reference materials available to students and to support staff wishing to increase their knowledge.
* Provision for one-to-one guidance in the sixth form, in addition to the post-16 choices and careers IAG that is a statutory element of the curriculum.
* Information, advice and guidance about the benefits of higher education and how to access the opportunities that it affords.
* Development of links with either local or other relevant Higher Education Institutions in order to support training of teachers and advisers and to offer students experience of higher education.

When is guidance required and what is the annual pattern for such guidance in relation to the UCAS and applications cycle?
Guidance should not begin in the sixth form. The statutory guidance concerning IAG places a responsibility on all secondary providers to have in place a curriculum addressing the six key principles set out in the DCSF *Statutory Guidance on Information, Advice and Guidance 2009.* These are central to our concepts of what guidance aims to achieve and affirms that effective guidance:
* empowers young people to plan and manage their own futures;
* responds to the needs of each learner;
* provides comprehensive information and advice;
* raises aspirations;
* actively promotes equality of opportunity and challenges stereotypes;
* helps young people to progress.

From year 9 onwards, the emphasis of a school's IAG curriculum should be moving towards preparing students for decisions about post-16 and post-18 choices. Depending on the nature of one's student body, involving HE institutions in some way in the programme is excellent practice. Visits to nearby universities and visiting speakers from a university help to cement the idea that higher education is one of the progression paths to be seriously considered. Having said that, the focus of this chapter is on the post-16 area so below is a suggested pattern for a two-year programme of HE-related guidance beginning at year 12 Induction.

Term	Activity	
Year 12 autumn	• Outline to students entering sixth form the general calendar of the two-year process. • Identify potential and interested Oxbridge and Medicine/Vet Science applicants. Meet with these groups and individuals to outline the process and establish 'reading' groups (Early Applicants Group). • Train year 12 tutors in the HE applications process. • Review contents of your HE library and other online resources so that reordering can take place.	

Year 12 spring	• Introductory session on HE application for all year 12 students. Focus on "why apply?" and how to research courses and institutions at this stage. • Inform students about open days and how to get the best from them. • Invite a speaker from a university to speak to year 12 – ideally to take place in March/April of year 12. • Involve parents and carers in the process. A formal evening event gives added status to the process the young people are now beginning. • Involve alumni at the start of their Easter vacation in a focused activity introducing their institutions and courses and the transition from school to university. • Early Applicants Group to continue meeting and preparation through reading and debate. • Begin 1:1 meetings with year 12 students
Year 12 summer	• Train tutors/reference writers in the UCAS Apply system and reference-writing process. • Seek provisional subject reports and reference material to support guidance of students post-AS level. Keep your whole staff team up to date on HE issues. • Train students in the "How" of applications: the UCAS process; personal statements. • Organise visit to an open day. • Begin preparing Oxbridge and medicine references. • Continue 1:1 meetings, particularly in June–July period.
Year 13 autumn	• Ensure students' decisions regarding banking or dropping (usually) subject(s) is consistent with their university choices. • Ensure students are all aware of final in-house deadlines for completion of forms and of your system for processing applications. • Ensure teaching staff finalise predicted grades in the light of AS results and that these are shared with students. • Review training of tutors/reference writers so all are primed for the busy weeks ahead. • Finalise Early Applicants' References: UCAS deadline is 15 October. • Process all other applications: the sooner the better! • Prepare those who have interviews for this and ensure those with work to submit (Oxbridge) or pre-admissions tests are prepped and entered for the tests: deadlines usually end of September.
Year 13 spring	• Remind students of university finance issues and show how to apply for loans + implications. • Advertise key deadlines and explain UCAS Extra; Firm and Insurance choices; applications for student finance.
Year 13 summer	• Review the cycle of the last 18 months – ready for the next cycle, which is already underway. • August Results Day: have a small guidance team on hand for advice and individual support with clearing, decisions regarding reapplications, re-marks.

Where should guidance take place?
Establishing a specific area in the school for a higher education resource and reference library and, depending on geographical and physical constraints, having a space that can be used for meetings with individual students, provides further evidence of the seriousness of your institution's aspirations for your students.

The resources for a higher education library will embrace those accessible online as well as some hard-copy items such as:
* university prospectuses;
* UCAS publications;
* Good University Guides (The Times and The Guardian both publish excellent guides annually);
* Student-focused guides to universities and gap years
* *What Graduates Do* and similar publications

Keep the stock up to date by reviewing annually and supplementing it with key articles from newspapers on higher education-related issues.

The key to high-quality provision lies in the calibre and expertise of those who offer guidance, whether it be the Head of Sixth Form and his or her team or the Careers and Higher Education Adviser. Having an identifiable location, however, enables reference materials to be overseen and used more effectively.

The spring and summer terms of year 12 will be the crucial times for the adviser to meet with students on a one-to-one basis, but do allow for the needs of students in the autumn of year 13 as final choices and tactical decisions are being made, and in the spring when students need support and guidance regarding Firm and Insurance choices, dealing with rejections, arranging finance and considering options such as UCAS Extra. Many of the issues that crop up during the UCAS calendar require the whole cohort to be informed, so the effective use of assemblies, meetings, tutorial sessions and electronic communication is going to be key to a programme being viewed as relevant and helpful by your student body.

How does a school or college go about improving existing guidance processes and practices and monitor the quality of the service offered to its students?
The structure and annual cycle outlined above is one that many schools and colleges follow. Whatever stage or level of development your institution's provision is at, now is the time for a precise audit, together with reflection on the philosophy that will underpin your future arrangements for post-16 IAG.

To end, then, some key questions for you to ask:
* Are the relevant post holders in the sixth form sufficiently knowledgeable about all progression issues?
* Looking at the examination results of your students over the last three years and your progression statistics for higher education, does your institution achieve a level of success that can be significantly improved on?
* Who should form the key members of your guidance team? What additional training do they need?
* What role does an impartial adviser have within your plans for effective IAG?
* Look at your resources and the location of your HE literature. How can this be further improved?

- What will be the measurements of success when you review again next year? These may be progression statistics, student satisfaction surveys, parental feedback or student recruitment.

It may also be useful to look at Higher Education Related Learning, a programme developed by the Specialist Schools and Academies Trust that integrates with Work Related Learning:
https://www.ssatrust.org.uk/community/highereducation/Pages/HERL.aspx

2. How to gain the knowledge you need

Giving advice on higher-education choices can be problematic: many people have access to the necessary information, but they may not always know how to use it wisely. HE advisers need to identify *original* sources of information so that their advice is as *empirical* as possible. The following ideas are suggestions that could help you improve your knowledge so you can advise your students in an informed way.

Take the Adviser's Certificate: Applying to Higher Education This unique course is validated by London South Bank University and offered by LSBU and the Specialist Schools and Academies Trust around England. See section 9 by Dr. Michelle Stewart.

Know how UCAS Apply is administered Read the information on the UCAS website and if possible attend UCAS Apply training or even better take the Wise Adviser course at UCAS headquarters, visit www.ucas.com/advisers/training

Know how the various application processes are administered These include the post-application supplementary form used by Cambridge; art foundation courses; additional tests such as BMAT, LNAT and UKCAT; and various tests for Oxford and Cambridge. See further sections in this book.

Go to the CRAC higher-education conference This is a three-day residential course that normally takes place at the end of the spring term. It includes a wide range of visiting speakers and provides an opportunity to network. For more information, visit www.crac.org.uk

Visit universities In your first year as an HE adviser, you should aim to visit five to ten universities to improve your level of knowledge (you could combine this with taking groups of students). Be sure to visit a range of universities and courses – not just those in your personal comfort zone. Use the university and course checklists in *Appendix A*.

Target your research Get to know the kinds of students you are dealing with and the structures of the post-16 courses. Are some subjects particularly popular? If so, directing your research in terms of courses, universities and employers could save you time and energy in the future.

Build up relationships with appropriate university staff Universities have schools-liaison officers and staff members charged with widening university participation. Get to know some of these people – they will help you build up your knowledge levels (you will probably be useful to them too).

Join your local Aimhigher network These can be useful forums for sharing and distributing information. They can also be a focus for joint activities with other schools. At the time of writing it is unclear what the future of the Aimhigher network will be. If funding ends, informal networks of schools, HEIs (Higher Education Institutions) and local authorities may still exist.

Improve your knowledge of graduate employment prospects You will face endless questions on this subject. Find out more by: visiting students on work experience (you might try to meet the human resources contact); keeping in touch with alumni (recent graduates and those established in a wide range of careers); visiting the website www.prospects.ac.uk; doing some wider reading about the future of work (see *15. Graduate employment*).

Read the UCAS monthly email Make sure you look at this *every month*. Important changes to the UCAS system are included, and useful training events are often advertised.

Allocate time to look at relevant publications, prospectuses and websites

Join the Institute of Career Guidance Higher Education Advisers Community of Interest This is free with membership of the ICG. It is the only national group of practitioners doing this type of work in the UK. People can keep in touch virtually, there is an annual conference and useful information is placed on the ICG website. www.icg-uk.org

The value of alumni
With modern IT and data systems, tracking success across years is an effective weapon/tool in helping successive generations of students. This can be used, for example, to put them in touch with alumni and also to raise the profile and sing the successes of institutions. Alumni are particularly effective in helping the next generation of students. Bringing them back to talk to future students not only provides them with a sense of pride in their education and their school/college; they also provide a valuable up-to-date set of eyes on what is currently happening in the institutions of higher education.

3. An HE adviser's timetable

The following is a guideline only. All schools and colleges operate differently and yours may already have an established and workable schedule for providing HE advice. This timetable, however, is a useful checklist for making sure all the ground is covered within the time limits. It could also be incorporated with the HERL programme (Higher Education Related Learning) which integrates with compulsory careers education and guidance (CEG) and work-related learning (WRL) programmes. HERL was developed by the Specialist Schools and Academies Trust https://www.ssatrust.org.uk/community/highereducation/Pages/HERL.aspx

WHEN	WHAT	HOW
Year 9 – spring or summer term	• Give advice on GCSE options including STEM and foreign language choices	• Talks, booklets, parents' event, relevant websites (Kudos, Prefinio etc)
Year 10	• Promote awareness of higher education	• Talks in school • Visits to well-targeted higher-education institutions
Year 11 – winter or spring term	• Give general information about choosing sixth-form subjects • Possibly hold individual interviews about sixth-form subjects	• Booklets, talks, website information • One-to-one with HE adviser
Year 12 – winter term	• Check that students' sixth-form subjects and GCSE results meet their aspirations • Make sure students understand AS/A2 system • Give advice on work experience	• Check records at time of sixth-form/college enrolment • Talk in school • Talk in school
Year 12 – spring term	• Provide initial information about higher education: how to choose your course; understanding UCAS; information sources and useful websites • Encourage visits to a higher-education	• Introductory talks in school • Possibly hold HE parents' evening • Hand out booklet to all students about applying for higher education or direct to relevant Blog/Fronter information • Go to an UCAS-sponsored event

	convention (or arrange one in school)	
	• Possibly hold individual interviews about higher-education choices	• One-to-one with HE adviser
Year 12 – summer term	• Encourage students to: visit HE institutions; apply for summer schools; apply for masterclasses/gifted and talented classes related to HE courses	• Set up organised visits or encourage students to act independently
	• Give advice on drafting a personal statement	• Talks, booklets, help from tutors
	• Possibly hold individual interviews about HE choices (especially early applicants: Oxbridge, medicine, dentistry, veterinary science)	• One-to-one with HE adviser
	• Check that applicants for highly selective courses are doing appropriate work experience or wider reading	• Talks, one-to-ones
	• Encourage students to put basic details on UCAS Apply	• Take tutor groups to IT suites
	• Give advice on AS results (i.e. which subject to drop)	• Provide a "results service" or give advice at year 13 enrolment
	• Collect relevant information for UCAS reference	• Liaise with tutors/subject teachers
Year 13 – winter term	• Hold individual interviews about HE choices	• One-to-one with HE adviser
	• Ensure early applicants meet 15 October deadline; ensure applications for highly selective courses are sent by half-term; ensure all other applications are made on time	• HE adviser needs to ensure subject references are completed early and that early applicants act with a sense of urgency

	• Sign off personal statements	• Only after much checking with individual students
	• Prepare students for interviews (where necessary)	• Talks, mock interviews
	• Give advice on student finance and graduate employment	• Talks in school
	• Discuss applying for art foundation courses	• Group discussions
Year 13 – spring term	• Give advice on responding to UCAS offers, UCAS Extra and Adjustment	• Talk in school; handouts
	• Give detailed advice on applying for student finance (this may be combined with UCAS Apply in the future)	• Talk in school; handouts
Year 13 – summer term	• Deal with confirmation and clearing	• Provide a "results service"

Part Two: One-to-one interviews

4. Conducting individual HE interviews: the guiding principles

Probably the single most important part of the HE adviser's role is to hold one-to-one interviews with students to guide them through the higher-education decision-making process. Practice varies, but each student should be offered at least one, and in some cases several, of these interviews, between the spring term of year 12 and the winter term of year 13. These interviews should be offered, but they should never be compulsory: guidance works best when the student is there voluntarily! By this time, students should (hopefully) have carried out some independent research into university courses and careers. Some may have a clear idea about what interests them, others may be as yet unfocused. In either case, they will need expert advice and information to help them clarify their ideas and put their plans into action.

If possible, each individual interview should be allotted a half-hour time slot. But what is the best way to structure such an interview? And what kind of advice should be given?

Sadly, there is no one magic formula for HE advisers to follow. On the contrary, the best advisers are able to mix and match from a number of overlapping strategies. Remember that the aim is to give non-directive advice in a coherent and systematic manner. The guiding principles described in this chapter are intended to achieve this.

4.1 The FIRST framework

The FIRST framework, developed in 1982 by Tol Bedford of the Department of Employment's careers service branch, is a very useful starting point. The mnemonic, which neatly covers the key elements of a successful interview, is as follows:

- **Focus** To what extent has the student *narrowed down* his or her options?
- **Information** How *well-informed* is the student?
- **Realism** Is the student being realistic about his or her own *capabilities*, given the constraints of university entrance and the jobs market? We may also have a role in encouraging ambition. The student may be capable of more than they imagine.
- **Scope** Is the student aware of the *range of options* available?
- **Tactics** Does the student know how to put his or her plans *into action*?

Let's take these ideas one by one, but not necessarily in the FIRST order.

Focus It is very difficult to make a decision when there are too many things to choose from. It is therefore essential to narrow down the options to a manageable short list. It is quite some task, however, to reduce the thousands of course options available down to a list of just five UCAS choices. This is the real nitty-gritty of the decision-making process and students will need guidance on how to do it (see *6.1 Focus: how to help students narrow down their options*).

Scope "Scope", paradoxically, goes hand-in-hand with "focus". Students' knowledge of possible degrees and careers may be limited, and they must be made aware of all the opportunities available. For example, if a student comes to you wanting to do a degree in information technology, but also really enjoys biology A level, is he or she aware of the possibility of doing a degree in bioinformatics? If a student is interested in physiotherapy but is doubtful about gaining the necessary A-level grades, does he or she know that occupational therapy is usually easier to get into and may be just as interesting?

There will be much alternating between "focus" and "scope" – periods of reducing the list of options and periods of expanding it to include new and exciting ideas – before the final university choices are made. In order to be able to offer useful advice, the HE adviser needs to be fully acquainted with information sources such as *UCAS Course Search (www.ucas.com)*, *Degree Course Offers* by Heap and ratings tables such as www.thecompleteuniversityguide.co.uk Many interest guides such as Centigrade and www.ukcoursefinder.co.uk will serve the dual functions of focusing ideas down and also scoping ideas out. Students should be encouraged to widen their own horizons by reading prospectuses and reference books and using the internet. See also section *6.2 Scope: an ideas generator* for useful information.

Realism Of course we should follow our dreams, but there must also be some attachment to the real world. The notion of realism, though, is somewhat problematic. An HE adviser should never tell students they are being unrealistic because they are aiming high, or because they want to do something difficult. Rather, students should be encouraged to "go for it" if they can, provided they know the odds and have constructed a safety net for themselves if they fail. Realism is as much about making sure one achieves what one is really capable of, as it is about accepting limitations. One can be underambitious as well as overambitious.

To be realistic, students need to consider two things:
- *Is it realistic for me?* What kind of person am I? Am I really interested in this, will I be satisfied by it, am I capable of something better?
- *Is it feasible, in the circumstances?* For example, if I am unwilling to move from my local area, my options will be restricted.

The five choices of the UCAS system allow applicants to spread their chances. For example, it might be possible to include maybe two choices that are slightly risky, while the other three are safer bets. In order to be sure about this aspect of their decision, however, students may need advice on understanding course entry requirements, and should be encouraged to research the career prospects and jobs market in their chosen field.

Information As we have already seen in "focus", "scope" and "realism", accurate and up-to-date information is a vital component of any decision. Information, by its very nature, relates to all the other areas of FIRST. Understanding where all the information sources are and knowing how to direct your students to them, is an art in itself, made even more complicated by the growth of social media. We will try to deal with this issue in chapter 10.

Don't forget, though, that it is just as important for students to build up information about themselves – to be self-aware – as about the opportunities available. For example, students need to consider how their GCSE results, AS results and A level predictions might affect their choice of course or career. Have they thought about whether they have the right personality for a particular subject or career? Have they thoroughly researched their career idea to make sure it will suit their aspirations? Have they tried to understand their own strengths and weaknesses by weighing up their personal interests, abilities, values and attitudes?

Tactics So, finally, your student interviewee has achieved a *focus*, developed from an awareness of the *scope* of what is available, is *realistic* about the jobs and higher-education market, and has all the necessary *information*. All that remains is to put ideas into practice.

Helpful "tactics" from an HE adviser might include: advice on filling in UCAS Apply to maximise chances (particularly for popular courses); ideas about what to say in a personal statement; help with gaining appropriate work experience; interview preparation; information on financing your studies.

4.2 Giving non-directive, non-judgemental guidance

Before you start advising other people, it is essential to acknowledge that you bring your own baggage to any situation. So, as the inscription on the temple of Apollo at Delphi reads: "Know yourself"!

How did you get to where you are now? What adversities did you overcome? What help did you get? How was your own experience different from that of the students you are now advising? What are your weaknesses? What are your strengths? Who were the main people who influenced your career? There is an interesting take on these issues in *Outliers* by Malcolm Gladwell.

This may sound like so much touchy-feely psycho-babble, but until you have the necessary self-awareness, you are likely to find yourself influencing students in unforeseen ways. Below are some issues to bear in mind.

Information abuse It is not a new idea to observe that information is a powerful tool, especially when it is abused. Experts rely on the fact that they have more information than the people they are dealing with. And they can use this imbalance to their advantage.

Information abuse can take many forms. Here are some examples:
- If a student is talking about a subject on which you lack knowledge, you redirect the conversation to your personal comfort zone.
- You emphasise the options available in your own sixth form, even though you know other options could be more suitable.
- You fail to admit that you need to find out further information before you can make any judgement or recommendations.
- You give advice to your students that you would not be happy to give to your own children if they were in the same position.

Your own levels of knowledge Until you have high levels of knowledge about university courses and careers, you may not even *realise* that you are being directive and judgemental in your guidance. For example:

- You might be telling students they are unable to do a particular course, when in fact they can.
- You might direct a student towards a particular degree related to a career, when in fact it is not necessary to specialise at such an early stage.

See section *2. How to gain the knowledge you need*, to find out ways to improve your knowledge levels.

The need to challenge flawed reasoning Some students might easily come to decisions about their futures based on faulty thought processes. The HE adviser's job is to recognise and challenge such flawed reasoning. I have based the examples below on the ideas in Nigel Warburton's *Thinking from A-Z*.

- *Seductive reasoning errors (such as "the Van Gogh fallacy")* This is the thinking: Van Gogh was poor and misunderstood in his lifetime, yet he is now recognised as a great artist; I am also poor and misunderstood, so I, too, will eventually be recognised as a great artist. For example: "My sister was lazy in her year 12 but still got good A-level results. I am lazy in year 12 and I am still going to get good A-level results." Alarm bells should start ringing: this student may not now be able to make up the points in year 13; she may be less able than her sister.
- *Correlation confusion* This is when a student connects two sorts of events, even though there is no correlation between them. For example: "I want to do an English degree because I want to become a journalist." But you do not need to do an English degree to become a journalist. In fact, postgraduate journalism courses normally look for evidence of a commitment to journalism, such as writing for a student newspaper.
- *Psychological factors that can be obstacles to clear thought, such as wishful thinking* Or believing that because it would be *nice* if something were true, then it must *be* true. For example: "I really want to become a dentist. I've done my work experience and spoken to dentists, therefore I'm going to become a dentist." Hang on a minute … What about getting a good grade in chemistry A level?

The need to respect students' hopes and dreams Whatever aspirations students have – however unobtainable their dreams may seem – I will always talk through the ways that they might achieve their goals. *But*, I also make them aware of the difficulties they will face getting there. I like to use this analogy: if a friend asked me the way to the best swimming pool in my area, I would tell him the route. However, I might also ask him if he knew how to swim! If he answered no, I could tell him where to go to get lessons. It is a question of combining honesty and ambition.

Cultural issues Religious and ethnic background can play a part in HE guidance. For instance, a student might reject a university in a provincial city because the area is "not multi-cultural enough".

Obviously, it is hugely important that students are happy with their university and course, both academically and socially. However, students also need to know that if they try to stay within a narrow social grouping (for example, living at home and not participating in the wider community of the university) they may be disadvantaged, particularly when applying for jobs in highly competitive fields. Employers want cosmopolitans and this may be a criteria in the assessment process they use. This applies to class, too: graduates with very narrow class experiences may be disadvantaged.

It is for us as HE advisers to help our students, whatever their background, to achieve their goals and maximise their opportunities. Sometimes we may need to challenge some firmly held beliefs to do this.

The "guidance community" By "guidance community" I am referring to the whole range of people students may speak to and be influenced by: parents, teachers, other family members, family friends, their peer group and people they meet doing work experience. HE advisers have to accept that students will absorb a range of advice and then compare it with what they find in websites and prospectuses. Our main role is to help them sift this advice and, if it is wrong, then to challenge it.

4.3 The importance of emotional intelligence

Students need to know that in order to be successful – in the sixth form, at university, throughout their careers – they will need more than just academic knowledge and intelligence. Daniel Goleman, who writes about emotional intelligence, has identified some key abilities. These are:

* the ability to motivate oneself (can the student push him or herself to achieve deadlines?);
* the ability to persist in the face of adversity (can the student keep going in spite of a poor mark?);
* the ability to control impulse and delay gratification (can the student balance work and social activities?);
* the ability to regulate one's emotions and think clearly (can the student remain calm if someone disagrees with him, responding with a clear counter-argument?);
* the ability to empathise (can the student understand and respond to how other people might be feeling?);
* the ability to hope (does the student have ambitions to follow a particular career or university path?).

In my experience, the students who have most of these key emotional abilities in place are the ones who go on to get very high A-level grades and excellent degrees. HE advisers need to make their students think about this. Do they possess these qualities? Can they work on developing them?

What most concerns me, though, is the ability to hope. I want to know this from my students: is there something that they are looking forward to in the future? A career, perhaps, or a university course, or simply going to university. From what I can see, people who have goals to aim for are often highly motivated and happy.

If you would like to find out more about these ideas, try reading *Emotional Intelligence* by Daniel Goleman.

4.4 General interview techniques

The basic interview techniques outlined here should be second nature to qualified careers advisers, careers officers and personal advisers. However, teachers involved in giving HE advice may not have received training in these matters. I therefore feel it is appropriate to spell out some general principles.

The different types of questions

- *Open questions* These encourage the flow of information and will usually begin with words such as "what", "why", "when", "where", "tell me about" or "how". The point is to encourage an expansive answer. Interviewees usually respond well to open questions.
  For example:
  o "What subject do you enjoy most?"
  o "Tell me about the work experience that you did."
- *Closed questions* These are direct and focused questions. Some people believe they lead only to "yes" or "no" answers and should therefore be avoided. However, closed questions are useful for contracting and summarising a discussion, confirming ideas and controlling the flow of information. They are also helpful for reining in an over-talkative interviewee.
  For example:
  o "Have you visited the university?"
  o "Are these the issues that you want to cover?"
- *Probing questions* These are follow-up questions for drawing out more detailed information about specific points. Look for depth rather than breadth of information.
  For example:
  o "You say you are interested in whales, but which whales interest you most and why?"
  o "You say you did work experience in a geriatric ward. What health problems particularly affect the elderly?"
- *Linking questions* These summarise the discussion so far, confirm that issues have been correctly understood and make a transition to a new subject.
  For example:
  o "I can see that you like chemistry. Can you think how this subject might be relevant to your interest in dietetics?"
  o "It's interesting to hear that. On a related subject I'd like to ask…"
- *Hypothetical questions* These are open in style and suggest a "what if…" scenario. They are useful for analysing interviewees' knowledge and attitudes, and seeing how they react to situations. Answers can also be a useful indication of creativity and speculative thinking. However, in suggesting a scenario, you need to be very careful that the interviewee understands the conjectural nature of the question.
  For example:
  o "If you don't make it as a singer-songwriter after your degree in commercial music, what will you do?"
  o "You are looking at a worst-case scenario. What about a best-case scenario?"
- *Behavioural questions* These seek evidence from the past as an indicator of future interests. They are similar to hypothetical questions in that they can

measure knowledge, attitudes, reactions, creativity and thinking – but on the basis of something the interviewee has already experienced or done.
For example:
- o "When you have a lot of homework and coursework to hand in, how do you cope?"
- o "When you walk out of a lesson and think, 'I didn't get any of that,' what do you do?"

- *Leading questions* These should simply be avoided.
  For example:
  - o "You really should be applying for Oxbridge. You are going to, aren't you?"
  - o "I expect you'll prefer to stay at home rather than move away."
- *Multiple questions* Several questions joined in a series. These are best kept to a minimum, as they tend to confuse the interviewee and produce limited information (often only the first question is answered).

The process
Your aim is to help students talk freely and with relevance. The best way to achieve this is to ask *open questions*, followed by *probing questions*. An effective way of probing is to keep asking for specific examples from the student's own experience to back up an assertion or claim.

Good listening is vital if the interviewer is to probe effectively. Think of the process as a funnel, with the open questions at the top and the probing questions gradually narrowing down the discussion to the concrete evidence.

At the end of the funnel process, the interviewer should briefly summarise the student's answers (to make sure there are no misunderstandings) before starting the process again with a new area of questioning.

5. Interview structure

By Penny Thei, Senior Lecturer Career Guidance, London South Bank University
theip@lsbu.ac.uk

Structuring an interview helps to keep the focus on the student and identify what they need and want, not what you may assume they need and want from you. A structure will help to guide the process forward to a conclusion and a plan for action. You are less likely to miss crucial pieces of information and they are more likely to go away with what they came for.
"Without this firm base, the interview will resemble a cosy chat … Without a structure, both the [student] and the adviser will feel lost and flounder without direction, with a consequent raising of levels of stress and dissatisfaction for both."
Ali and Graham (1996) *The Counselling Approach to Careers Guidance,* Routledge.

A three-stage framework
A simple three-stage model can provide a useful structure. It is based on the work of Professor Gerard Egan, author of widely used counselling text *The Skilled Helper.*
(*The Skilled Helper – A Problem Management and Opportunity Development Approach to Helping,* Wadsworth.)

Stage 1: Exploration – Building a picture of current thinking and situation
Stage 2: New Understanding – Finding solutions and deciding goals
Stage 3: Action – What to do to achieve those goals

5.1 The skills you will need
Skills for Stage 1 (Exploration):
- *Attention giving* – give the student your attention, use some eye contact and smile appropriately. This will help to build and maintain trust.
- Questioning – use clear open questions to help the student tell their story and tell you what you need to know.
- *Listening* – questioning is pointless unless you are actively listening to the answers. Listening actively means listening with both your ears and your eyes, responding to their body language as well as the words that are spoken. To ensure that both you and the student understand what is being said, take time to reflect back to them what you have heard, ask clarifying questions where what is said seems unclear, and summarise from time to time to check you have heard what has been said accurately.
- *Summarising* – this can also provide a breathing space when you're not sure where to go next and an opportunity for your student to add to or correct information they have given you.

Ten Commandments for Good Listening

1. **Stop talking** You cannot listen if you are talking.
2. **Put the talker at ease** Help them feel they are free to talk. A friendly facial expression and an attentive but relaxed attitude are important, as well as the occasional grunt.

3. **Show them you want to listen** Look and act interested. Don't read your mail or doodle. Use some eye contact.
4. **Remove distractions** Don't shuffle papers or fiddle with paper clips or pens. Divert your calls, turn off your mobile and put a "Do Not Disturb" notice on the door.
5. **Empathise with them** Try to put yourself in their place so you can see their point of view, but remain impartial and non-judgemental.
6. **Be patient** Allow adequate time. Don't interrupt, or jump in to fill a silence – this may be valuable thinking time for the interviewee.
7. **Hold your temper** Emotional involvement will only make it more difficult to find out what is really being said, however much you disagree or feel challenged.
8. **Don't argue or criticise** Even if you win, you lose.
9. **Ask questions and summarise them from time to time** This encourages and shows you are listening. It also helps to develop points further and gives the student a chance to restate facts and ideas if they feel you haven't quite grasped the point.
10. **Stop talking** This is the first and the last because all other commandments depend on it.

Skills for Stage 2 (New Understanding):
All the skills from Stage 1, plus:
- *Challenging* – don't be afraid to challenge if what you have heard seems inconsistent, inaccurate or contradictory. The student may be experiencing some confusion and by challenging you will be able to help them think more clearly.
- *Information giving* – you should be prepared to share information at this stage. If you have identified what they already know (the 'I' of the FIRST model) you can be more selective about what you need to tell them during the discussion. Information should be accurate, up to date, unbiased and timely. If you don't know the information, be honest and say so, and signpost where the information may be found. Don't bluff, as you do neither the student nor yourself any favours.
- *Decision making* – you should be helping the student to start making decisions about what they want to do and where they want to go through questioning, brainstorming and information-giving. You should also be helping them clarify their goals.

Skills for Stage 3 (Action):
All the skills above, plus:
- *Action planning* – the skill is in giving ownership of the plan to the student and ensuring actions are clear, concrete and timely.

5.2 Contract and agenda

Before embarking on the three stages of Exploration, New Understanding and Action, it will be useful to set out a **contract** and an **agenda** for the interview.
The importance of contracting
You may know the student sitting in front of you and they may well know you, but do they know the role you have as an adviser about HE? This needs to be clear, as do the issues of:
- confidentiality (and its limits);

- impartiality, crucial to helping the student make the best decisions for them – and not necessarily for you or your institution;
- negotiating an agenda for the discussion without making assumptions
- not giving information immediately, without the facts and issues that lie behind what is presented.

What will the contract look/sound like? You might try writing it down and trying it out on a colleague. You should aim to cover the following:

- Introduce yourself and your role in this context. For example: "My role today is to help with any questions you may have about applying to university."
- Purpose of the interview. For example: "The aim is to clarify any ideas you may have already or perhaps suggest some you hadn't thought of and to help you find any information you may need. I'm not here to tell you what to do."
- Confidentiality and its limits. Don't forget that there are always limits, such as: school or college policies on sharing student information, record keeping, any issues of child protection or illegal activities that might be revealed (don't assume this won't come up.)
- Impartiality. You may have your own ideas but your role here is to be an unbiased listener and guide. You may advise but you must never impose your ideas.
- Any boundaries. Questions and issues may arise that are beyond your field of expertise or experience, so you should mention the possibility that you may need to refer to someone else.
- Possible outcomes – a plan of action, further discussion.
- Time allocated for the interview.
- Checking this has all been understood.

Now you are ready to find out what the student wants and/or needs from you. In taking a couple of minutes at the start to ensure that the student is clear about the purposes and boundaries of the interview you are helping to build up trust, a vital ingredient if the outcome is to be successful for the student.

The Agenda

This is the start of your exploration of the student's current ideas and circumstances and will set the tone for what is to come. It is all too easy to *assume* you know what is wanted, particularly when you know the student well – or think you do. You may think they are of course going to look only at Oxbridge/Russell Group universities: they're too good for anything else. But maybe, just maybe, they have other, to you, more surprising ideas.

Your job is to **listen** to and **explore** these ideas briefly and identify what the student's wants and needs are from the rest of the interview. You may suggest other avenues to explore but it's up to the student to agree. Summarise all these ideas and suggest these may form the basis of discussion for the time remaining. Show that you are listening!

Don't fire off information. It may turn out to be inappropriate in the light of your subsequent discussion, which may uncover some sound reasons why your choices for the student are not appropriate. Show that you are listening!

It is not unusual to be confronted with a long list of wants at this stage, too long to cover in the time you have to offer them. Get the student to prioritise what is most important to them and focus on these in the subsequent discussion.

Based on the FIRST model, **Focus** and **Information** questions will help your understanding of the student's thinking and determine what will be the most useful topics for discussion in the time available:

- How long have you had the idea(s)?
- What gave you the idea(s)?
- How definite are the ideas/plans?
- What do you know already?
- How much research have you done to date? It is really important to find this out, as what they "know" may not be correct, or they may know everything, or nothing. Please note, however, that this is not the time to give the information. You can do this later on in the interview, once you have a greater sense of what information is needed and wanted.
- What would they like to take away from the session that will be most helpful to them?

What about the student who comes with no definite ideas or plans of their own? This is still no reason to tell them what to do based on your own preconceived ideas about them. You can start by asking questions such as:

- Do they have any vague ideas, or ones they have dismissed as being unrealistic for them? For example, they would like to apply for medicine but don't think they stand a chance.
- What makes them think that?
- Are they aware of what the possible options might be?
- Have they any particular career goals in mind?

Whatever you do, don't start giving them information or lists of possible alternatives. Just **LISTEN**, summarise and negotiate with them as to what will be most useful for them to leave the session with. This might be a plan for researching the options available or information about entry routes to a particular career.

5.3 Using the three-stage framework

You are now ready to put the three-stage framework into action.

Stage 1: Exploration
There are a few things it will be helpful to find out first, however well you think you know the student sitting in front of you. You will be trying to ascertain **Realism** (as in the FIRST model) through gathering this information.

- Check what subjects they are doing.
- How well do they think they are doing? Strengths and weaknesses.
- If the subject in mind is a current course, how well are they doing, and what is their interest in taking it further? Do they have any doubts about it?
- Any areas of weakness and any reasons for this? Are they struggling, or is it just not what they hoped?
- Any grades already achieved, including GCSEs. These are really important for competitive courses at competitive institutions. Do they have both maths and English at C or above?
- Predicted grades. How realistic do they think these are?

- Any particular interests that might have a bearing on subject choices and that could be included in a personal statement or open up avenues they had not considered.
- Any relevant work experience. Again this will be useful for their personal statement and may be essential for some courses.
- Are there any constraints to any choices they may make, be it subject or location, for instance family circumstances, personal choices or financial issues?

If you ask good open questions and listen to the answers you should gather a lot of useful information. Make sure you summarise from time to time to ensure you have got the picture right and summarise clearly the key information you have before moving onto Stage 2. Remember the Ten Commandments for Good Listening.

Stage 2: New Understanding

The aim of this stage is to help your student reach some decisions and clarify their goals, after you have discussed new ideas/options and given them some information. This stage involves the FIRST principles of **Information**, **Realism** and **Scope**.

At this stage you will want to help them:

- think realistically about the choices they may have already made, based on the information you have from Stage 1;
- broaden their ideas or even narrow them down where the student has lots of disparate ideas but doesn't know how to choose between them.

The issues may vary from "I don't know which subject to choose from these three" to "I don't know which is the best university for the subject I want to study".

You may find you need to gently challenge preconceptions about the courses they are considering, the institutions that are offering them and even about themselves and their abilities and interests, using the information they have given you already. For instance, in discussing architecture, have they expressed any interest in buildings or in design? Do they have the required GCSE subjects/grades? Are they likely to achieve the grades required for the courses they are interested in?

This is where your initial Stage 1 exploration is so important. You will need to draw on it to help keep focus on what is important for the student to know: not just what they want to know but also what they need to know.

- Have they thought about the issues they might consider in choosing a suitable course at a university that will meet their needs for three years? These might include location, facilities and assessment methods.
- Are they aware of the variety of courses on offer in their chosen area of interest?
- Do they have any long-term career goals that might mean some courses are more suitable than others?
- Do they know about the resources available to help them in making decisions?
- What might be realistic alternatives or options? What if they don't achieve the required grades?
- Might there be any financial issues that need explanation?

Please note – you do not need to know all the answers, but it is important to know where to get the answers and be able to explain this accurately. You need to keep asking questions but this is also your opportunity to fill in the gaps in information by signposting to the resources available and sharing information gathered from your experiences of past students, visits you have made and information you have read.

You may need to help the student consider the best options for them, but without telling them what to do or completely destroying their dreams. You should be able to help them come up with more realistic alternatives if what they are proposing is likely to prove unrealistic, based on the evidence gathered so far. In the end they will make the decisions about their future goals – you can only try to help them make the best ones in the light of the information and feedback you give them.

Your role:
- It is vital that the information you give them is accurate, up to date and unbiased.
- Your skills in this stage are questioning, challenging when necessary and giving information.
- And of course you need to keep **LISTENING.**

By the end of this part of the interview the student's goals, be they short, medium or longer-term, should be becoming clearer and some decisions about how to proceed now need to be made. In other words, you are ready to move into Stage 3: Action.

Stage 3: Action

Here you will look at short, medium and long-term action, covering the FIRST principles of **Scope** and **Tactics.**

It is all too easy for you to tell the student what they should be doing next. Don't, because you can be sure they won't. The student has to see the relevance of what needs to be done in a way that allows them to take ownership. A useful strategy is to ask the student to summarise what they think are the decisions made in the discussion so far. A useful technique at this stage is Egan's "prompt and fade". You can prompt if you think they have omitted something they or you felt was important for them to research further, such as:
- What about the need for sports facilities, or access to good transport links that you mentioned?
- Have you thought about contacting the admissions tutor with your query? (Then withdraw and leave the student to think about their response to this prompting.)
- What do you think you need to do next? This will help them sort out their priorities. They may, for example, decide the most important action is to seek additional help with a subject they need to do better in to ensure they get to the course at the institution of their choice, then to do some more research into courses and go to open days.

Having established their priorities and actions needed, help them to formulate a SMART (Specific–Measurable–Achievable–Realistic–Timely) action plan, preferably written. This will act both as a reminder and a useful tool for reviewing progress should any follow-up be required. Timing is crucial in HE planning and applying and you can help them get it right by ensuring their actions are timely and realistic: what needs to be done in the short or medium or longer term?
- The key question is: "WHEN are you going to do this by?"
- But you also need to make sure they know HOW to do it, WHO and/or WHAT may be involved and HOW to reach that person/information.
- What are the pros and cons of the various approaches or actions they may be considering?
- Do they know how to make contact with an admissions tutor?
- Are they aware of how to access the resources that will help them choose, for example, between different courses?

Finally, what if they need more help? A useful way to end is to remind them of when and where further help is available: your availability and external sources of help if appropriate. You will have covered a lot of ground and it may need further discussion before decisions can be finally made and put into action.

The action plan will only be as useful as the information written on it. Your job is to ensure the student can go away feeling they want to act, and can act with confidence. That confidence will come from taking the time to use the structure and work through the stages of the interview, asking questions, listening to the answers, helping to generate ideas and options with sound information and ensuring the student can go away and act on the decisions made.

6. The FIRST principles in detail

6.1 Focus: how to help students narrow down their options

The first step for students is to settle on the subject they wish to study. Some may know already; others may have no idea. In fact, although there are thousands of different higher-education courses at hundreds of colleges, the system for narrowing down the choices – the "focus" of the FIRST mnemonic – can be relatively simple.

Initially, students should be made to ask themselves the following questions:
* Are they interested in continuing to study a subject they are currently enjoying in the sixth form?
* Do they want to do something that leads to a certain career?
* Do they want to study something new that they feel they might be very interested in?

Whichever of these three paths the student takes, the HE adviser will need to make sure he or she is aware of any relevant issues or considerations.

Choosing a subject based on sixth-form study: points to remember
* There will often be marked differences in content between the degree course and the A level (or equivalent) of the same subject. For example, an economics degree will involve far more statistics; a biology degree will include far more chemistry.
* Some arts subjects, such as English, are incredibly competitive. AAA is the standard offer from most traditional universities. Would a degree in some other subject, such as philosophy, cultural studies, American studies or modern European studies, be equally appealing?
* Science degrees, on the other hand, in the subjects studied at school (chemistry, physics, biology and maths) are much more flexible in their entry requirements, especially at the clearing stage.
* It is still important to look at the career implications.

Choosing a subject based on a career idea: points to remember
* A large number of careers have graduate-only entry – either officially or unofficially (teaching, professional surveying, professional engineering, chartered accountancy and medicine are some examples). Some careers require a specific degree (for example, pharmacy, hotel management) while others will accept a degree in any subject (for example, chartered accountancy, retail management).
* If a degree is specific to a particular career, then it must match the student's own personal profile. Does it reflect his or her interests, abilities, values and attitudes? The student needs to find out by doing some research: work experience; talking to people working in the career area; information from libraries and the internet.
* What happens if you change your mind? How easy will it be to gain entry to another career field? This will vary, but very often core skills gained in one degree can be useful for another career area.
* Be wary of newer degrees related to career areas such as popular music or forensic science, as there may not be a clear career path at the end of the degree. On the other hand, some newer degrees such as computer animation can have some clear career paths following graduation.

Choosing a subject based on a new interest: points to remember
- These subjects can be split into two categories: degrees with no obvious vocational link and degrees with a vocational link.
- Examples of degrees with no clear career link include anthropology, philosophy and classics. Students need to find out more about these courses through prospectuses, further reading and their own personal interest. People often worry about the employment prospects of graduates in these subjects; in fact, their levels of employment tend to be the same as for other non-vocational graduates.
- Examples of degrees with a career link include psychology (although only a minority of these graduates become professional psychologists) and media studies (although these graduates are in no way guaranteed a job in the media). Students must want to study these subjects simply because they are very interested in the content of the course. What may follow in terms of a career is a bonus.

Once the student has settled on a subject, how is it possible to narrow down the number of options available to the five choices allowed on UCAS Apply? The main factors to consider are: course content; predicted grades; the reputation of the university/college; the location of the university/college; finance.

Course content
- Many degrees will be very similar from one university to another, *either* because they have to meet the requirements of professional bodies (for example, law, medicine, psychology, electrical engineering), *or* because past practice has led to degrees in certain fields having similar content (for example, business studies).
- When course content is fairly similar, students might find it worthwhile to look at the methods of assessment each university uses (exams, assessments, modules) as a means of narrowing down the options. Different methods of assessment suit different people.
- On the other hand, some degrees with the same title can vary greatly in content (for example, geography, history, media studies and languages). Students must study the course information in depth to make sure they will be getting what they want.
- Some courses provide great variety through the range of options on offer. Some universities have an in-built system for providing a range of choice, for example through faculties or schools. Students must consider what is best for them.

Predicted grades
- Universities state their entrance requirements for each course in their prospectuses (published in the spring of year 12 for entry in the autumn after year 13). Students need to make sure their predicted grades match the requirements for their chosen course.
- The more popular the degree course, the higher the predicted grades need to be. Take, for example, the cases of medicine and veterinary science, which will normally be looking for A grades. If the student is not predicted to get these grades then the application will probably fail.
- Degree courses in the STEM field, such as chemistry or mechanical engineering, may offer an opportunity to take more risks. For example, if the course requires BBC, and the student is predicted CCC, he or she may still have a chance of being made an offer.

- It is worth pointing out that some universities may also take GCSE grades into consideration and will only make offers to students with a certain number of A or A* grades. AS grades are also likely to have an influence on the offers received.
- Students should be aware that if they do get higher grades than predicted, they will be free to apply again the following year.

Reputation of the university
- Students may want to judge similar courses at different universities according to their teaching quality. The place to look for this information is www.unistats.direct.gov.uk This has ratings for teaching, student satisfaction and graduate destinations from each course.
- Ratings websites such as The Guardian University Guide, www.thecompleteuniversityguide.co.uk and The Sunday Times University Guide contain subject-based tables, but the information is collated differently so the results are not identical.

Location of the university
All kinds of issues come into play here and it really boils down to students' personal preferences. Here are some points for them to think about:
- Would they prefer a greenfield site, redbrick university or city campus?
- Do they want to go away or stay at home?
- If they go away, how far is it from home?
- Is the university large or small? Some have more than 15,000 students, others have 6,000.
- Is it new or old? Some institutions are centuries old, others were built in the 1960s, some are new.
- What are the costs of being a student in a particular city?
- Does the university provide accommodation?
- Is there a good ratio of male students to female students?
- Some universities have several sites and separate franchised colleges, often miles apart. Is the student sure about which site the course is being taught at?

Finance
At the time of writing, the Browne Review has not been enacted. If many of its elements are taken on board by the Government, then the financing of studies may well become an increasingly important issue:
- Will the university charge the £9,000-per-year fee or will it charge the more typical £6,000-per-year fee?
- Is there a private higher-education option that could work out to be cheaper in the long run?
- Is it all worth it? Is there another work-based route that will allow you to achieve your goals?
- Is part-time study an option?

6.2 Scope: an ideas generator

The previous section of this chapter concerned the "focus" element of the FIRST mnemonic. But what about "scope"? How do you ensure that students consider the full range of options available to them?

The ideas generator below is designed to ensure that students are aware of all the possibilities open to them. Ask them, "What's your favourite subject?" Then refer to the table here. It includes 45 different sixth-form subjects and, for each one, lists the full range of university courses that might be worth considering. If one of these ideas sparks an interest, students will need to identify possible university courses. They can do this by visiting www.ucas.com, going to "Course search", then "Subject search" using the keyword that interests them. Most importantly, they *must* check that they will have the appropriate qualifications for the course they want to apply for.

Accountancy	Accountancy; actuarial science; banking; building management; business administration; business studies; commerce; economics; estate management; finance; financial services; forensic computing; health administration; hospitality management; insurance; management sciences; marketing; quantity surveying; retail management.
Applied art and design	Advertising; animation; architecture; art (teaching); art therapy; bookbinding; ceramic design; computer animation; conservation; costume design; creative arts; digital and lens media; display design; fashion design; fashion promotion; fine art; film and video; floral design; furniture design; garden design; glass design; graphic arts; illustration; industrial design; interior design; jewellery; landscape architecture; media studies; model design; photography; print design; product design; sculpture; stage management; textile design; theatre arts; typography. • Some of these courses may require students to do a diploma in foundation studies (art and design) after their A levels. • Some courses may require extra A levels.
Applied science (single, double award or diploma)	Agriculture; audiology; anthropology; beauty therapy; countryside management; dental technology; environmental studies; golf course management; health promotion; horticulture; human communication; ICT; music technology; nursing (adult, child health, community health, learning disability, mental health, midwifery); occupational therapy; paramedic science; psychology; physical education; speech therapy; surveying; radiography. • This list presumes that the student is doing no other maths or science subjects. • Students taking applied science (double award), or a BTEC national in science, should look at the lists in this table for biology, chemistry or physics, depending on which is their favourite science subject.
Art	Advertising; animation; archaeology; architecture; art (teaching); art therapy; bookbinding; ceramic design; computer animation; conservation; costume design; creative arts; digital and lens media; display design; fashion design; fashion promotion; fine art; film and video; floral design; furniture design; garden design; glass design; graphic arts; heritage management; history of architecture; history of art; illustration; industrial design; interior design; jewellery; landscape

	architecture; media studies; model design; photography; print design; product design; sculpture; textile design; theatre arts; typography; valuation (fine arts). • These courses will probably require students to do a diploma in foundation studies (art and design) after their A levels (see *13.4 Why do an art foundation course?*).
Art history	Anthropology; archaeology; art and design; art history; arts management; book binding and restoration; church history; classical civilisations; conservation; costume design; film studies; fine art valuation; French; heritage management; history of architecture; history of modern art; Italian; oriental studies; Russian; Spanish.
Biology	Agriculture; anatomy; animal behaviour; animal science; animal welfare; anthropology; biochemistry; bioinformatics; biology; biology (teaching); biomaterials science; biomedical sciences; biotechnology; botany; brewing and distilling; cosmetic sciences; countryside management; dental hygiene; dental technology; dentistry; dietetics; ecology; environmental health; environmental sciences/studies; equine science; exercise and health; food science; forensic science; genetics; golf course management; health promotion; herbal medicine; horticulture; human biology; human communication; human sciences; immunology; learning disabilities; life sciences; marine biology; medicine; microbiology; midwifery; natural sciences; neuroscience; nursing; nutrition; occupational therapy; ocean science; optometry; orthoptics; osteopathy; paramedic science; pharmacology; pharmacy; physical education teaching; physiology; physiotherapy; podiatry; polymer science; prosthetics and orthotics; psychology; radiography; speech therapy; sports science; veterinary nursing; veterinary science; zoology. • This list is also relevant to students taking applied science (double award) or a BTEC national in science, and whose favourite subject is biology. However, some courses may require extra, relevant science A levels.
Business studies/applied business	Accountancy; advertising; arts management; banking; building management; business administration; business information technology; business law; business studies; commerce; countryside management; e-business; e-commerce; economics; estate management; fashion marketing and merchandising; finance; financial services; health administration; hospitality management; human resources; insurance; land economy; management sciences; marketing; public administration; public relations; quantity surveying; retail management; travel and tourism; management; transport management. • Many of these courses will include economics, accounts and finance, human resources, marketing and IT – whatever the course title.
CACHE	Care management; childhood studies; community care; criminology; deaf studies; disability studies; early years

	education; health promotion; nursing (adult, child health, community health, learning disability, mental health, midwifery); occupational therapy; physiotherapy; psychology; psychosocial studies; radiography; social work; sociology; speech therapy; youth work. • Many primary teaching courses will require an A level in a National Curriculum subject as well (this may not be the case with Early Years teaching). • Some of the health-related courses above may require a science A level.
Chemistry	Agriculture; animal science; biochemistry; biology; biology (teaching); biomaterials science; biomedical sciences; biotechnology; botany; brewing and distilling; chemical engineering; chemistry; cosmetic sciences; dental hygiene; dental technology; dentistry; dietetics; earth sciences; ecology; environmental health; environmental sciences/studies; equine science; exercise and health; food science; forensic science; genetics; geology; golf course management; horticulture; human biology; human sciences; immunology; life sciences; marine biology; materials science; medicine; microbiology; natural sciences; neuroscience; nursing; nutrition; ocean science; optometry; osteopathy; pharmacology; pharmacy; physiology; physiotherapy; podiatry; polymer science; veterinary nursing; veterinary science; zoology. • This list is also relevant to students taking applied science (double award) or a BTEC national in science, and whose favourite subject is chemistry. However, some courses may require extra, relevant science A levels.
Classical civilisations	Ancient history; ancient world studies; anthropology; archaeology; classical civilisations; classical studies; ancient Greek; English literature; history; history of art; Latin; medieval and renaissance studies; philosophy; theatre studies.
Classical Greek	Ancient history; ancient world studies; anthropology; archaeology; classical civilisations; classical studies; ancient Greek; English literature; history; history of art; medieval and renaissance studies; philosophy; theatre studies.
Dance	Alternative theatre; acting; arts management; American theatre arts; choreography; community dance; dance; directing; drama; events management; education; English literature; music theatre; performance arts; physical education; stage management; theatre arts.
Design and technology	Architecture; art therapy; biomedical engineering; bookbinding; ceramic design; computer animation; conservation; costume design; creative arts; dental technology; design and technology (teaching); digital and lens media; display design; engineering (all types); fashion design; fashion promotion; film and video; floral design; furniture design; garden design; glass design; graphic arts; history of architecture; history of art; illustration; industrial design; interior design; jewellery; landscape architecture; media

	studies; model design; photography; print design; product design; stage management; textile design; theatre arts; typography. • Some of these courses may require students to do a diploma in foundation studies (art and design) after their A levels.
Drama and theatre studies	Alternative theatre; acting; arts management; American theatre arts; broadcasting; classical civilisations; dance; directing; drama; events management; education; English literature; music theatre; performance arts; public relations; stage management; theatre design; theatre arts.
Economics	Accountancy; actuarial science; agriculture; banking; building management; business administration; business information technology; business administration; business studies; commerce; development studies; economic and social history; economics; estate management; financial economics; finance; financial services; health administration; hospitality management; human resources; insurance; land economy; management sciences; marketing; mathematical economics; money, banking and finance; public administration; planning; politics; quantity surveying; social policy; sociology; statistics.
Engineering (double award, BTEC national or diploma)	Architecture; building management; building surveying; construction management; dental technology; broadcasting (electronics); building; computer science; cybernetics; earth science; engineering (aeronautical, automotive, biomedical materials, chemical, computer, electrical, electronic, mechanical, music systems technology, software, telecommunications); facilities management; hazards; horology; media technology; motorsports technology; music technology; quantity surveying; safety and health; special effects; stage management. • This list presumes that the student is doing no other maths or science subjects.
Engineering (single award)	Architecture; building management; building surveying; construction management; dental technology; facilities management; hazards; horology; media technology; motorsports technology; music technology; quantity surveying; safety and health; special effects; stage management. • This list presumes that the student is doing no other maths or science subjects.
English	Advertising; American studies; Anglo-Saxon; broadcast journalism; classical civilisations; communication studies; creative writing; cultural studies; drama; English literature; English (teaching); history; history of art; information studies; journalism; languages; linguistics; media studies; philosophy; public relations; publishing; sociolinguistics; theatre studies.
Film studies	American studies; communication studies; cultural studies; creative writing; drama; English literature; European studies; film studies; journalism; media studies; scriptwriting.
French	African languages; Asian languages; east European Languages; European studies; French; French (teaching);

	history; international business studies; international finance; international hospitality management; international management studies; international marketing; international relations; Italian; languages for business; law with French; linguistics; literature; oriental studies; Scandinavian languages; Slavonic languages; tourism management; travel management.
Further maths	Accountancy; actuarial science; astrophysics; banking; building; cognitive science; computer science; economics; engineering (acoustic, aeronautical, automotive, chemical, civil, communications, computer, electrical, electronic, environmental, marine, mechanical, mining, music systems technology, integrated); insurance; investment; management science; mathematics; naval architecture; operational research; philosophy; quantity surveying; robotics and cybernetics; statistics; surveying.
Geography	African studies; agriculture; anthropology; archaeology; countryside management; development studies; earth sciences; ecology; economics; environmental studies; estate management; geographical information systems; geography; geography (teaching); geology; human geography; land economy; landscape architecture; meteorology; oceanography; planning; politics; surveying; town and country planning; transport studies; urban studies.
German	African languages; Asian languages; east European languages; European studies; German; German (teaching); history; international business studies; international finance; international hospitality management; international management studies; international marketing; international relations; languages for business; law with German; linguistics; literature; oriental studies; Scandinavian languages; Slavonic languages; tourism management; travel management.
Government and politics	American studies; development studies; economics; education studies (not teacher training); European Community studies; European studies; government; history; industrial relations; international relations; law; parliamentary studies; peace studies; philosophy; political economy; politics; public administration; social administration; social policy; sociology; war studies.
Health and social care/health, care and Early Years	Beauty therapy; care management; childhood studies; community care; criminology; deaf studies; disability studies; Early Years education; health promotion; nursing (adult, child health, community health, learning disability, mental health, midwifery); occupational therapy; physiotherapy; psychology; psychosocial studies; radiography; social work; speech therapy; youth work. • Many primary teaching courses will require an A level in a national curriculum subject as well (this may not be the case with Early Years teaching). • Some of the health-related courses above may require a science A level.

History	American studies; ancient history; Anglo-Saxon and Norse; archaeology; economic and social history; classical civilisations; east Mediterranean history; European Community studies; European studies; Egyptology; government; history; history (teaching); industrial relations; international relations; Irish studies; Islamic studies; Jewish studies; law; medieval studies; oriental studies; parliamentary studies; peace studies; philosophy; political economy; politics; public administration; social administration; social policy; sociology; war studies.
ICT/IT and computing	Artificial intelligence; bioinformatics; business computing; business information systems; business information technology; business studies; cognitive science; computer studies; computer games design; computer modelling; computer systems engineering; e-commerce; finance information systems; forensic computing; geography; information science; information systems; internet computing; management studies; mathematics; multimedia computing; networks; robotics.
Italian	African languages; Asian languages; east European languages; European studies; Italian; history; international business studies; international finance; international hospitality management; international management studies; international marketing; international relations; languages for business; law with Italian; linguistics; literature; oriental studies; Scandinavian languages; Slavonic languages; tourism management; travel management. • Many degrees involving Italian ask for *any* foreign language A level.
Latin	Ancient history; ancient world studies; anthropology; archaeology; classical civilisations; classical studies; Latin; English literature; history; history of art; medieval and renaissance studies; philosophy; theatre studies.
Law	Business law; commercial law; criminology; estate management; European Parliamentary studies; European law; government; history; international relations; land economy; law; philosophy; police studies; public administration; social policy.
Leisure studies	Adventure tourism; air travel management; amenity management; arts management; coaching; culinary arts management; events management; fitness; football studies; hospitality management; leisure management; music management; physical education; public relations; outdoor pursuits; sports marketing; sports journalism; sports studies; sports science; tennis coaching; tourism management; travel management; travel journalism; travel operations.
Mathematics	Accountancy; actuarial science; astrophysics; banking; building; cognitive science; computer science; economics; engineering (acoustic, aeronautical, automotive, chemical, civil, communications, computer, electrical, electronic, environmental, marine, mechanical, mining, music systems

	technology, integrated); insurance; investment; management science, mathematics; mathematics (teaching); naval architecture; operational research; philosophy; quantity surveying; robotics and cybernetics; statistics; surveying.
Media/media studies	Advertising; arts management; broadcasting; communication studies; cultural studies; fashion promotion; film studies; information studies; interactive media; journalism; marketing; marketing communications; media studies; media writing; public relations; publishing; scriptwriting; sports marketing; sociology; television and video.
Music	Acoustics and music; acting; actor musician; band musicianship; commercial music; creative music technology; digital music; electronic music; jazz studies; music; music composition; music informatics; music industry management; music production; music (teaching); musical theatre; performing arts; stage management; world music.
Music technology/popular music	Acoustics and music; band musicianship; commercial music; creative music technology; digital music; electronic music; music; music composition; music informatics; music industry management; music production; music (tuition); stage management.
Performing arts	Alternative theatre; acting; actor musician; arts management; American theatre arts; band musicianship; broadcasting; choreography; commercial music; community dance; creative music technology; dance; directing; drama; events management; education; music theatre; performance arts; stage management; theatre design; theatre arts.
Philosophy	Classical civilisations; classics; cognitive science; economics; education studies (not teaching); government; history; law; mathematics; peace studies; philosophy; philosophy of science; politics; psychology; religious studies; theology.
Photography	Broadcasting; digital and lens media; documentary photography; fashion photography; film and video studies; history of art; imaging; interactive media; photography; photojournalism; radiography; television studies.
Physical education	Adventure management; adventure tourism; coaching; dance; equine studies; exercise and health; football studies; golf studies; health education; leisure management; nursing; occupational health and safety; occupational therapy; outdoor activities; physical education; physical education (teaching); physiology; physiotherapy; psychology; sport and exercise science; sports equipment; sports management; tennis coaching.
Physics	Acoustics; architecture; astronomy; astrophysics; broadcasting (electronics); building; computer science; cybernetics; earth science; engineering (aeronautical, automotive, biomedical materials, chemical, computer, electrical, electronic, mechanical, music systems technology; software, telecommunications); geology; laser systems; materials science; mechatronics; metallurgy; meteorology;

	microelectronics; naval architecture; oceanography; optometry; physics; physics (teaching); pilot studies; planetary science; robotics; radiography. • This list is also relevant to students taking applied science (double award) or a BTEC national in science, and whose favourite subject is physics. However, some courses may require extra, relevant science A levels.
Psychology	Advertising; animal behaviour; anthropology; artificial intelligence; behavioural science; business studies; childhood studies; cognitive science; community studies; counselling; criminal justice; criminology; education; gender studies; health studies; human sciences; human resources management; management sciences; marketing; medicine; mental health nursing; natural sciences; occupational therapy; psychology; psychosocial studies; public relations; robotics; social care; social work; sociology; speech therapy; women's studies.
Religious studies	Ancient history; Anglo-Saxon and Norse; anthropology; archaeology; biblical studies; church history; classical civilisations; comparative religions; cultural studies; divinity; education studies; history; history of religion; Islamic studies; Jewish studies; philosophy; religious studies; religious studies (teaching); sociology; social anthropology; social policy; theology.
Sociology	Advertising; anthropology; architecture; behavioural studies; business studies; communication studies; consumer studies; criminology; development studies; economic and social history; economics; geography; government; history; human resources management; industrial relations; management; marketing; media studies; philosophy; police studies; politics; psychology; public administration; public relations; social administration; social policy; social work; sociology; town and country planning; urban studies; women's studies.
Spanish	African languages; Asian languages; east European languages; European studies; Hispanic studies; history; international business studies; international finance; international hospitality management; international management studies; international marketing; international relations; languages for business; Latin American studies; law with Spanish; linguistics; literature; oriental studies; Scandinavian languages; Slavonic languages; Spanish; Spanish with TESOL; tourism management; travel management.
Travel and tourism/ travel and hospitality	Adventure tourism; air travel management; amenity management; arts management; business studies; culinary arts management; events management; hospitality management; human resources management; leisure management; management; marketing; public relations; tourism management; travel management; travel journalism; travel operations.

6.3 Information, realism and tactics

So by now, we hope, your student interviewee will have settled on a possible university subject. At this stage, you need to move on to the other three elements of the FIRST mnemonic. In fact, much of the rest of this book – all of *Part Three: Essential information about applying for university* as well as *Appendix A* – is about information, realism and tactics!

Information
Is the student well informed about:
- the different types of courses available within his or her chosen subject?
- the kind of jobs this subject might lead to?
- the issues raised in the "focus" and "scope" sections of this book?
- the costs of their university education?

Realism
Is the student:
- already studying the necessary subjects at AS level?
- going to get high enough grades?
- doing (or has he/she done) relevant work experience?
- aware of where their course will leave them in the graduate employment marketplace?

Tactics
Does the student need to:
- find out more about his or her chosen subject through wider reading?
- research courses and job prospects by visiting websites associated with this career area/profession?
- think about what to put in a personal statement that will impress admissions tutors for the chosen subject?
- prepare for interview by being knowledgeable about the chosen subject and course?
- look for work experience or a part-time job relevant to the chosen subject?

Relevant information, including useful websites, is listed on a subject-by-subject basis in *Appendix A: An A-Z of university subjects with essential information for students*. Simply look up the student's chosen subject to make sure all the ground has been covered.

6.4 Which AS level to drop at the end of year 12

This is a tactic that the student has to get right because it has a bearing on their higher-education options. They must think carefully about it. Moreover, there are a number of misconceptions about what is the best thing to do. Here are a few pointers that might help students reach a decision.

Grades at AS level
- If a student's AS-level results are AAAE, then it is fairly obvious which one of their subjects they should drop. For most people, of course, things will be less clear-cut than this. Nevertheless, AS results can be a clear indicator as to what to do.

Career or university entrance requirements
- Students who have a firm idea about the career or university course they want to apply for must make sure they are taking the appropriate AS or A2 levels. For example, some medicine degrees require chemistry at A2 level, while others will accept an AS level in chemistry. Some engineering degrees will consider students with an AS in maths, while others will only look at those with maths at A2.
- It is therefore vital that students look in detail at the university prospectuses when they come out in the spring/summer of year 12. For a general guide, they can look up their subject in *Appendix A*.

"Traditional" or "core" A levels
- A student whose AS levels are, for instance, maths, physics, French and psychology, may be pressurised to drop what seems to be the least "traditional" A level – in this case psychology. But this may *not* be good advice.
- The most important thing, in fact, is to choose the three subjects in which the student can achieve the highest grades. This is because when university courses are assessed, one of the many things taken into consideration is the A-level *results* of students when they join the course, not what A-level *subjects* they have. Therefore most universities would rather take, for instance, someone with a B in psychology than someone with a D in English.

Enjoyment of subjects
- Surely one of the most important reasons for carrying on with a subject is that you enjoy it. Students should consider, however, whether they will enjoy it so much when it becomes more difficult at A2 level.

Teachers' advice
- Teachers will have seen how students have coped with their AS levels for a year and will therefore be able to offer advice about whether it is worth progressing to the A2.

Students taking three AS levels
- Some students may be taking three AS levels only, having dropped one already. There are a number of possible solutions. They could start a new AS (if available) in year 13; they could do two A2 levels and a new AS; they could continue to A2 with the three subjects they did at AS.
- Students in this situation should ask themselves the following questions. How can I achieve maximum results for myself? If I know what I want to do, what do I need to get in? Can I get in with three A2s and no stand-alone AS? Can I get in with two A2s and two stand-alone AS levels? Above all, they must do the research!

6.5 Understanding university entrance requirements

For students applying for a course, the big issue is: "What do I need to get in?" Unfortunately, they might well get three different answers.

- **Some universities make offers based on A-level grades** This is the old-fashioned method. To take an example, a student applying to study geography might be required by the university to get BBC at A2 level and a C at AS level or BBC at A2 somewhere else.
- **Some universities make offers based on the UCAS Tariff** To take the same example, a student applying to study geography might be asked by the university for a tariff of 320 (this is the equivalent of BBC at A2 and a C at AS). According to this method, numerical values are given to the different qualifications taken in the sixth form (that is, AS levels, A2 levels, EPQ-extended project qualification etc.). The higher the grades, the higher the points. The totals are added up and this is the tariff. A table of the tariff points can be found on the UCAS website: www.ucas.com
- **Some universities make offers based on the UCAS Tariff, but students have to achieve certain grades and/or certain subjects within this**

Tactically, when the student makes their five choices they need to think about what may constitute an offer, and they may find it easier for whatever reason to apply for some courses which are likely to make offers based on the UCAS Tariff because these are more achievable.

7. Strategies and useful lines of questioning

Any number of different scenarios may arise when a student walks into the interview room, but HE advisers should have well-defined strategies for dealing with:
* students who have no idea what they want to study at university;
* students who have two or three ideas;
* students who have a definite idea.

They must also ensure that they know how to deal with students from across the ability range, from AAA candidates to EE candidates. These grades presume that you are working with school-age students. You may be working with older clients such as adult career changers who only have work experience. You will still need some strategies.

7.1 Questions for a student who has no ideas

This situation calls for some exploratory questioning. The examples below may prompt some interesting discussions.

* ***How do you see your life developing in the next ten years?*** This sort of very general question can establish, if nothing else, whether the student really wants to go to university or not. The student may have thought about a gap year or working before going to university (which would then beg the question, "What sort of work?") In my experience, this question often causes the student to become reflective and to come up with interesting ideas.

* ***If you are not sure what you want to do, do you know what you*** **don't** ***want to do?*** A colleague of mine once likened the university choice process to the work of a sculptor: "When you get rid of the bits that you don't want, you get left with the bits that you do want!" It is enormously helpful for students to be clear about what they *don't* want to do, as this leaves us with something much more manageable.

* ***If you are not clear about your university ideas, what about career ideas?*** Sometimes this works. For example, Andrea decides her career aim is to get onto a training scheme in fashion retail management. Recruiters in this field, you tell her, are looking for graduates from a wide range of disciplines, plus retail work experience. So Andrea decides to do a degree related to the A level she enjoys most, which is geography. You tell her that it is possible to do a degree in fashion management, but she says she would like to do geography out of pure interest.

* ***Which of your current studies do you enjoy the most? Which are you best at?*** In my experience, most students who say they want to go to university but have no idea what they want to study, end up basing their choice on the A level they enjoy the most or the one they are best at. Generally, this decision has the soundest evidence to support it. If a student has no career ideas or strong interests in other things, there may be nothing else to go on. In this case, it would definitely be worth looking at the ideas generator in section 6.2 above.

* ***Do you have any reading interests/hobbies/activities that occupy you outside of your studies?*** This question may lead to some interesting answers. However, I always ask myself: "Is there enough evidence in the answer to make me feel that this interest could be the basis of *three years* of study?" It is also important to explore whether the student's interest matches the content of the degree. For example, we may decide in the interview to consider sports studies because the

student is an excellent sportsperson, but is he or she also interested in physiology, psychology and the business of sport?

- ***What do members of your family do?*** Opinions vary, but there is general consensus that genes do influence intelligence in some way. We have to be careful here. I would never come to any conclusions based on this question alone and in reality I hardly ever ask it. When I do, it is usually because a lot of evidence seems to be pointing in a certain direction but for some reason the student doesn't want to follow that path.

- ***Have you had an idea that you have then rejected?*** I ask this question quite a lot. This is because students sometimes reject an idea through flawed reasoning ("My brother couldn't get onto this degree course, therefore I won't"), or a lack of information (they didn't know that they could do a degree in forensic computing), or misinformation (they had been told by someone in their peer group that they needed economics A level to do a management studies degree).

- ***What work experience have you had? Do you have a part-time job?*** This could lead to explorations of degree ideas. The big issue here is whether students found out enough about the career to base their choice of degree on it. Also, does the area of work correspond with their interests and aptitudes? Can it sustain their interest for three years at least?

As well as the questions above, a useful strategy for students with no ideas is to suggest they take a psychometric test or interest test, the results of which may provide the necessary evidence for making a degree choice. Some to consider are:
- the Morrisby Profile (www.morrisby.com);
- the Stamford Test and Centigrade (www.ucas.com);
- UKCourseFinder (www.ukcoursefinder.co.uk);

There is a range of products that try to help students with their HE choices. Most are available from:
Prospects Education Resources (www.prospectseducationresources.co.uk)

7.2 Questions and strategies when a student has two or more ideas

The strategy here is to weigh up all the evidence, and *perhaps* look at joint courses. Most of the discussion will be based around two initial questions:
- What are the student's ideas?
- Why is the student considering these subjects?
Once you have established these points, the following issues should be taken into account.

- **How many ways forward?**
It is important to give the student a very clear picture of *all* the different ways forward, encompassing their ideas for both degrees and careers. For example, the student may be considering law and engineering (two quite contrasting *degree* areas) but is thinking of a *career* in law. If the student takes a law degree, he or she will save the possible expense of doing a GDL (Graduate Diploma in Law). However, doing engineering might make it slightly easier to get into one of the more selective universities (many employers in the law field take into account the university a

candidate went to). Finally you might want to look at future career prospects in the areas of engineering and law. These issues have to be considered on top of the actual degree content the student would prefer.

- **Sometimes courses can be similar but have different titles**

The clearest example of this is in the life sciences (degrees based on biology and organic chemistry), where a student might put down five different courses on their UCAS application: biochemistry; biomedical sciences; biomolecular sciences; medical biochemistry; microbiology. Students on these courses would find that their first year and much of the second would be very similar, whatever the course title, and that admissions tutors would be happy with a personal statement that established their interest in biology studied at a molecular level. Business and management is another field with many different course titles but similar course content.

- **Sometimes it is possible to apply for courses that have some differences, but also some similarities**

Admissions tutors only know about the course or courses that the student has applied for at their own university – they do *not* know what courses the student has applied for at other universities. The only clue admissions tutors have, therefore, is the personal statement. So students could apply for different but similar courses, such as history and politics, and concentrate in their personal statements on the areas these subjects share, such as political history and ideology. Another example would be theology and philosophy, which can both cover ethics. Another would be English and American studies, which can both cover modern literature.

Applicants for medicine, dentistry and veterinary science are limited to four choices in their particular field. Admissions tutors for the other course listed on UCAS Apply are often happy for their course not to be mentioned at all on the personal statement (unless it is another highly selective course). Sometimes the other course will contact the student and request an extra personal statement that is sent direct to admissions staff for that course.

- **What to do when the ideas are both related to A-level subjects**

It is essential to find out which subject the student is stronger at, and which subject he or she enjoys more. Students often pick up received wisdoms about a particular subject that may not be accurate. For example, a student who prefers theology to English, and wants to become a journalist, may think that she needs an English degree to get into journalism – this is *not* the case.

It is also important to explore issues such as:

o entry requirements (students may be able to get the grades for one subject, such as theology, but not another, such as English);

o course content, which may differ from A level (for example, English A level might concentrate on modern texts while an English degree course might look at literature from Anglo-Saxon times onwards).

- **What to do when one idea is based on an A level and the other on a career idea**

Students must explore their career ideas thoroughly through research and work experience in order to make an informed choice. Most importantly, students must find out whether their career idea requires them to do a specific degree: some do, some don't. For example, a career as a TV researcher does not require a degree in media and communications. On the other hand, a student who wants to become a clinical psychologist should do a degree in psychology accredited by the British Psychological Society.

If a specific degree is required, then the issue is decided. If the chosen career area will consider applicants from a wide range of degree choices, students might need to consider the following issues.

o   Some employers, such as in some areas of investment banking, may show a preference for degrees that offer evidence of numeracy and problem-solving ability.

o   Some employers (such as for graduate fast-track schemes) will consider a wide range of degrees but will only look at students who achieved very high A-level grades. They will then send candidates to an assessment centre to make their final choice.

o   Students should be aware of postgraduate conversion opportunities if they decide to do a degree based on an A-level subject. Some are well known, such as journalism and law; others less so, such as for chartered secretary and occupational therapy.

- **What to do when one idea is based on an A level and the other on a new interest**

At least with the idea based on an A level there is some definite evidence that the student knows what is involved. It is difficult to be certain that he or she has a clear idea about what the new interest involves. So crucial questions will be: "Why do you want to study this?" and "What does it involve?"

- **What to do when one idea is based on a career idea and the other on a new interest**

Again, the HE adviser has to be sure the student is making informed choices. Why does the student want to do these subjects? What do they involve? How much do these ideas relate to the student's academic strengths? Work experience and wider research will be vital in this situation. And if the student has done a psychometric test such as the Morrisby Profile, the resulting information will be very useful.

- **How do joint degrees work?**

There are two types of degrees that link two specific subject areas:

o   the *equal combination* (for example, mathematics *and* computer science) where approximately half the courses are studied in each subject area;

o   the *major-minor combination* (for example, chemistry *with* management studies) where about two-thirds to three-quarters of the courses are studied in the major department.

Students should also be aware of the Scottish system where, for the first year of your four-year degree, you join a faculty and can take courses in a very wide range of subjects before you specialise in a single subject or joint degree (often different from the course that you originally applied for).

7.3 Questions to ask once the student has decided on a subject

Once a student has settled on a subject or subjects, the HE adviser's questions will tend to be based on five main areas:
- course content;
- entry requirements;
- location and other social issues;
- ratings;
- career prospects.

The first four of these issues are dealt with in detail in *6.1 Focus: how to help students narrow down their options*. The fifth is covered in *15. Graduate employment*. Below is a list of possible questions relating to these five areas that might be useful. Remember that the end goal is that students are happy with their five UCAS choices and are able to justify logically why they have made their decisions.

Content of course
- *What does this degree involve?* This question can throw up a frightening lack of research on the part of the student.
- *What does the prospectus say about this course?* Another way of asking the same question. With either of these, you should be able to establish whether students do have a clear idea about what they are committing themselves to for at least three years.
- *What is it about this course that interests you?* Again, we are checking for flaws in their reasoning. Is there a mismatch between what they want to do and what the course actually is?
- *Do you do better in exams or coursework?* Students who prefer coursework should ask the universities about this issue. It may be a shock for them to do a course that is mostly assessed by exam.
- *Does the course stay general or does it allow you to specialise?* Many students are unaware of this issue. For instance, a course such as business studies will probably mean specialising in, say, human resources by the end of it.
- *Do you prefer to learn through lectures and seminars or through more practical experiences?* For example, there is both the traditional approach for medicine and the "problem-based learning method" (PBL) of medicine education. Or for someone who is good at maths and physics it might mean comparing a physics degree with an engineering degree. Or for someone who is interested in working in TV, it might mean the difference between a more academic media and communications degree or a more practical foundation degree in broadcast operations and production.

Entry requirements
- *Do you know what grades you are going to be predicted?* We need to check that predictions match entry requirements. The more popular/selective the course is, the less likely it is that admissions tutors will consider applicants who have not been predicted the required grades. Therefore someone predicted BBC, applying for a popular history course requiring AAB, is likely to be rejected. However,

supply and demand can have an effect – sciences, engineering and languages may be more flexible.

- ***What is a best-case/worst-case scenario in terms of your grades?*** This question can indicate the range of courses that ought to be considered. The student may have a very positive or very negative outlook on life, so it is important to see the bigger picture. It is possible that the student will end up looking at a spread of courses, reflecting the best-case to the worst-case scenarios (for example BBB to CCD).
- ***What points did you get at AS level?*** (see *18.3 How students can maximise their A-level grades*) Students may be considering courses for which they cannot realistically achieve the grades. They might be able to resit an AS unit, but they could be relying on getting very high scores at the harder A2 level, which may be beyond them.

Location and other social issues

- ***Do you want to stay at home or leave home?*** It is important to establish this with the student. Some students may, in fact, decide to include some local choices and some away from home. Some students may be wanting to stay at home for unclear financial reasons, which ought to be explored. Others may be unaware that, if they stay at home, their experience of student life may be limited. Will they regret this in later life? Whatever students want to do, it is good to know what geographical areas they are considering, as this will help you and them to define the search.
- ***Do you think you will need to work part time through your course?*** If so, students need to explore the likelihood of gaining work in the locations they are considering. University visits and talking to current students are often the best ways of finding out. This question can often bring up other financial worries that the student may have, which can then be explored further.
- ***What do you want from the university you go to?*** A general question such as this can identify issues such as religious beliefs or sporting ability, which may affect choice.
- ***Do you want a campus (greenfield) or city (redbrick) type university?*** There *are* differences. Manchester University is a different type of environment from Royal Holloway. The University of Winchester is a different type of environment from London Metropolitan University. Students do need to think about where they will be happy for at least three years. They can confirm their choices through open-day visits before they decide on their first and insurance choices.

Ratings

- ***Do you know the best university for the course you are interested in?*** A very difficult question to answer, because there is no consensus on what we mean by best. An obvious next step is to look at ratings websites such as The Complete University Guide, The Sunday Times University Guide or The Guardian University Guide. An applicant could also look at the Unistats website (though this site normally needs an HE adviser to interpret its meaning). Be aware that if you are looking at best for teaching and best for graduate employment, you could get two very different answers. It will be very interesting to see the effect of the new student finance changes on how courses are viewed. I'm speculating here, but will measures of graduate career destinations become much more important?
- ***Do you know the best course you can get into with the grades you are likely to get?*** Students may identify the best courses according to the tables, but they may

be unable to get the grades required to get in. It is important to have a realistic picture of students' A-level predictions to ensure they are considering appropriate courses. (Incidentally, it is probably unnecessary to ask this question in such brutal terms. However, it still needs to be asked, perhaps in a more subtle form!)

Career prospects

- ***Do you know what graduates with this degree go on to do?*** This question can open up many issues. For subjects that do not lead to a specific career (arts and humanities in particular), I try to impress on students that they will have to take responsibility themselves for deciding on a career, and that they will need to do this *before* they graduate. The HE adviser's knowledge of graduate employment trends is very important here. For example, if a student wants to get a training contract with a large firm of chartered accountants, and is looking to get accepted for an accountancy degree with CCD at a modern university, he or she needs to know that this firm is probably looking for graduates with at least AAB at A level and will not mind what the degree subject is. See also *15. Graduate employment*.

8. An example of an interview

Finally, to put all of this into perspective, here is a model of an individual guidance interview done at the start of year 13.

Jo has done AS levels in English literature, history, sociology and economics. She is currently taking English, history and sociology at A2. Her predicted grades are BBC or BCC. As yet, Jo has not given any thought to what she wants to do – either at university or as a career.

The contract

Jo and her HE adviser begin by discussing her current situation: how she is getting on with her A levels, her interests and her work experience. They go on to discuss her future plans, and it becomes clear that Jo has no idea about her long-term future but that, in the short term, she likes the idea of going to university. They agree that her academic abilities point towards her going on to higher education, and that she should try to decide on a subject based on:

- her A levels;
- a career idea; or
- a new idea that interests her.

They also agree to look at the results of a Kudos Online interest guide test she has recently taken, to see if it throws up any ideas.

The process

Jo knows there is no new subject that interests her and in any case she doesn't want to take such a risk; she feels that as she does not read beyond her syllabus it is better to stick with what she knows. She has done some work experience in a nursery and knows that she does *not* want to work with small children. She has a Saturday job in a shoe shop and thinks she might like to go into retail management, but she is really not sure as yet. However, she very much enjoys history A level and she decides she might like to continue her history studies at university. This is *focus*.

Jo and her HE adviser now need to ask the following questions (covering *realism, scope* and *information*):

- Why?
- Does her academic record so far show enough evidence of her aptitude for history?
- How will a history degree course be different from (or the same as) the A level?
- Is it a popular subject that is difficult to get into?
- What career options would be available to her with a degree in history?
- How would employers view the sort of university she is likely to get into with her A-level grades?
- Are there any similar subjects (archaeology, American studies?) she should consider?
- Does she want to do joint honours with another subject?

Jo looks up history in *Appendix A* of this book and finds a number of career areas that interest her that she has never thought of before, such as human resources and public relations. She is becoming clearer that she wants to study history. She now needs to think about the following (more *focus*, more *information*):

- How do her predicted grades match the entry requirements for history courses at different universities?
- How does the course content vary from one university to another? Are there any courses that particularly appeal to her?
- Does the history course that interests her get good ratings and what do these ratings really mean?
- Does she want to go away to university or stay at home? Are there any other personal or social issues to take into account?

Summary
- Jo has come to a definite conclusion that she would like to study history.
- She has a realistic idea about which universities she will get into.
- She has thought about wider issues such as the location of the university and the career implications of her degree choice.

Written action points
- To read carefully the prospectuses of the courses she is thinking about applying for, checking that the course content interests her and the entry requirements are achievable.
- To research the ratings of her possible choices, through websites such as The Guardian University Guide.
- To research the employment opportunities for history graduates from the sort of university she is likely to get into with her grades.
- To do some wider reading on history to help with her personal statement.

9. The Advisers' Certificate: Applying to Higher Education

By Dr. Michelle Stewart, Senior Lecturer in Careers Education and Guidance, London South Bank University
stewarm3@lsbu.ac.uk

Introduction

The Advisers' Certificate: Applying to Higher Education is an accredited gold-standard professional development course for those who advise young people and adults about applying to Higher Education (HE) and the possible outcomes of those decisions. This article reflects on why and how it was developed at London South Bank University (LSBU) and how it is regarded by those who have undertaken it.

Why it was developed

Following the publication of the Government's White Papers on skills (HMSO 2005, TSO 2006), the Higher Education Funding Council for England (HEFCE) re-emphasised the vital role HE has in making the country more competitive by promoting the knowledge-based aspects of our economy and, through improving skill levels, driving up productivity and growth. It also developed a workforce-development strategy to support the sector to work more effectively with employers to maximise the benefits for learners, employers, employees, the economy and society. As part of this strategy, in 2007 London South Bank University Employer Engagement Unit (EEU) received three years' funding to investigate the design and delivery of HE courses in partnership with employers, and to increase the number of learners in the workplace supported by their employers.

As the UK responds to a rapidly evolving society and globally competitive economy and working lives lengthen, workers are having to re-skill. For people to consider improving their skills, *"They need access to good quality, impartial information on local learning opportunities and their relevance in the labour market"* (Leitch 2006, p.106).

Nevertheless, *Fair access to the professions* (2009) was highly critical of the advice that HE applicants receive. Many note how difficult it has been to make informed choices. Issues such as entry requirements, course and university choice, graduate employment opportunities and student finance can be overwhelming, especially alongside programmes of study, pressures of work, managing a family or contemplating a career change.

Thousands of people of all ages apply to HE every year to improve their skills and career prospects. However, research by the Higher Education Statistics Agency (2011) reveals that as many as one in eleven (more than 28,500 a year) students who start university leave without completing their studies, with many blaming schools for encouraging them to take inappropriate degrees. The overall cost of a degree to the student was calculated as £34,740 in 2007 (Nat West Student Money Matters). Access to good-quality impartial advice about HE has become even more critical following the Government's decision to allow universities to charge up to £9,000 per year tuition fees from 2012, raising the cap from the 2011/2012 level of £3,375. It is important that students choose the degree that is right for them and have a realistic idea of what career paths may be open to them afterwards. It is not only encouraging young people to remain in education and training that is important. Information and advice about the labour market and employment opportunities are equally essential.

This advice about HE can make a vital difference. It can help to reduce university drop-out rates and enable a successful transition from learning to meaningful employment, offering economic benefit to both the nation and the student. However, the former Department for Children, Schools and Families advised that:

> *"High-quality IAG [information, advice and guidance] depends to a considerable degree on the skill and commitment of the professionals who offer it on the front line. It is therefore important that those who specialise in this area of work receive training, support and career development to do the best possible job"* (Quality, Choice and Aspiration, DCSF, 2009a, p.45).

Being one of only nine universities in England offering careers guidance training accredited by the Institute of Career Guidance, clearly a question was being asked of the EEU. What training and career development could the Institute offer, drawing on its expertise in careers education and guidance, to those who specialise in this area of work? Working in collaboration with employers, practitioners and academics, the EEU responded by investing in the development of a short accredited professional development course called The Advisers' Certificate: Applying to Higher Education.

How it was developed
During 2008, the EEU's careers and workforce development adviser held meetings with key employers in the career guidance sector, career guidance practitioners and career guidance academics in and around London, to ensure that the course met the needs of the workforce in terms of structure, content and affordability. Feedback was also provided by a focus group of guidance practitioners providing HE advice in schools and colleges in London and the South East. Following consultation, the course was developed using the expertise of the Postgraduate Diploma in Career Guidance team at LSBU, Sue Holden (former Head of Professional Development at the Institute of Career Guidance) and Andy Gardner (practising HE adviser and author of *The Higher Education Advisers' Handbook: practical steps for one-to-one guidance*).

The findings of research into the qualifications, skills and roles of careers coordinators undertaken by the National Foundation for Educational Research and the National Institute for Careers Education and Counselling on behalf of the former DCSF (McCrone *et al* 2009) were taken into account. In particular, with the support of the EEU's education learning technologist, e-learning materials and a dedicated virtual learning environment using Blackboard were developed. Research undertaken on behalf of Lifelong Learning UK by Trends Business Research to develop a new qualification strategy for career information, advice and guidance was also considered, especially, the need to provide rigorous underpinning knowledge and application of theory within the learning programme (Johnson 2009). In addition, a bid for funding to cover the costs of a course manual was approved by South East London Lifelong Learning Network.

Having established a successful business case for introducing a new course of study, the programme of learning was submitted to the university's Quality and Standards Committee for validation. Early in 2009, the university accredited the Advisers' Certificate: Applying to Higher Education, a unique course designed for professionals called upon to offer information, advice and guidance about the steps that lead to HE and the outcomes of those decisions, and to maximise the productivity benefits of training to the employer (Lambert 2003, Leitch 2006).

Aim

The course aim is to broaden professional practice in supporting applicants to HE beyond the UCAS process. It has three key objectives for participants:

- Through the development of guidance interviewing skills to be able to identify what clients/students need and want to know, and to be able to access a wide range of resources relevant to the client group, in order to keep up to date with current practices and current information.
- Through practical tasks, including visits to universities and a job study, to develop information-gathering skills and understanding of what the requirements of universities and courses within them might be, as well as an understanding of the graduate labour market.
- Through reflective practice to be able to identify areas of individual and organisational practice that can be further developed.

Crucially, the course aims to empower and enable professionals in the front line to provide impartial, high-quality information, advice and guidance for all wishing to enter HE and succeed in the modern labour market.

Level

The level of study was determined in line with the Qualifications and Credit Framework Level 7 indicators (QCF 2008) and underpins the need for front-line professionals to:

- critically analyse, interpret and evaluate complex information;
- address problematic situations that involve many interacting factors;
- take responsibility for planning and developing a course of action that underpins change or development;
- exercise broad autonomy and judgement.

The course is worth 15 credits.

Typical participants are already qualified to at least the equivalent of the Qualifications and Curriculum Framework level 4/5 (equivalent to 1st/2nd year undergraduate). However, applications have also been welcomed from those without this level of qualification who possess the life/work skills that make them suitable to study at this level. All participants must have regular client/student contact.

Structure

The course is delivered over 13 weeks excluding holidays through a mix of workshops, on-line material available on Blackboard and self-directed learning. This structure facilitates networking and combines work-based training, face-to-face delivery, and assessments based on real-life scenarios (McCrone *et al* 2009). On average, participants undertake ten learning hours a week and are invited to attend three one-day learning events which take the form of lectures and workshops. Each participant is allocated an academic supervisor to provide support and advice by e-mail and telephone.

Content and learning outcomes

The course content has been broken down into four main sections:

1. An introduction to the course and factors around going to university.
2. Conducting HE Interviews: guiding principles and review of the interview structure.
3. Labour Market Information: what graduates do, graduate recruitment and the graduate labour market.
4. Careers Education: advising on HE in schools and colleges.

The learning includes rigorous underpinning knowledge and application of theory to practice (Johnson 2009) and promotes the six "principles" of good-quality impartial careers education (DCFS 2009b) – that it:

- empowers young people to plan and manage their own futures;
- responds to the needs of each learner;
- provides comprehensive information and advice;
- raises aspirations;
- actively promotes equality of opportunity and challenges stereotypes; and
- helps young people to progress.

It increases the knowledge and understanding of a variety of sources of information, HE Institutions and their requirements, the UCAS process and specialist course entry requirements, student finance and the graduate labour market.

It enables professionals to review their skills as guidance interviewers using theories and models of practice, identifying strengths and areas for further development. It also provides them with an opportunity to reflect on the learning and its impact on practice.

The course improves the ability to carry out effective HE advice and guidance interviews, access and explain the UCAS process, write reports on visits to universities and specific courses, write effective UCAS references and carry out a graduate job study.

Assessment

The final assessment of the course consists of three pieces of work:

- A case study based on an actual or typical client/student, with accompanying materials: university visit reports, graduate job study, UCAS application form and reference, and research references.
- A recording of a client/student interview and a written reflection on the process, content and skills involved with reference to theories and models of practice and reflection on the participant's own skill development.
- A written analysis and reflection on how the learning from this unit can be taken forward in the participant's own context.

Once this structure for the course had been established, the next stage was to run a pilot to evaluate it further and assess the viability of a new employer-co-funding model. Importantly, the use of additional student numbers allocated by HEFCE to the

EEU meant that a pilot could be sanctioned without drawing on the funding of student places.

How it has been regarded
The course was promoted in a variety of ways including the websites of career professional bodies, company e-mails and electronic newsletters, attracting sufficient response to run two pilots in 2009: one in the spring and another in the autumn. Both included three non-consecutive one-day learning events held at LSBU. In addition a further pilot took place during the summer in partnership with Connexions Cumbria. This involved running the three one-day learning events off-site on consecutive days. The course was modified slightly in response to feedback during the pilot phase. In particular the number of recorded interviews was reduced from four to three and a planning guide was created to assist participants in organising their learning activities. Also, examples of good practice and sample assignments were placed on Blackboard to demonstrate the standard that participants should be working towards.

Recognising that the course complemented the Specialist Schools and Academies Trust (SSAT) Higher Education Related Learning programme, it was agreed that LSBU and SSAT would run some further off-site courses in partnership. Building on SSAT's links with schools and colleges across England, the course has subsequently been run with workshops in Manchester, Wolverhampton, Newcastle, Blackburn and Cambridge. In addition to running a third course at LSBU during the spring of 2010, the course has also been run with learning events in north London, Somerset, Canterbury and Worcester, all in direct response to requests from a sixth-form consortium, a careers company and two Aimhigher Partnerships.

By the end of 2009 more than 100 participants had successfully undertaken the course and gained accreditation, and more than 140 were on target to complete the course by September 2011. All are evidence of the value and robustness of the course content and the suitability of its flexible structure in meeting the needs of learners in the workplace.

> *"The best thing about the course was the fact that it was delivered in only three days – and that required me to only take a few days off work"* (Aimhigher coordinator).

Participants come from a range of backgrounds and include teachers and personal tutors in schools and colleges, heads of sixth forms, university admissions staff, careers advisers and independent careers consultants, Connexions personal advisers, Aimhigher advisers, learning mentors and career leaders/coordinators in schools. Some have funded themselves, others have been part funded. The majority have been sponsored by their employers who have recognised the worth of having HE specialists as part of the guidance services they offer. This is especially valuable in terms of strengthening the organisation's business case in order to secure contracts to provide careers information, advice and guidance in education.

Feedback from participants has been extremely positive, with the majority experiencing an improvement in their understanding of the higher education adviser's role, entry qualifications and access routes into HE, including the UCAS application process and student finances. For example:

> *"Although I initially resented what I felt was the scrappy nature of the case study assignment, it has really been useful. I have realised how much research is needed for some courses, particularly if students are progressing with non-traditional qualifications"* (careers adviser).

> *"The course has shown me the importance of university visits. The visits have enabled me to speak to/see presentations from admissions tutors talking about their subject, what they are looking for in students and their entry requirements. This has improved my confidence that information that I am giving students is up to date"* (Connexions personal adviser).

Importantly, evidence demonstrates that the confidence of participants in conducting a guidance interview on progression to higher education increases. This finding is supported by statements such as:

> *"Feedback on my interviews has been useful as I had picked up some bad habits over the years that I was not aware of"* (careers adviser).

> *"I feel much more confident in conducting careers interviews"* (teacher).

The on-going appraisal of the three one-day learning events has found them to be consistently "good" to "outstanding" or "excellent". Phrases such as "inspirational", "thought provoking", "interesting" and "informative" have repeatedly been used to describe the standard the programme and the content delivered. For example:

> *"The presentations and content were extremely good. I found the team to be both professional and extremely supportive"* (careers consultant).

The course manual has also been regarded as well put together and extremely useful:

> *"The course manual has become my bible – it travels around with me and I add bits and pieces to it all the time"* (Connexions personal adviser).

The events provide opportunity to network, discuss post-16 issues and share good practice with each other. This has been valued by the participants:

> *"Really good to be able to discuss and query with other professionals"* (careers consultant).

> *"Among the best things about the unit was networking"* (school senior manager).

However, the use of a virtual learning environment (Blackboard) for assessment and feedback and to provide access to learning materials has generated a more mixed response. Some have found it easily accessible, citing being able to upload assignments and recorded interviews as some of the best things about the course, while others struggled and found navigating the system quite difficult:

> *"Blackboard was good when I wanted to access information about the unit. However, it was poor when I wanted to upload my interviews"* (Connexions personal adviser).

Critically, in terms of its aims, the course has caused professionals to reflect more on the outcomes of those deciding to enter HE:

> *"The course has given me a better understanding of the need to consider and plan for post-degree options and clarified the fact that HE goals are longer term – to complete a university course well rather than just getting in"* (careers adviser).

Undertaking the course has also been shown to have brought added personal benefit and better HE guidance in schools and colleges:

> *"Since completing the course I have applied and been appointed HE specialist. Studying Applying to HE has definitely helped make this possible"* (Connexions personal adviser).

> *"It was only once I had begun the course that I realised how lacking in structure my efforts had been before. This course has provided me with greater levels of confidence and has helped my school in its strategic plans to develop this often-neglected area"* (head of sixth form).

> *"I feel that the course has given me the confidence to challenge things within my organisation in terms of the lack of attention we give to HE and the lack of resources that we have. The course has put me in the position of being able to make recommendations as to how things can be improved and to implement these changes"* (a Connexions adviser).

Conclusion

Overall, the success of the course has justified the investment of HEFCE employer engagement funding and the commitment of the university to provide flexible and responsive learning provision, and has demonstrated how an HEI can work more effectively with employers to support them in up-skilling their workforce. Moreover, by offering training, support and career development to IAG professionals on the front line, it has increased access to good-quality information and expert advice about the steps that lead to HE and the outcomes of those decisions, which will maximise the benefits for learners, employers, employees and the economy and society. What better way to conclude than with the words of an IAG professional?

> *"Studying on the course has had a significant impact on my professional development in relation to HE work. It has significantly increased my confidence in this area, has provided me with valuable resources and has improved the guidance process in relation to HE. I fully endorse the course and shall recommend the programme to colleagues"*

Building on this success, Applying to Higher Education is now one of five short accredited professional development courses in careers education offered by LSBU and culminating in a new Post-Graduate Certificate. Should you want more information about Applying to Higher Education or any other careers education course, please contact Dr. Michelle Stewart: stewarm3@lsbu.ac.uk or 020 7815 8358.

References:

DCFS (2005) *14-19 Education and Skills* London: HMSO

DCFS (2006) *Further Education: raising skills, improving life chances,* London: TSO (The Stationery Office)

DCFS (2009a) *Quality, Choice and Aspiration,* London: DCFS

DCFS (2009b) *Statutory Guidance: Impartial Careers Education,* London: DCFS

Milburn, A., (2009) *Fair access to the professions,* London: The Panel on Fair Access to the Professions, Cabinet Office

HEFCE (2006) *HEFCE Strategic Plan 2006-11* www.hefce.ac.uk (accessed January 2011)

Higher Education Statistics Agency www.HESA.ac.uk (accessed January 2011)

Johnson, C., (2009) *Developing a new qualification strategy for career information, advice and guidance*, London: Lifelong Learning UK

Lambert, R., (2003) *The Lambert Review of Business-University Collaboration Report: Final Report*, London: Her Majesty's Treasury, HMSO www.lambertreview.org.uk

Leitch, S., (2006) *Prosperity for all in the global economy – world-class skills,* London: TSO (The Stationery Office)

McCrone, T., Marshall, H., Reed, F., Morris, M., Andrews, D., Barnes, A. (2009) *DCFS RR171: Career Coordinators in Schools,* London: DCFS

QCF, (2008*) Regulatory arrangements for the Qualifications and Credit Framework,* London: The Office of the Qualifications and Examinations Regulator

Part Three: Essential information about applying for university

10. Researching universities, their courses and careers

By the spring term of year 12, students should be starting to research their ideas about higher education, and by the end of the summer term they should ideally have a shortlist of courses and institutions that interest them. Research can take a number of forms: the internet, reference books, higher-education fairs and university open days.

There is now so much information available to applicants and their advisers that I think simply giving out lists of websites, books and visits, is no longer appropriate. In fact I think we can apply a model of guidance to our research method, and guess what? That model is FIRST.

When thinking about the resources we could use, four points should be kept in mind:

- The use of information should fit within a guidance framework.
- The use of information should fit relevant timescales.
- When contracting with the student you must agree with them where they are on the decision-making spectrum.
- You or the student cannot use all the resources that are available, so spend time researching the most important for you.

10.1 The decision-making spectrum

For the purposes of making an application through UCAS Apply we have to identify with the student where they are on the decision-making spectrum. One end of the spectrum is someone who has no idea of the course or courses they want to study, no idea of the job they want to do after higher education and no idea of where they might want to go to university. They may well still be unsure if higher education is what they want at all. The other end of the spectrum is someone who has decided on virtually everything. They know what course/courses they want to study, they know where they want to study and they know what job they want to do and which organisation they want to work for.

Most students will be somewhere on this spectrum and of course if you follow the guidance in other parts of this book, you may question some of their decisions and they may move in one direction or the other along the spectrum. For many of us this will be connected to a process, which is using UCAS Apply. So we will be thinking about the decision-making spectrum in terms of using information and resources with the FIRST model to help a student who may have no ideas – and is presented with 50,000 possible course choices at 300 higher-education institutions – focus down to the five choices in UCAS Apply.

It is really important when contracting with the student to know roughly where they are on the spectrum. Do they have any ideas? Do they know what they want to study but have no idea where they want to do it, or do they know what they want to study and where they want to do it? Ascertaining this means you can use the appropriate resources at the relevant time. For example, there is not much point directing people to a website all about what different universities are like if they haven't decided on their course choice. The course they eventually settle on may not be available at the university they are exploring through this website.

If you are involved with a higher-education careers education programme in your institution as well as doing one-to-one guidance, I would recommend you think about the timescale of when you tell your students about various resources. For example, if you are doing a presentation on resources to help with university interviews, doing it in February year 12 may not be appropriate when so many students have not even made their course choice yet. It may well be better to leave this until the end of year 12 or start of year 13, when the issue might be more relevant for a larger number of students.

You or your students cannot use all the information available to them – there are simply too many. Below I explain how I use information resources according to the FIRST model. These are some of the resources I use; you may prefer others and that is absolutely fine! The important thing is that there is a method to using them.

10.2 Applying the FIRST model to information resources

FIRST stands for Focus-Information-Realism-Scope-Tactics. We will use F-R-S-T to help us sift through all the I available.

Focus There are two stages to this part of the process.

Stage 1 – Choosing what you want to study
- **If your choice is based on what you are currently studying/have studied – i.e. A-level subject**
  Suggested resource: University websites.
  You can compare the course content of the subject you want to study (history, for example) with the course content of your history A level.
- **If your course choice is based on a career idea.**
  Suggested resource: www.prospects.ac.uk/ and go to Types of Jobs. This will allow you to explore the job you are interested in, including what it involves, salary and entry.
- **If your course choice is based on something new** (that you haven't studied before and isn't related to a career idea)
  Suggested resource: Get Set for University series from Edinburgh University Press.
  This series is really useful in that it explains in understandable language what it is like to study, for example, philosophy and what all the terminology means.

If after looking at these resources we are still none the wiser, the student may want to go away and do an Interest Guide such as www.ukcoursefinder.co.uk or The Stamford Test/Centigrade which are available through the UCAS website.

Stage 2 – Choosing where you want to study

- **Comparing course content**
  Suggested resource: Degree Course Guides from CRAC.
  Unfortunately, while these are still available, they do not seem to be being revised. Many students are now cutting and pasting course content information from university websites into their own unique document for easy comparison. Some may use UCAS Entry Profiles but the quality of information is variable.
- **Who does the course and what grades do they want?**
  Suggested resource: UCAS Course Search then straight to university online prospectus.
- **Ratings**
  Suggested resource: I tend to use www.thecompleteuniversityguide.co.uk but there are others.
  Ratings tables should always come with a warning, just like school league tables. Advisers should take some time to understand what is behind the league-table position.
- **Will the university really take me with the grades I'm likely to get?**
  Suggested resource: www.unistats.com
  Here you can find out what UCAS Tariff points students on the course you are considering actually have, not what the university says it wants in its prospectus. This information is really useful to know if you are considering applying for a course whose normal conditional offer is above what you are predicted. It can help you work out the odds! Beware, most students find using Unistats very difficult and need assistance.
- **Location**
  Suggested resources: www.push.co.uk and www.whatuni.com
  Deal with the issue of "what is this place like?"
- **Extra Finance**
  Sometimes extra bursaries/scholarships can be available, however these may change after the Browne Review in England.
  Suggested resource: Bursaries section in Course Search www.ucas.com
  In reality I have found very few students have chosen their courses because of the offer of bursaries.

Using Social Media

Students and their advisers now have access to a vast array of information. Many of these resources are traditional in the form of a printed prospectus, a printed league table or a university website, but students and their advisers can also tap into social media to help them in their choices. Examples are:

- www.thestudentroom.co.uk – where *"GCSE and A Level and university students share academic and social knowledge: from study help, to choosing a university, careers and student life."* The main issue for me when someone contributes to this website is: "How do they know what they know?" Some of the content is absolute rubbish, but sometimes there are useful nuggets of information and opinion. My worry is how does the untrained eye sift it all? Also, content such as the Personal Statement Library can clearly cause problems with plagiarism.

- www.yougofurther.co.uk – *"It's the website where you can meet people doing your course, or going to your university or college of choice, before you leave."* Gone are the days of worrying about whether you will make friends when you get to university, you can have them all lined up before you go!

To see what a university looks like, there will now be virtual campus tours on university websites, official films placed on Youtube and unofficial and official films placed on www.whatuni.com.

Clearly social media is here to stay, but is it any good and where does it fit into the guidance process? I think much of it is very useful, but one must never forget that a lot of the content is opinion, and opinions can change if, for example, someone has been accepted or rejected for a course. In helping students to focus ideas I think social media has very little use in the first stage – choosing what you want to study. In my experience it is used and is helpful in the second stage of choosing where you want to study, narrowing down your choices and helping with the transition to university.

Scope There are a range of resources that can help make the student aware of other courses, HEIs and careers they hadn't thought about previously. Many students left to their own devices will consider a very narrow range of courses and universities. Suggested resources:
- www.ukcoursefinder.co.uk is one way to widen ideas. This is a free resource that gets you to fill in a questionnaire and then suggests courses.
- Centigrade and Higher Ideas are useful, although they carry a cost.
- Many university online prospectuses will make suggestions of alternative courses in course information sections.

To widen ideas about universities and higher education institutions to be considered, see the section further down on types of university.

Realism Two questions that constantly come up in the guidance process are:
What sort of job will I get from this degree?
Do my predictions match up with what the course I want to apply for really wants?

What sort of job will I get from this degree?
Suggested resources:
- www.prospects.ac.uk then Options With Your Subject shows the range and scope of careers that graduates with the subject you are considering often go into.
- www.unistats.com has graduate employment information on a specific course you are considering. N.B. Advisers need to spend time understanding this site. You may need to guide your students to the relevant information personally.
- www.bestcourse4me.com shows the link between what people study and their employment record afterwards.

Do my predictions match up with what the course really wants?
Suggested resource: www.unistats.com
Once you have selected the subject at a specific university, you can go to UCAS points and entry info and see the range of UCAS Tariff points that students on this course have. Sometimes many people on the course in reality have a lower UCAS Tariff than is stated in the usual entry requirements for the course; but you can also

often see that many people have a much higher tariff/grades than is asked for in entry requirements. This information can be extremely useful when fine tuning choices.

Tactics Especially for competitive courses, getting your tactics right can be advantageous.
- Personal statement (See section *11.1 Personal statements*)
  Suggested resource: There is an industry devoted to helping people with personal statements! The resource I am going to recommend is Alan Bullock's *Creating Your UCAS Personal Statement*. It's really cheap so you can buy copies for your students and doesn't include any examples of statements, just tips.
- Interviews
  Suggested resource: *University Interviews Guide* by Gardner and Hamnett. (I suppose I would say that, wouldn't I!)
- Work experience/taster days/internships
  Suggested resource: www.accessprofessions.com
  A one-stop shop where, once you are registered, you will be notified of activities that relate to your interests. This site will be especially helpful for people who do not have access to the social networks that would normally help.

10.3 Types of higher-education courses for undergraduates

Bachelors' and masters' degrees
These can have various titles, such as:
- Bachelor of Arts (BA);
- Bachelor of Science (BSc);
- Master of Arts (MA);
- Master of Science (MSc);
- Bachelor of Engineering (Beng);
- Master of Engineering (Meng);
- Bachelor of Law (LLB);
- Bachelor of Medicine and Surgery (MBBS).

Generally, a bachelor's degree is three years long and a master's degree is four years long.

Single or combined degrees
The following are possible:
- Single (for example, Bsc in geology);
- Equal combination (for example, BSc in mathematics *and* management studies);
- Major-minor combination (for example, BSc in mathematics *with* management studies);
- Triple combination (for example, BA in philosophy, psychology and physiology);
- Cross-disciplinary and interdisciplinary (the student takes a wide range of courses across a range of disciplines, for example, BA in economic and social studies).

Foundation degrees
- These are normally two years long.
- They are work and career related.
- They can be studied at the university or at a local franchised further education college.
- An optional top-up year will convert the qualification to an honours degree.

- These courses are gradually replacing Higher National Diplomas.
- They are often marketed at non-traditional higher-education applicants, such as adults.
- For more information, visit www.fdf.ac.uk

Sandwich degrees
- These are normally four years long.
- They can include a single (thick) twelve-month work placement or two (thin) six-month work placements.
- The placement is normally paid work.
- Sometimes placements are found for the student, sometimes students have to find them themselves.
- Universities such as Aston, Bath, Surrey and Ulster have a policy of encouraging most of their students to take a work-placement year.

Extended degrees
- These offer an initial preliminary year at college and are common in engineering and science.
- There are a few art and design courses offered as an alternative to art foundation courses.
- Preliminary years for medicine offer an alternative route, but they still require very high A-level grades.

10.4 Types of university

Here we will look at:
- University groupings
- Futuretrack paper on classifying universities by UCAS Tariff scores
- Sutton Trust 13

If we are researching universities and HEIs we will soon become aware of the sheer range of different institutions. Interestingly, most universities (but not all) have formed themselves into like-minded groups. This is helpful to new advisers, as it gives us an indication of how a university might view itself.

The groupings are (these include their own descriptions – my own comments are in italics):

94 Group www.1994group.ac.uk
Established in 1994, the Group brings together 19 internationally renowned, research-intensive universities.
These are most of the universities that were not polytechnics but are also not members of the Russell Group – you must not assume they are inferior to the Russell Group; in fact it is often assumed that some of the universities below are in the Russell Group.

University of Bath
Birkbeck, University of London
Durham University
University of East Anglia
University of Essex

University of Exeter
Goldsmiths, University of London
Royal Holloway, University of London
Lancaster University
University of Leicester
Loughborough University
Queen Mary, University of London
University of Reading
University of St Andrews
School of Oriental and African Studies
University of Surrey
University of Sussex
University of York

Association of Colleges www.aoc.co.uk
The Association of Colleges was created in 1996 as the single voice to promote the interests of further education colleges in England and Wales.
Colleges provide 38% of entrants to higher education. Half of all foundation degree students are taught in FE colleges. 63% of colleges teach foundation degrees. Colleges deliver 78% of HNCs and 59% of HNDs. Around 168,000 students study higher education in a college. 272 colleges provide higher education in the UK.

Colleges in England (2010):
227 general FE and tertiary colleges (GFE)
95 sixth-form colleges (SFC)
16 land-based colleges
4 art, design and performing arts colleges (ADPAC)
10 special designated colleges

GuildHE www.guildhe.ac.uk
Many member institutions share key characteristics, specialist mission or subject focus, being smaller than the average university in the UK but some being major providers in professional subject areas including art and design, music and the performing arts; agriculture; education, health and sports. Within GuildHE are a number of older HEIs with their roots in Victorian philanthropy and interest in education and crafts. These include specialist institutions and those founded by the churches. These sources of inspiration have an impact on the interest in values and social justice visible within GuildHE as a whole, and inform its positions on inclusion and support for difference.

Arts University College Bournemouth
Bishop Grosseteste University College Lincoln
Buckinghamshire New University
Harper Adams University College
Leeds Trinity University College
Newman University College
Norwich University College of the Arts
Ravensbourne
Rose Bruford College
Royal Agricultural College

St Mary's University College Belfast
St Mary's University College Twickenham
Liverpool Institute for Performing Arts
University College Birmingham
University College Falmouth
University College Plymouth St Mark & St John
University for the Creative Arts
University of Cumbria
University of Winchester
University of Worcester
Writtle College
York St John University

Associate Members

American InterContinental University
Anglo-European College of Chiropractic
Bradford College
Glyndwr University / Prifysgol Glyndwr
Leeds College of Art
Plymouth College of Art
Regent's College
The British School of Osteopathy
The Tavistock & Portman NHS Trust

Million+ www.millionplus.ac.uk

This is a think tank representing the universities below. It must be stressed that many of the courses that are offered in these universities can have extremely high levels of employability. You must not make lazy assumptions about these universities and you should take the time to research the courses and outcomes of what they offer.

University of Abertay Dundee
Anglia Ruskin University
Bath Spa University
University of Bedfordshire
Birmingham City University
The University of Bolton
Buckinghamshire New University
University of Central Lancashire (UCLan)
Coventry University
University of Derby
University of East London (UEL)
Glasgow Caledonian University
University of Greenwich
Kingston University
Leeds Metropolitan University
London Metropolitan University
London South Bank University (LSBU)
Middlesex University
Napier University
The University of Northampton
Roehampton University

Southampton Solent University
Staffordshire University
University of Sunderland
University of Teesside
Thames Valley University (TVU)
University of the West of Scotland
The University of Wolverhampton

Russell Group www.russellgroup.ac.uk
The Russell Group represents 20 leading UK universities committed to maintaining the very best research, an outstanding teaching and learning experience and unrivalled links with business and the public sector.

University of Birmingham
University of Bristol
University of Cambridge
Cardiff University
University of Edinburgh
University of Glasgow
Imperial College London
King's College London
University of Leeds
University of Liverpool
London School of Economics & Political Science
University of Manchester
Newcastle University
University of Nottingham
Queen's University Belfast
University of Oxford
University of Sheffield
University of Southampton
University College London
University of Warwick

University Alliance www.university-alliance.ac.uk
The University Alliance, previously convened informally as the Alliance of Non-Aligned Universities, was formed in 2006 comprising a mixture of pre- and post-1992 universities. The member institutions have a balanced portfolio of research, teaching, enterprise and innovation integral to their missions and represent a strong voice from the middle sector making a vital contribution to the prosperity of the country.

Aberystwyth University
Bournemouth University
University of Bradford
De Montfort University
University of Glamorgan
University of Gloucestershire
University of Hertfordshire
University of Huddersfield
Institute of Education

University of Kent
University of Lincoln
Liverpool John Moores University
Manchester Metropolitan University
Northumbria University
Nottingham Trent University
Open University
Oxford Brookes University
University of Plymouth
University of Portsmouth
University of Salford
Sheffield Hallam University
University of Wales Institute, Cardiff
University of Wales, Newport
University of the West of England

Futuretrack paper on classifying universities by UCAS Tariff scores
Purcell, Elias and Atfield, IER 2009 in Futuretrack Working Paper 1 argue that we
could classify universities not by their groupings but by the UCAS Tariff scores that
they use on entry. Therefore universities are divided into the categories of:
Highest tariff
High tariff
Medium tariff
Lower tariff

I have two main comments to make here. Firstly that you will always get outliers, so
for example, a course may be at a Medium tariff university but has a national
reputation i.e. Media Studies at Westminster. This would need to be discussed with
someone who is thinking about media studies who may be expecting to achieve a high
UCAS Tariff. Secondly, the Browne Review and student finance changes in 2010
have pushed many tariffs upwards.

Sutton Trust 13
The Sutton 13 Universities are based on average newspaper league-table rankings and
comprise: Birmingham, Bristol, Cambridge, Durham, Edinburgh, Imperial, LSE,
Nottingham, Oxford, St Andrews, UCL, Warwick and York.

This grouping came from the Sutton Trust paper – University Admissions By
Individual Schools 2008

10.5 Research using the internet

Much of the information you or your students will need is available online. This is
not a comprehensive list

For information about universities, courses and how to apply
•   www.ucas.com This site allows students to search for courses on the basis of
    subject, university/college or location. In many instances, the course information
    includes entry requirements. The site also provides links to individual university

and college websites. Much useful information on a specific course is now grouped into Entry Profiles.

Once students have applied through this site, it then allows them to check on the progress of their application through UCAS Track. It also clarifies the rules and regulations surrounding UCAS application.

- www.push.co.uk A quick and often humorous insight into the different universities.
- www.whatuni.com Video and written reviews.
- www.unistats.com This site brings together key sources of official information and is intended to help students compare institutions and subjects. It has statistics on: entry qualifications, drop-out rates, awards obtained and subsequent occupations of graduates. It also includes the results of national student surveys on student satisfaction.
- www.coursediscover.co.uk This is a comprehensive advice programme that allows searches by course and tariff points. It also has bursary information, dates for open days, course content and sample personal statements. Note: this is a subscription service.
- www.hotcourses.com A course database with search facilities. www.opendays.com A directory of university and college open days.
- www.skill.org.uk This is the website of the National Bureau for Students with Disabilities. It allows users to search for universities and gives a guide to facilities and access. At the very least, it gives the relevant contact name for disabled students at each university.
- Online league tables – Could be international (Shanghia Jiao Tong, QS World Rankings or THES Global Institutional Profiles) or national (The Sunday Times University Guide, The Guardian or The Complete University Guide).

What to study?

Stamford Test and Centigrade within www.ucas.com
www.ukcoursefinder.co.uk
Also paid services such as Higher Ideas and Prefinio

For information about careers and graduate opportunities

www.prospects.ac.uk – go to 'careers advice', then 'options with your subject'.
www.graduate-jobs.com
www.get.hobsons.co.uk
www.targetjobs.co.uk
www.milkround.com
www.sectorcareersinfo.co.uk – the Sector Skills Council portal
www.icould.org.uk
www.notgoingtouni.co.uk
www.careersbox.co.uk

Admissions Tests

www.spa.ac.uk
www.ukcat.ac.uk – medicine
www.lnat.ac.uk – law
www.admissionstests.cambridgeassessment.org.uk

Professional Scholarships

www.bconstructive.co.uk/scholarship

Institute of Physics Undergraduate Bursary Scheme www.iop.org

Institution of Engineering and Technology www.theiet.org

Institution of Civil Engineers www.ice.org.uk

Institution of Mechanical Engineers www.imeche.org

Gap Year

www.gapyear.com

www.csv.org.uk – Community Service Volunteers

www.yini.org.uk –Year in Industry paid work placements before university

www.gogapyear.com – hints on planning travel

www.vinspired.com – volunteering opportunities

Study Abroad

www.britishcouncil.org/erasmus – British Council

www.fulbright.co.uk – USA

www.braintrack.com – international index

www.ukcosa.org.uk – advice for UK students studying abroad and for international students studying in the UK

Finance

www.ucas.com – click on 'student finance'.

www.direct.gov.uk/studentfinance

www.funderfinder.org.uk

www.push.co.uk

10.6 Research using books

There are many books published about entry to higher education, what it is like when you are there and what careers you can get into afterwards. See the websites below for some of the main organisations that can get you the books that you need:

www.prospectseducationresources.co.uk

www.ucasbooks.co.uk

www.lifetime-publishing.co.uk

10.7 Higher-education fairs: getting the best out of them

Higher-education fairs are great places to get information and ideas: endless aisles of stands, shelf-loads of prospectuses and lots of friendly university staff intent on promoting their particular institution to every passing sixth-former. But for many students the experience can be overwhelming and confusing. So how do you help them get the best from the event?

Here are some hints to give students *before* they set out for the fair.

- Make sure students do *not* intend to wander around aimlessly for hours, picking up piles of prospectuses they will never read from universities they aren't in the slightest bit interested in.

- Instead, encourage them to do some research beforehand. They should identify a small number of institutions (say up to ten) they know they are interested in. On arrival, they should find out where these stands are and make straight for them.
- It is a good idea to have two or three questions ready to ask at each stand. They will then be able to compare answers. Questions could be about:
o the course content (is there a course booklet?);
o the entrance requirements;
o whether there will be interviews;
o how students' work is assessed;
o career opportunities for graduates of a particular course.
- Universities often employ recent graduates on their stands. Encourage students to think of questions to ask these people, perhaps to do with money, accommodation or social life (they can give a really good and up-to-date picture of what student life is like at their institution).
- Discourage students from spending more than an hour going round the fair (or, if it takes them longer, they should at least have a break).
- Make sure students see the fair as just one part of their research, not as the whole answer to it.

10.8 Open days

The best advice is for students to try to see some of the universities that interest them in the summer term of year 12 – that is, *before* they make their application. In any case, most universities hold their organised open days in the summer term.

Students can find details of when open days are being held from prospectuses or university websites. For some, it may be necessary to book in advance; for others, students may simply be able to turn up. Institutions that do not have formal open days may be happy to arrange visits when students can see the department of their choice and talk to the admissions tutor. Students should not be afraid to pick up the phone and arrange this.

It would be impossible for students to visit every university that interests them. However, they should be encouraged to see a good cross-section so they can compare, for example, old with new, large with small, campus with non-campus, city with countryside.

Hopefully, students who attend open days will come back with an overall impression of the institution and an instinctive feel for whether it's the place for them. Specifically, it is helpful to consider the following:
- Were the facilities good (particularly for lab-based subjects)?
- Will the course content and exam structure suit them?
- What was the accommodation like? Will they get university accommodation in the first year? How much will it cost?
- Was the open day well organised? Were they made to feel welcome?
- Were the lectures interesting?
- Were the undergraduates they met enthusiastic about the place?
- Is it an exciting prospect?

Students can find out about open days by visiting www.opendays.com.

10.9 Higher-education opportunities outside the UK

A wide range of useful information on this subject is to be found on the Directgov website in the section *Studying at an overseas university*:
http://www.direct.gov.uk/en/BritonsLivingAbroad/EducationAndJobs/DG_071571

Because of the fees change, many students are looking to explore opportunities outside the UK. Possible options could be:

European Union
http://ec.europa.eu/youreurope/citizens/education/university/index_en.htm
A book worth getting is *Study Abroad Guide for School Leavers*
(ISBN: 9780956784506).
This is the only complete Study in Europe Guide for school leavers to the 400+ undergraduate degree programmes in continental Europe that are taught through English and now accessible to Irish and UK students.

It includes: country profiles of principal destination countries in Europe; selected university profiles; directory of courses; selected course profiles; admission processes and an overview of opportunities in Australia, Canada, NZ, and USA.

United States
www.fulbright.co.uk – the official source of information on applying to American universities from the United Kingdom
www.petersons.com – the US equivalent of UCAS Course Search
www.collegeboard.org – prepare for and take the SAT

Australia and New Zealand
www.studyoptions.com – Study Options is a free, independent, expert service for people looking to study in Australia and New Zealand

UK universities abroad
Bizarrely, it may work out cheaper to study at an English university with a campus abroad, for example the University of Nottingham in China:
www.nottingham.edu.cn

However, many of the above options outside the EU will want fees paid up front!

11. The university application process

11.1 Personal statements

Along with making the (probably) five choices on UCAS Apply, the personal statement is the one thing the student will have to think about. They will need to think creatively and they have to own and believe in what they are writing about themselves. Who would have thought that writing 47 lines of text (or 4,000 characters) could be so problematic, but schools, sixth-form centres and FE colleges up and down the country are creating a small industry in helping their students to produce this mini-document. It is an invaluable opportunity for students to influence admissions tutors in their favour. But how can you ensure that students will impress?

First, it is worth remembering that admissions tutors (or centralised admissions teams) use the personal statement to:
- help them decide who will be made offers;
- decide which candidates to interview;
- develop lines of questioning during an interview;
- test whether the student understands the nature of the course they are applying for.

Students faced with a blank sheet of paper or screen may struggle to decide what to write about. However, there is a basic model – a five-point plan – that they could follow, but do not have to!

Their choice of course Students must explain their reasons for choosing a particular course at university, and the background to their interest in the subject. This is the section that admissions tutors are most interested in, so it usually forms at least the opening paragraph. Remember: *what* do they want to study?; *why* do they want to study it?; what *evidence* have they got that proves this?
Their work experience Placements through school, part-time jobs, voluntary work. Students need to explain *what they learnt* from their work experience, and make this relevant to the course they are applying for.
Their school experience Students should include any particular interests they have in their current studies, as evidence that they *enjoy* aspects of study.
Their interests and experience outside school What do they do outside of their studies – sporting, social or other activities?
A concluding statement

Bearing the five-point plan in mind, here are some ideas about what to include: sports (playing/watching); work experience (part-time, voluntary); field courses; summer schools; lectures; conferences; university visits; book/magazine articles they have read; politics/current affairs; environmental issues; music (playing/listening); travel (done/planned); career ideas.

It is also helpful to bear in mind what admissions tutors want to see in a personal statement. They will be looking for:
- an idea of why the student wants to do the course, backed up with evidence (this is by far the most important issue);
- evidence of a well-rounded personality;

- a well-written statement (correct grammar and punctuation, interesting and expressive vocabulary, avoidance of clichés);
- a well-presented statement;
- details of relevant work experience (especially for vocational courses);
- evidence of broad key skills;
- examples that demonstrate a willingness to work hard and persevere;
- anything distinctive about courses the student has taken;
- positive explanations of unusual A-level combinations or reasons for taking a vocational course.

They do not want to see:

- repeated information (for example, the student's name, A-level subjects) that is evident from the other parts of UCAS Apply.

Here is an example of the opening section of a personal statement, dealing with the student's choice of course. The student wants to study English. The statement must say:

- *what* the student wants to study (in a general way: sometimes you can be applying for courses with different titles. You do not need to list these);
- *why* the student wants to study it;
- what *evidence* there is that he or she is genuinely interested in the subject.

What, why and the evidence? "I enjoy the reading, analysis and criticism of poems, plays and novels. The analysis of a play such as George Bernard Shaw's *Arms and The Man*, for example, can cover so many topics – the historical context, war, emotions and our unwillingness to come to terms with them. Such detailed examination of literary texts is for me the most appealing aspect of studying English. As part of my A-level course I have particularly enjoyed the poetry of Wilfred Owen and *Bleak House* by Charles Dickens. Away from set texts I read widely, especially enjoying Patrick Hamilton, Stella Gibbons and Ian McEwan. I have recently read *The Iliad* and have been amazed to notice its influence on other works of literature."

Resources for personal statements

Excellent information for writing personal statements is contained on the UCAS website. There is also a short film in the UCAS TV section, which can be shown in tutor periods to help students get started. If you are looking for more resources, one I think is useful for students to look at is:

Creating your personal statement (Alan Bullock; Trotman Education 2008).

If you are looking for a book to read yourself, and I must admit I haven't read them all, then a good start is:

Personal statements: How to write a UCAS Personal statement (Paul Telfer; Iris Books 2005).

Helping students to start their personal statement

Over the years, just getting started has proved hugely problematic for my students. This then begged the question, are there common themes in how students start their personal statements? I looked at approximately 300 personal statements done at both of my schools in one year's application cycle. Of course I was worried that students may be starting personal statements in certain ways because they have been influenced by me. In one school I am heavily involved in the tutorial/careers education programme surrounding personal statements and in my other school I had nowhere near as much involvement. So I had at least one group of students who could act as a control group. Nevertheless, in both schools some clear themes were observed in how students start their personal statements:

The click moment

This is when the student is describing the moment they decided, "This is the course for me." Examples included:

The music, lights and atmosphere at a fashion show – fashion management degree
Reciting a poem while at the top of a mountain – English literature
Observing a hospital consultant interact with a patient – medicine

The heritage move

This is when the student is relating their course choice to their background/heritage. Examples included:

Linking the economic situation in Nigeria to her interest in studying economics and relevant reading on the oil industry.

Relating the experience of a relative who was a holocaust survivor to the student's own interest in history.

Having family members who have worked in the building industry in craft/technical careers and how this has influenced the student in wanting a management career and wanting to study civil engineering.

The quote

Some institutions ban the use of quotes, some encourage it. While I am wary of students using quotes, some of my students do use a quote to start their personal statement. I have these provisos:

Does the quote really encapsulate in just a few words exactly why you want to do this course? If it doesn't, then why put it down?

Do you really understand what the quote means and the original context in which it was used? The student can look an idiot if they do not understand the meaning and context of the quote.

Is the quote connected to the rest of the text? It may seem obvious but the quote must relate to the rest of the text in the personal statement.

The dream

I have always dreamed of studying this, becoming this, etc. While to a lay observer this may come across as a bit cheesy, some of my students genuinely want to put this because it is heartfelt. If the student then backs up the dream with evidence as to why they want to study the course, who am I to criticise? Many people who were using this theme, I noticed, were applying for courses in professions allied to medicine and creative areas such as drama.

The intellectual

Not so much a theme as an approach. This student seems to have swallowed a dictionary and almost seems to be pleading, "Trust me. I'm really clever, like you." The question we have to ask ourselves is, "Is the student painting an accurate picture of themselves?" If they are, then fine. If they understand exactly what they are saying, and why they are saying it, with some evidence, then who are we to criticise? My problem is when students feel they need to over-intellectualise their statement and do not really understand what they are writing. I would then step in because the statement is not an honest picture of them and they would almost definitely be unable to withstand rigorous questioning on the content if it came to an interview.

This is what I want to study, this is the evidence!

The "Ronseal" type of personal statement, most commonly used by science, engineering and maths applicants. Very little waffle is used. They will like (for example) physics, because of what they have studied at A level, because they have done a taster course or because they have seen physics used in real-life examples. This will be fine as most of the admissions tutors in these areas will not like waffle either and are very happy with a factual approach.

Plagiarism and personal statements

It is very important that you read the information about the Similarity Detection Service on the UCAS website. This is from the UCAS website 2011:

"What the Similarity Detection Service does

Each personal statement is checked against:

- *a library of personal statements previously submitted to UCAS*
- *sample statements collected from a variety of websites*
- *other sources including paper publications.*

Each personal statement received at UCAS is added to the library of statements after it has been processed.

What happens if a personal statement has similarities?

- *Any statements showing a level of similarity of 10% or more are reviewed by members of the UCAS Similarity Detection Service Team.*
- *Applicants, universities and colleges are notified at the same time by email when an application has similarities confirmed.*
- *Admissions tutors at individual universities and colleges decide what action, if any, to take regarding reported cases."*

What if the personal statement is not plagiarised but is written by someone else?

A student could apply for five courses with a statement that has been written by somebody else. This statement might help them to gain their place. This could still have consequences:

- They have an interview and they clearly do not understand what they have said in their personal statement, leading to rejection.
- The language in the statement does not tally with the qualifications profile of the applicant, leading to rejection.
- The sending institution knows that the statement does not reflect the applicant so they refuse to endorse the statement.

11.2 Personal statements: subject-specific advice

Students may well ask for advice on how to impress admissions tutors for their particular subject. The list below gives subject-specific advice and ideas for personal statements. This is just a snapshot covering a few popular areas. More detailed points on what could be included in a personal statement are in *Appendix A: An A-Z of university subjects with essential information for students.*

Architecture	Ideas to include: visits to modern and historical sites; work experience in an architect's office; evidence of reading on the history of architecture; preferences among 20th-century architects; a favourite building and why. For more ideas, students should visit www.greatbuildings.com
Business, management, finance and economics	Students should read *The Economist* and the business pages of the broadsheet newspapers. They will need to show: evidence of coping with a wide variety of subjects; evidence of interest in economics, finance, marketing, human resources and IT; a high level of numeracy; evidence of working in teams on projects. AGCE/BTEC National business students should identify specific examples. It is a good idea to focus on some particular economics issues, for example, EMU.
Computing, IT	Courses can vary in their content, so students must make sure they know what they are applying for. Some courses will be concerned about maths ability, some may be more concerned about design or business skills. Students should try to think about all the experience they have had with computers and programming, inside and outside of school. What did they learn from it?
Education, teacher training	Include any work experience/observation in schools and describe what was learnt from it (for example, mixed-ability teaching, testing, special needs). Students should mention any work with young people and what problems they encountered.
Engineering	The purpose of engineering is the design and manufacture of the "hardware" of life. Students should show evidence that they can relate maths and physics to a "hardware" issue (for example, relating the study of electricity in physics to how a car ignition works). They could write about an engineering issue that interests them.
English	Reading beyond the syllabus is essential. Students might: write about their favourite authors, poets and dramatists and why they like them; mention theatre visits; show that they understand the link between literature and history (through knowledge of a historical setting). Most degrees are literature based, so it is not a good idea to go on about creative writing or journalism too much.
Geography	Ideas include: describing visits or field trips to any specific region; reading geographical magazines and describing any special interests and why; showing an awareness of world issues and an interest in their own locality.
History	Students need to show a passion for the past above and beyond schoolwork. They can prove it by writing about books and magazines on history, saying why they interest them. It is a good idea to show an interest in the wide sweep of history – not just Europe between the wars! If they have a joint interest in history and literature, they should exploit it.
Languages, European studies	Students should include visits to relevant countries, noting the cultural and geographical features of the region visited. Students should give evidence of interest in the history and literature related to their language. A good idea is to read newspapers, magazines and

	websites in the appropriate language.
Law	It is a good idea to: visit law courts and take notes on cases heard; follow legal arguments in the press; read law sections in broadsheet newspapers; read *Learning the Law* by Glanville Williams or *Understanding the Law* by Geoffrey Rivlin. Some admissions tutors are concerned about students' interest in law as an academic discipline, rather than as a career. Students might include evidence of work experience/work shadowing/career research.
Maths	Students should include anything that proves their love of maths: wider reading, entering competitions, maths clubs. They could mention other interests related to maths, such as IT, chess or philosophy, and explain how they would like to use their maths degree in their future career. It is a good idea to include any evidence of maths they have had to learn by themselves, or maths problems they have solved through determination.
Media studies	Students should describe their work experience/shadowing and say what they learnt from it (for example, job roles, how media organisations differ). They should include evidence that they have shown initiative outside of the syllabus (for example, creating their own website). It is important to show that their reasons for applying correspond to the content of the course, and that they are not just doing it to get a job in the media.
Medicine, dentistry, veterinary science	Admissions tutors are looking for evidence of: work experience and what the student learnt from it; scientific interest; interest in the welfare of others; communication skills; stability and stickability. Students could try to gain a more in-depth knowledge of one or two medical issues outside of their A-level syllabuses (for example, about the roles of health professionals, or social factors which influence health and disease). They could think about which disease interests them most and why.
Music, drama	Even though universities may hold auditions, many will take a student's talent as a given and are more concerned about an interest in the academic issues. They are looking for evidence of intellectual curiosity and an interest in the cultural background and construction of the subject matter. Therefore wider reading and concert and theatre visits are essential.
Natural sciences (biochemistry, biology, chemistry, physics)	Students need to show that their interest goes beyond their A-level syllabus, through wider reading of scientific journals, for example. It is a good idea to become more knowledgeable on one or two issues. Students could say what they have enjoyed most in their relevant A levels and why. They could relate something they have learnt to a practical use. They should find out more about the careers these degrees can lead to (all the relevant institutes have careers sections on their websites).
Professions allied to medicine	These include speech therapy, occupational therapy, physiotherapy, radiography, dietetics and nursing. Admissions tutors are looking for evidence of: work experience and what the student learnt from it; scientific interest; interest in the welfare of others; communication skills; stability and stickability. Students could try to gain a more in-depth knowledge of one or two medical issues outside of their A-

	level syllabuses (for example, about the roles of health professionals, or social factors which influence health). Those applying for physiotherapy, occupational therapy or speech therapy must show that they understand the differences between the three subjects.
Social sciences (politics, psychology, sociology)	Students need to show evidence of: reading current affairs avidly; wider reading that shows an interest in society, political issues and human behaviour; an understanding of how these are all interrelated. Those who *have not* studied the subject before must provide evidence of reading an introductory book (especially for psychology). Those who *have* studied the subject might identify part of the syllabus and say why it interests them.
Sport and physical education	Students need to be clear about what sort of course they are applying for. Most sports courses will be looking for evidence of interest in physiology, psychology, sports performance, coaching and the business and administration of sport.

11.3 UCAS Apply: how to complete it

The home page of the UCAS website is set out very logically: on the left side are three main areas which you and your students will enter constantly. Firstly there is the Course Search section, then there is the Apply section, then there is the Track Progress section where they can see what offers and rejections they have received and respond to them.

UCAS Apply has been designed to be as user-friendly as possible, with drop-down menus and help options at every step, though as my fellow careers adviser John Beckett says, "We now live in the world of the drop-down menu" where life-changing decisions can be confirmed in a few clicks. Those HE advisers who are monitoring the UCAS Apply process have a vital role in making sure that the clicking has been properly thought through. UCAS Apply cannot usually be submitted before a date in September (which varies over the years), but students can enter information into the system before this in that June/July period after AS levels/year 12 exams.

I am not going to replicate masses of information which is freely available on the UCAS website on the process of completing UCAS Apply. Rather I will point out a few issues that can make life a bit easier as you guide your students through the process. If you are new to this process, I would recommend taking one of the UCAS training courses.

Students will need to gather up a certain amount of information before they think about sitting down to fill in UCAS Apply. They need to make sure they have the following to hand:
• their school or college's buzzword;
• the county or borough they live in;
• the fee code (normally 02);
• dates of their school or college attendance from the age of eleven (to the nearest month);
• details of exams taken or to be taken (including the exam centre name and number, exam board and grade for each exam);

- their personal statement (they will need advice on how to place this on the form);
- their payment details (it is possible to pay by credit/debit card or through the school);
- their five course choices (for each course they must know the course code and college code so they do not click on the wrong course; these are available from the Course Search section of the UCAS website).

They can then get started by:
- going to www.ucas.com and clicking on "Apply";
- registering using their school/college buzzword (they will be issued with a user name and password which they *must not lose*).

Most importantly, HE advisers need to ensure that the list of five courses each student puts down on UCAS Apply is *consistent* in a way that is acceptable to admissions tutors. Let us look at some examples.
- This is acceptable: two electronic engineering courses and three electrical and electronic engineering courses. Why? Because nobody would be in any doubt about what the student wanted to do and the personal statement would be straightforward in expressing an interest in engineering.
- This is also acceptable: two English courses, two English and history courses, one English studies course. Why? The core theme running through these choices is English. History is very compatible with English, so it would be perfectly easy for the student to express an interest in both in the personal statement.
- This is also acceptable: three management studies courses and two business studies courses. Why? Management and business studies are very similar, just with different titles. One of the few differences is that business studies courses are more likely to contain a sandwich year. It would be acceptable for the student to express an interest in both business and management studies in the personal statement.
- This is *not* acceptable: three philosophy courses and two nursing courses. Why? Because the admissions tutor would not know what the student was most interested in doing. It shows a lack of commitment to a particular subject that would be obvious in a personal statement.

11.4 Writing effective UCAS references

By Barbara Hamnett MBE, HE Consultant (former Principal Deputy Headteacher, JFS School, north London)
hamnett@jfs.brent.sch.uk

In an age of mass applications to university (the previous Labour Government had a target of 50% of 18-year-olds proceeding into higher education), it is evident that not all institutions, nor even admissions tutors within institutions, can possibly grapple with the sheer volume of forms and information they receive about applicants. This section, therefore, attempts to consider the most effective way of preparing references to best help individual students succeed in their chosen applications.

Painting a picture of individual students

This is very important. Firstly, we owe it to them to get it right. This will clearly take time but it will be time well spent as it will focus on the output of each of our institutions, the education system as a whole and of the success of individuals within that. Spending time will help students secure appropriate course choices and prevent dropout.

Secondly, we owe it to our colleagues who teach the students, and who also have a strong vested interest in their success. So many students proceed and succeed in higher education because of an inspirational motivated teacher who put their interests first.

Thirdly, not to be forgotten, we owe it to our colleagues in the institutions of higher education who are doubtless drowning in the number of applicants and application forms they now receive. Additionally, there are current pressures on the universities to be more cost effective as well as the cuts currently being imposed. One must be realistic and expect that not all personal statements will be read on first sifting; the reference is, therefore, crucial.

The four main elements in a reference

1. Predicted grades. One must always work on the assumption that, given the sheer volume of applicants, the key element in any selection process will be the predicted grades of individual students. They are arguably the most important factor in the initial perception that a selector has of a form. We all know of students who argue and cajole us into raising the prediction because of the particular demands of the course they wish to apply for. It is also important to recognise that many institutions monitor predictions and indeed the schools or sixth-form colleges from which those students come.

It does no one any favours, least of all the student, to over-predict in order to "help" an individual student at the point of application. Invariably, an institution will become known for over-prediction and whilst an individual student may, or may not, receive an offer if they under-achieve dramatically in their results, they could realistically turn round and confront us about why we allowed ourselves to be convinced.

In very high-demand courses such as English or medicine, where most of the applicants will have high predictions, these will be a vital first step in the "accept" or "reject" initial sifting. Clearly different institutions will consider the method of predicting results based on practice and individual subject areas. The oversight of a senior manager/leader in considering the potential of students in their care will be crucial in overall quality control.

The arrival of the A* further complicates the accuracy of predictions. See the section on the A* at A level (and whether it can be predicted) for more on this topic. One thing our research shows is that individual subject A* predictions are unreliable. At the time of writing each subject in the UCAS Apply reference has a drop-down menu inviting you to predict an A*. This should be looked at by UCAS so that a more holistic prediction can be made i.e. "We think they can get A*AA, but we are not sure what the A* will be in."

2. Comments from the teachers who actually teach the students. Using quotes from these teachers is a very effective way of painting a picture of an individual because these are the teachers who actually know them best, especially in a subject they may wish to go on to read.

Many selectors at universities have told us that it is often difficult to differentiate students, and difficult to differentiate a student reaching their peak at A level versus those with more potential yet to be tapped. An indication of potential and even comparators with previous students or students in the same year group are very effective in order to help selectors (though this is difficult with open references – as the student themselves may not be discreet). For example, *"the best student I have taught in economics for the last 20 years"* makes a statement that is stronger than merely "excellent" or "outstanding" used in the narrative.

The referee overseeing the final reference will, of course, need to recognise that there may well be differences between performance in different subjects and attempt to portray the student in an honest light, representing strengths and areas for development/weaknesses. Having surveyed the practice in a number of post-16 institutions it is evident that different methods are used for the gathering of predictions and comments – this will make the task of a selector at the university very difficult indeed.

3. Portraying the talents of a particular student for a particular course. This is the importance of other information in the referee's statement. Key elements in considering suitability of a student for the subject and the institution will be such components as *"teachability", "potential", "motivation and enthusiasm", "reflection", "analytical and flexible thinker"* and so on.

This may well be a point at which to cross-reference information in the student's own personal statement as a means of reinforcing key attributes of particular students.

4. Assembling the final reference from all the contributors. It is evident from our survey of various types of institutions (see table at the end of this section) that the person pulling together the final reference will vary considerably. In a small grammar school it may be a teacher who will know a student extremely well and can paint a very powerful picture. In a college of FE or consortium where students are travelling between different institutions, a personal tutor may have limited knowledge about an individual student or, indeed, their personal circumstances where relevant. Thus a selector reading references in these two very different cases will find it quite difficult to make a judgement, even though they will have contextual information about the institutions on which to base some of their decision making.

Fundamental to any referee pulling together a final comprehensive and coherent reference is (I believe), a meeting with the student. This might take some 15 or 20 minutes but is an opportunity at the end of a student's school career to pull together all the strands of information available on that student, to question the student finally about their intentions and to very effectively dot the i's and cross the t's of pulling together an effective reference.

A coherent structure

Finally, you need to put this information into a coherent structure. The following is an example:

- Paragraph 1 could give a preamble including his/her educational background.
- Paragraphs 2/3/4 could be based on subject reports with an account of the performance and potential in each subject.
- Paragraphs 4/5 could comment on non-academic qualities, emotional intelligence and issues relating to disadvantage.
- You could finish with an encouraging declaration on their appropriateness.
- You should include all predicted A-level grades.

Confidentiality in an age of open references

It is evident from our survey of institutions that most students either see, have read to them, or are actually given a copy of their actual references. Whilst this is laudable and open, it can sometimes compromise a situation in which confidential information is known, for example, about a student's family circumstances. Such information might enhance their chances of achieving a place but where the student, being intensely private, has no desire for this information to be reflected in a reference, it poses questions about how best to support that student. Obviously one would need to discuss this with him or her as to the benefits or not of raising particular confidential information. This is further complicated if students and their peers share their references – which may well happen and peer pressure is powerful. Clearly, with the student's permission, it is possible to contact individual higher-education institutions after the initial form has been despatched, to add additional information that can be treated with confidentiality. In our experience institutions are only too willing and helpful in responding to such matters, though issues of data protection and confidentiality pose a number of potential minefields and need to be handled with care.

Making sure HEIs know if the student has faced difficult circumstances

Examples of the following could be included in the reference:

- Family living in local authority housing or in an area of acknowledged social deprivation.
- Parents/parent in receipt of benefits.
- Student in receipt of free school meals.
- Lack of study area at home.

As mentioned above, it is important that you gain the student's permission to share this information with HEIs.

Significant staff changes

It is not uncommon for students to have complete changes of staff between AS and A2, thus grappling with different styles of teaching. This may be by design or in response to crises. Different approaches can be difficult for a student to adjust to in what are, effectively, the final two terms of their study. Individual teachers may be ill and even students studying the same subject in the same institution may well have very different experiences.

It is important that higher-education institutions are made aware that there is not a level playing field even within one's own institution, let alone across different institutions. Quality control is fundamental in ensuring not only the reputation of a particular institution, but of ensuring all students have the right to have an effective and thorough reference produced with rigour and with the student at centre stage.

It is clear from our survey work that in the vast majority of institutions, personal tutors now compile, collate and "top and tail" the references. In the majority of institutions, quality control is effected by a senior manager, usually a head of sixth form or a senior careers teacher/adviser or, indeed, somebody from the Senior Leadership Team sampling a percentage of the references. Whatever the particular system, some form of quality control is critical.

The problematic reference

There will be, however, some students for whom it is difficult to say much that is meaningful. This may mean that they haven't done anything and there is little to say, or it may mean that s/he is a very private person and reveals very little. It is essential to probe here and sit down with this student to explain the difficulties you are having, in order to best help them. Your prompts will need to go further. For example, "Tell me what you do out of school", may also require:

- "Do you do any work for a youth club/charity?"
- "Do you help with an elderly relative?"
- "Do you help look after a brother/sister regularly?
- "Do you have a weekend/evening job?"
- "What do you do in this job?" and so on.

With such additional questions you will probably be able to extract such qualities as self-sufficiency, thoughtfulness to others, leadership and taking responsibility. These can be linked into, for example, "an ability to juggle conflicting priorities and still succeed academically" (at whatever level).

This process may be needed over and over again in response to other questions, which might include:

- "Tell me what you like best about studying …… at A level (linked to subject of HEI choice)."
- "Tell me about something you've read in this area."
- "What has helped to motivate you to apply for ……?"

There may be many sub-questions to these. The more references you write, the more these supplementary questions will come automatically.

Overcoming pitfalls

Writing a reference is never a level playing field, even within the same institution. So spare a thought for the poor admissions tutor trying to compare applicants from different types of institutions. Some institutions may even use banks of statements (as in school reports). In high-demand courses, HEIs are known to look at applicants from the same institution and compare what is said. For example, if you include a statement such as, "the best student I have taught in the last 20 years" from a subject teacher and the teacher says the same thing about another student, it could be spotted and dismissed.

Beware too, within your own institution, of five different types of student:
1. *High achieving, motivated, empathetic, modest* and don't see anything exceptional

in what they do. Potentially an easy reference to write but your task will be to précis in order to paint an accurate picture, as other students for these courses may well have a similar profile.

2. *Quite high achieving but bursting with confidence* and "talks the talk". Beware! Do not be seduced! Probe and paint a fair and accurate picture.

3. *Quite high achiever but, like the iceberg, two thirds is hidden.* You will have to work really hard with these students in order to paint a fair picture. They may well have considerable qualities and achievements but they themselves don't see them as considerable. These students are often really impressive when you probe.

4. *The average or low-achieving student who always has excuses* for things not done but paints a very inflated picture of themselves. To be fair to all the others, playing down their perceived reality about themselves will require some skill.

5. *The average or low-achieving student about whom there really is very little to say* except to reinforce the points made above about probing questions, and to ensure that s/he really is applying for the right course … or indeed any course, if they are not committed.

Survey of the different methods used by institutions to construct references

The UCAS procedure	Suburban Grammar School	Inner-City Sixth Form Centre	Provincial Sixth Form Centre	Inner-City Comprehensive	Inner-City Sixth Form Centre (many BTEC National Applicants)
What info on students is collected in order to compile the reference? How do you report on a) academic potential; b) contextual info?	Each teacher and each department gives overview of skills developed. Teachers make predictions. Teachers write reference (and some senior staff.) Specific staff involved for Oxbridge/ medicine etc. Students fill in sheet re extra curric	Each subject teacher writes a reference	All subject teachers write in September/October and add estimated A2 grades. 30 personal tutors add intro and conclusion (personal qualities etc). Tutors helped with model references	Academic information is sourced from three assessment points (APs) per year. Form tutors use this and AS results. Context information provided by each subject	a) Collect from tutors, ALIS and AS results for teachers to give predictions – end of summer term and update in September. b) Questionnaire that students complete with tutor – includes personal information
How is the information collected/collated/ assembled? When are predictions finalised?	Via SIMS – all staff see a shared area. Predictions end September – possible change to October half-term (review in progress)	Subject references entered online on intranet. Final prediction – mid September. Tutors collate (online) and write coherent ref and add own knowledge	Central online system. Reference template for every student. Teachers "paste" onto this and personal tutor tops and tails ①*	SLs write report at same time as final AP of the year – stored online. Predictions in second week autumn term Y13	Each student has folder on shared drive. Teachers of subject references and tutor references on this too. Tutor writes final reference*
What is your internal deadline for a) students; b) staff to complete their parts in the process?	a) For Oxbridge 1/10, rest 22/11. b) Oxbridge 16/9, rest 7/10. Oxbridge reference deadline 5/10, rest 25/11	a) Internal for students Friday after half-term break b) No specific deadline for staff but asked to complete by two weeks after student	a) For Oxbridge etc October, rest 1/12 but encourage earlier b) Do after seen teacher and personal statement ②*	a) 1st draft personal statement end of three-day UCAS event in July and finalise 1st week autumn term. b) 1st draft summer term and final 3rd week September	a) End of November b) 1/11
What are the roles of a) teachers and b) tutors in the process?	As above	a) Teachers write references in June and update in September b) Tutors collate	As above. Also have IB co-ordinator. Gifted + Talented co-ordinator does	Subject teachers produce insight/academic ability report. Form tutors put into	a) Teachers have 1:1 discussions re. progress and predictions b) Tutors input all

		into a complete reference as students submit forms	Oxbridge etc	context of whole student	references before summer holidays Missing referenc chased by SLT
What are the roles of a) careers specialists (both internal and external to the school) and b) other non-teaching professionals?	Careers advisers do advice and guidance re. choices and application, linked to expected work with sixth-form team on deadlines etc. Careers advisers also see references. UCAS administrator checks and sends forms (non-teacher)	Internal careers adviser and head of careers do final check before go to UCAS. Other non-teaching staff are not involved	Three qualified careers specialists plus Connexions (two to three days). Team of three oversee UCAS process – Head of Careers plus G+T + Support Manager. Lots of careers advice	To ensure students have explored all options and made good choices	Careers adviser l UCAS process, training re. UCA Apply/codes etc. Aimhigher to arr visits from HEIs help.
Who actually writes the reference? How are they trained to do this?	Form tutors and some SMT staff trained in summer term and led by experienced teacher in field	Tutors – using information from teachers and are trained by Head of Careers	Personal tutors and rotate Y12→Y13. Trained every September	Form tutors – no formal training, use UCAS information and publications	Tutors. Trained summer term – l career adviser an experienced tutor using past examp SLT check final reference.
Are students permitted to see the final reference before despatch? How is this carried out?	No – not shown at all	Yes. Tutor shows if student asks	Reference is read to them	Yes and get printed copy	Allowed to see b sent
How is quality control effected?	Head of Sixth Form sees all applications and references. References stored in staff area of SIMS	Sample checked by Head of Careers and SMT in June. Final reference seen by appointed teacher and/or Head of Careers	Three Administrators, Heads of Faculty and Head of Careers	Heads of Sixth Form read all references	Careers adviser
Is there a specialist team for Oxbridge/medicine etc (i.e. the 15/10 deadline courses)?	Oxbridge Co-ordinator and KS5 leader of learning look at all and work with careers specialist	As above but member of staff chases everyone to meet deadline	Yes	No – but need one	No – only a hand currently
What admin support does the whole UCAS process have?	UCAS administrator and support staff set up SIMS template for subject staff to input	None. Web/IT staff prepare online system.	Three Facility Administrators who check for errors	-	Careers adviser d Apply process. A chases HEIs
			①* Predictions updated when Apply finally sent. System above this to ensure consistency. ②* We allow some leeway for students who need more time		*Folder also incl all sixth-form rep written

11.5 Preparing students for interviews

The commonly held belief, it seems, is that universities do not interview applicants much any more. This is not true. While universities may certainly be looking to reduce the number of applicants they see, interviews are still happening in large numbers and students should be prepared for them. In fact, in the case of degree courses that train for a specific career, applicants are highly likely to be interviewed. And some universities still interview *all* applicants who make it past the initial selection process.

Students who have been invited to interviews will need help and advice on:
- what to expect;
- how to prepare themselves beforehand;
- how to present themselves.

A very good way to prepare students is to hold mock interviews in school. A useful book is the *University Interviews Guide* (Gardner/Hamnett), which contains sample interview questions for a wide range of subjects. This can be used both by students preparing for interview and by HE advisers conducting mock interviews.

What students should expect
- An interview can last anything between ten minutes and an hour.
- Interviews are usually conducted by one interviewer, but there could be two, three or even four of them.
- The greater part of an interview will be devoted to questions about the chosen course. Interviewers will be trying to discover: why students have applied for a particular course; how much they already know about the chosen subject; whether they have the aptitude and thinking skills to learn more; whether they have thought about what the degree course will involve.
- Students should feel reassured that the very fact that they have been invited for an interview means the university is interested in them, so their battle is half won. Also, there is no such thing as a perfect interview!

Preparation
- Students need to think beforehand about the kinds of questions they will be asked, and how they will answer them. They need to remember what interviewers are looking for (see above). They should look up their subject in the *University Interviews Guide*, which will prompt them to start thinking.
- It is important to read carefully any material sent before the interview.
- Students should reread the university prospectus and details about the course.
- They should photocopy or print off their personal statement and reread this thoroughly before the interview.
- It is a good idea to prepare some questions to ask (making sure these have not already been answered in information sent by the university).
- Students need to plan their journey. If an overnight stay is involved, they should plan for this as well. It is really unhelpful to be late or in a rush.

Presentation
- In any interview, as in any conversation, there should be a two-way interaction. Students should be prepared to participate and contribute.
- Those applying for a vocational degree (for example, medicine or hotel management) should dress smartly and appropriately.
- For most degrees, students should dress in clothing they feel comfortable with, and that will not distract the interviewer from the points being made.
- No one should chew gum – whatever course they are applying for!

- It is important for students to think about what their body language is conveying. Sitting slumped in a seat wearing a baseball cap is not a good idea! It is important to engage with the interviewer from the start.
- When it comes to handshakes, sitting down, starting to talk, and so on, it is best to follow the interviewer's lead.
- Students should work on making eye contact, regulating their voice levels and putting across an appropriate level of friendliness and warmth.

11.6 Responding to offers from UCAS: what students need to know

All the universities and colleges on your UCAS Apply entry have to make a decision one way or the other about whether to make your students an offer. Once all the institutions have come to a decision, UCAS will inform them through the UCAS Track service, detailing the offers they have been made.

It is definitely worth paying for the Adviser Track service that allows you to see what offers and rejections your students are receiving.

Normally, by a date in very early May (which will change slightly over the lifetime of this book, so see the UCAS website), your students have to make some crucial decisions about which offers to accept. They need to consider their replies very carefully. The decisions made are binding – they cannot change their minds at a later stage, for example when results come out in August.

A really important role for HE advisers and tutors is to check with their students around March/April these issues:
- That if the student is accepting offers, they can actually mathematically achieve the points required in their AS and A2 exams to reach the grades needed to meet their offers.
- That the student is choosing a genuine insurance choice they are happy to go to, and that is achievable in their circumstances.

What you and your students need to know
- The only official offers are those sent by UCAS through Track. Any verbal or written offers from individual institutions cannot be considered as confirmed until your students have heard from UCAS.
- They may receive offers without interviews but, if they do, they will almost certainly be invited to open days. They may well want to attend an open day before deciding whether to accept an offer.
- Their offers will almost certainly be conditional on A-level, AS-level or BTEC National results. Conditions may be stated in terms of exam grades or as a tariff score (see UCAS website). An offer may include conditions about GCSE maths or GCSE English language.
- There are three responses your students can make to the offers they receive:
  > Firm acceptance
  > Insurance acceptance
  > Decline
- They can hold two offers, one as firm acceptance, the other as insurance. Or they can firmly accept just one offer at the place they most want to go to. If they

satisfy the conditions of their "firm acceptance" offer in August, this is the course and institution they will attend.

- An insurance acceptance should normally be for an offer at lower grades or tariff score than their firm acceptance. Remember – if they do not make the grades for their firm acceptance, but satisfy the conditions for their insurance acceptance, they are committed to going to the university they accepted as insurance. It is therefore important to think very carefully about which offer they accept as insurance.
- If they decline all offers they will be eligible for clearing in August, and possibly for UCAS Extra.
- If they have any doubts about what to do, they must take advice. If as an adviser you are unsure, then ring the dedicated UCAS Adviser helpline.
- Through the Track service, UCAS will state the date by which they have to respond. This will be personal to them. The deadline for responding is likely to be in April or May, but UCAS will usually allow an extension into June, especially if they have some interviews to attend.

UCAS Extra
UCAS Extra was introduced in 2003, and enables students to make an additional choice of university course. It is aimed at two types of applicant:
- those who have not received any offers;
- those who are "non-committed" for any other reason and want to decline all their offers.

These applicants no longer have to wait until clearing to find a course to suit them.

The scheme normally operates from the end of February to the end of June. If an applicant is eligible to use Extra, a button will appear on their Track service. They can then apply for one course at a time using Track.

The aim of UCAS Extra is to reduce the numbers who use clearing.

11.7 Results time!

HE advisers can expect a busy few days when results arrive. You will need to set up some kind of "results service" to answer all the queries and have strategies for dealing with a number of scenarios.

Let us imagine that a student has entered UCAS Apply. They have just taken three A levels. They are holding a firm conditional offer of BCC and an insurance conditional offer of CCD. They could be faced with a number of scenarios.

Scenario 1: They exceed everybody's expectations They were aiming for BCC yet they get AAB. If this happens (and it is a rare occurrence) they are still committed to both their firm and insurance choices for this year's entry. Most people who fall into this category take a year out and apply again in the light of their unexpectedly good A-level results (though the fees situation in 2011 may change behaviour!) If they made a deferred application, they have a few weeks to withdraw after receiving their results and they can apply again the following year.

Please be aware of the new **adjustment period (information from UCAS)**: A five-day "adjustment window" in August has been agreed. For five days after A-level results come out, eligible applicants will be able to look for an alternative course that has places available whilst still holding their original choice. However, it is estimated that of the 500,000 or so applying annually, the number of applicants using this process will be in the hundreds (in 2010 it was less than 400). This is how it works:

- The applicant receives results and firm choice is confirmed.
- The five-day window is initiated through Track.
- Results are "better" than required by conditional offer.
- The applicant looks at available "aspirational" courses.
- The applicant contacts HEI to discuss a new application.
- The applicant receives a new offer of a place or remains with original firm choice.

Scenario 2: They get what they expected They get BCC. They do not have to do anything for a while. The university knew their results approximately four days before they did. They will soon confirm the place through Track.

Scenario 3: Near miss (the nightmare scenario) They get CCC and they needed BCC. They have not met the conditions of their firm offer. They should telephone the university immediately. When they finally get through (be patient) they will say one of four things:

- "Don't worry, we are still going to take you."
- "You are rejected." The student will have to go to their insurance university. If they have no insurance place, they will automatically enter clearing.
- "We haven't made our minds up yet and could take up to a week to decide, but no longer than that." If the student has an insurance place, they know they have this to fall back on. If they do not have an insurance place, this presents them with a dilemma: do they hang around and wait, thereby missing the best places in clearing, or do they ask to be rejected so they can go into clearing? Circumstances can be different depending on subject so they need to seek advice.
- "We are going to offer you an alternative course." The student does not have to accept this. It may be a very good course that is just right for them, or it could be a disaster waiting to happen. Again, they must seek advice. They should not be rushed into any snap decisions.

It is worth remembering that, if your students are holding a CF (Conditional Firm) or CI (Conditional Insurance) offer, universities should try to let them know their decisions by the Thursday following the publication of A-level results and really as soon as possible.

Scenario 4: They miss by a long way They get DEE! We can be fairly sure they will be rejected and they can enter clearing. Unless of course they were applying for science or engineering courses – strange things can happen here, and they may get some form of alternative offer.

11.8 Going through clearing

Clearing is the system that matches students without a place to university courses with vacancies.

Who is it for?
- If a student has entered UCAS Apply but does not hold any conditional offers, they will automatically be allowed to enter clearing.
- If they had conditional offers, but they were rejected because they failed to make the required grades, they will automatically be allowed to enter clearing.
- If a student did not enter UCAS Apply but decided after receiving their results that they would like to go to university, they still have to go through UCAS Apply to enter clearing.

How does it work?
- Clearing now starts the day A-level results are known.
- It is the student's responsibility to find out about vacancies, contact the universities and ask them if they will be accepted.
- They may get a number of positive responses, but the most important thing is that they only click on the one university they really want to go to.

How do they find out about vacancies?
- The Independent, Guardian and other daily papers.
- www.ucas.com provides an excellent vacancy service.
- University websites.
- Adverts that most universities place in a range of newspapers.

What about retakes and remarks?
- They need to discuss this with subject teachers/sixth-form managers (the issue has been further complicated by the Curriculum 2000 A-level system).
- Traditionally, most retake students have gone to further education colleges. For various reasons, schools are not normally keen to have people retaking.
- There is now so much remarking of units/exams/papers etc that you will need to have an institutional system worked out with your Exams Officer so you can provide a rapid response for your students.

12. The A* at A level (and can it be predicted?)

By Andy Gardner with contributions from Barbara Hamnett, Tim Miller and Helen Furman
gardner@jfs.brent.sch.uk

The reason for the introduction of the A* at A level seemed clear. So many A grades were being awarded that it was proving ineffective as a filter for selective/elite universities and courses. The proportion of students gaining A grades at A level had gone up steadily, from 16% in 1997 to 25.3% in 2008. The A* was introduced in response to complaints from leading universities that A grades were devalued and no longer enabled them to pick the best students. One way that universities have dealt with this issue to date is to introduce an extra test to filter applicants: examples include the BMAT and UKCAT for medicine and LNAT for some law courses.

It is therefore easy to understand why there has been pressure from the HE sector for a more robust means of filtering candidates. The current situation can also leave candidates applying for a variety of top institutions and courses with a mind-boggling number of tests to sit.

The Qualifications and Curriculum Authority (QCA), which oversaw the examinations system, awarded A levels to approximately 500,000 people in England, Northern Ireland and Wales in 2009. The A* is awarded to students who achieve a grade A overall at A level and also achieve 90 per cent or more on the uniform mark scale (UMS) across their A2 units i.e. 270+ out of 300 for a 3-unit A2 and 180+ out of 200 for a 2-unit A2. The A* grade was introduced for results published in August 2010.

N.B. If you are new to the A-level marking system it is very important that you understand the grade boundaries. You especially need to understand the concept of a high and low A grade at AS level, as we are using this as a possible predictor of A at A level.*

At the time of writing in January 2011, more and more universities and courses are now asking for the A* at A level, and it is pointless drawing up a current list as this will be added to all the time and will become out of date very quickly. Clearly we have a new benchmark to achieve for many courses, A*AA – though how long before A*A*A or even A*A*A* becomes common?

Many in schools, colleges and HEIs have called for a "wait and see" approach to allow the A* to bed-in, given the additional elements in the revised A levels of "stretch and challenge" and the new synoptic units. So where does all this leave teachers and lecturers making predictions, and advisers helping students through this minefield?

With funding from the Specialist Schools and Academies Trust, JFS School embarked on a small three-stage research project, looking at some of its own results.

JFS School Research – a three-stage process
- Stage 1 – 2009 – Could we have predicted the A* using the old system?
- Stage 2 – 2010 – Now we have A* results, can we predict from the available data?
- Stage 3 – 2011 – How reliable are teacher predictions based on AS results?

We are currently at stage 2 and will share stage 3 results with the wider community, hopefully late 2011/early 2012.

Stage 1 – 2009 – Could we have predicted the A* using the old system?
What did the 2009 research show?
- The students who scored 90%+ at AS were not always those who scored 90%+ at A2 to qualify for A* (using 2008 A2 cohort).
- Where a student would have achieved one A* it was not always in the subject most central to their university application.
- In one subject, 11 achieved 90%+ at AS but only one went on to achieve 90%+ at A2; in another, 6 out of 10 achieved 90% in both AS and A2.

Conclusion: Correlation between AS and A2 not proven.
Problem: How can one predict A* with confidence?

Stage 2 – 2010 – Now we have A* results can we predict from the available data?
- Eight subjects were used in survey of results from 2010 A2 cohort.
- We also looked at students' average GCSE point scores as well.
- Research focused on students who achieved A or B at AS level in sample subjects.
- Each result analysed was assigned to one of seven categories to aid comparison.
- Teacher opinion is not being considered here.
- Maths A level was not included in the research because there seems to be more agreement over its predictability.

Results were compiled in the following table.

	Humanities 1	Humanities 2	Humanities 3	Social Science 1	Social Science 2	Creative Subject 1	Science 1	Science 2
Total – A or B at AS Level	48	24	52	16	31	19	20	17
Category 1 (90%+ at AS and A* at A Level)	6	3	4	3	1	1	3	2
Category 2 (90%+ at AS and A at A Level)	14	3	9	2	0	3	3	1
Category 3	2	2	5	2	4	3	1	2

(80-89% at AS and A* at A Level)							
Category 4 (80-89% at AS and A at A Level)	14	7	17	3	12	5	5	7
Category 5 (B at AS Level and A* at A Level)	0	0	0	0	1	0	2	0
Category 6 (B at AS Level and A at A Level)	1	7	4	1	3	1	2	1
Category 7 (B at AS Level and B or lower at A Level)	11	2	13	5	10	6	4	4
Mean average GCSE point score of students scoring A* at A Level	7.5	7.2	7.4	6.5	7.4	6.5	7.5	7.7

What about those who got A*AA or above?
- 43 students got at least A*AA
- 75% of these had at least 7.2 at GCSE
- 22 got at least one high A and two As at AS level
- 20 got at least two high As and one A at AS level
- 11 got at least one high A and two low As at AS level and did not get A*AA (from the 8 subjects surveyed)
- Many students were getting the A* in a subject they had scored a low A in and getting an A in ones they had scored a high A in
- GCSE scores of those who got A*A*A*:
  8, 7.9, 7.9, 7.9, 7.6, 7.6, 7.6, 7.4, 7.3, **6.6** – the outlier!

What if we had invented a predictions policy based on the available data?
What if … we decided we will predict A*AA:
- **if** the student gets 7.3 at GCSE and one high A (90% UMS – 180/270+) at AS level;
- **or** the student gets two high As at AS level?
Of the 43 at JFS who got A*AA we would have got:
- 29 correct predictions
- 14 wrong predictions

Conclusion
Clearly, from this small sample, the correlation between 90%+ UMS at AS and getting an A* at A level is not strong when we are looking at making individual subject predictions. From our data, if you get a high A at AS level you are slightly more likely to get an A at A level rather than an A*. Looking at all the data – using

the three AS results and GCSE point score holistically – seems to be a better predictor, with two-thirds being correct using our invented predictions policy.

This certainly begs the question, should A* predictions be done by a person who has an overview of all the applicants' results, such as a Head of Year? Do we need to make some adjustments to UCAS Apply so we can indicate we think a student might be capable of getting A*AA, but we are not sure of the subject the A* will be in?

It is vitally important that institutions look at their own data. Just because we have identified these correlations, or rather a lack of them, doesn't mean this will apply to other institutions.

If, after taking into account teacher opinions in stage 3, predictions are still proving difficult, will this be a reason to move to PQA (post-qualifications application)?

13. Selective and specialist courses

HE advisers not only need to be approachable and friendly with good interviewing skills, they also need to be constantly updating their knowledge. One area the HE adviser needs to be sure of is selective and specialist courses. I have grouped these courses together because they often involve knowing extra information, and time needs to be invested in finding out about them.

In this section I have covered:
Oxbridge
Medicine
Additional tests
Art foundation
Dance and Drama
Music conservatoires

I have not covered dentistry or veterinary science here, though they are in *Appendix A*.

Getting the required A-level grades
Many courses are highly selective and the main tool that will be used for selection is grades (A*AA – AAB are common requirements). Students need to understand that getting high grades at A level is now mostly about meeting criteria set by examiners. Moreover, as the system currently stands, achieving high grades at AS level in year 12 will go a long way to ensuring high grades at A level (see section *18.3 How students can maximise their A-level grades*).

Students can do three things to help themselves:
* They need to make sure they are absolutely clear about what criteria they have to meet in exams and other forms of assessment. They should arrange meetings with their subject teachers to find out exactly what is required.
* They need to get down to some hard work *in year 12*, in order to get high grades at AS level.
* They should recognise how they themselves learn (for example, through understanding, or remembering, or both). They should try to identify their weaknesses, as well as their strengths, and do something about them.

13.1 Applying for Oxbridge – a realistic application using the GRIST framework

Never, in the history of education, has so much hot air been wasted on a single issue. Rather than adding to the global warming attributable to this subject, this is our attempt to deconstruct what is really going on. It is written presuming the reader is a teacher or careers adviser who has recently been given responsibility for students who might be considering an Oxbridge application.

A helpful acronym

In careers guidance, if we are trying to make something more understandable, our first tactic is to create an acronym. This will hopefully remind you of the issues you need to be aware of to help your possible Oxbridge applicants:

G	–	Grades
R	–	Reading
I	–	Interview
S	–	Subject
T	–	Tests

The phrase "grist to the mill" refers to turning something to one's profit or advantage. Turning the resources available in the sixth form to the student's advantage is exactly what is required for a successful Oxbridge application and is what will be addressed in this section.

Grades

We need to ensure that possible candidates have a realistic idea of what GCSE, AS and A-level (or equivalent qualification) grades or scores are typical of a successful Oxbridge applicant, and that they receive this information in time to act on it. Some would argue that by being specific about grades we could be putting off talented potential applicants. We would disagree. In practice we need clarity, not ambiguity.

• Typical GCSE grades

Both Cambridge and Oxford are now openly saying that the average applicant has 5-8 A*s at GCSE. Moreover, Cambridge is saying that even if the applicant has been to a challenging school they normally have 3-4 A*s – and quite often more. There can be exceptions, but the person doing the reference must be prepared to give comparative evidence as to why the student is an exception and refer to compensatory and contextual factors.

• Typical AS grades

Getting A grades at AS level is not normally enough. For Cambridge they need to be high AS grades, with applicants having 87-92% UMS scores in their three most relevant or best subjects. Oxford seems to be placing more emphasis on the performance in tests (see below) though in reality their applicants will have similar UMS scores. Please remember that Cambridge applicants have to declare their AS level UMS scores on the online supplementary form but Oxford applicants do not.

• Typical A-level grades

Cambridge asks in the main for a standard A*AA. A number of Oxford courses, mainly in the area of mathematics, physical and life sciences, will be asking for A* grades for students applying for 2012 entry. Always check details in the online Cambridge and Oxford prospectuses. If you want a real eye-opener, check UCAS Tariff scores for Oxford and Cambridge degrees in www.unistats.com

When writing a reference for an applicant you should place his or her academic ability in the context of where they stand in comparison to the rest of the year group. Any other contextual information could also be usefully added.

Reading

Possible applicants need to understand they will have to read more widely than for most other university interviews, be prepared to analyse what they have read and offer a critique. Some students may need help with choosing texts or, in maths and the sciences, practising problems. The more they read and do that is related to their subject, the more they will have to say in their personal statement.

It is essential:
- That the student learns that without wider reading or subject-related activity they will have very little evidence to back up their claim to be interested and engaged in their subject.
- That the student understands how the admissions tutor is likely to look for salient points in the personal statement as possible embarkation points for deeper questioning in the interview.
- That he or she learns that anything put in the statement can lead to a question that may be followed up with others on the same topic.
- That the student learns to talk and discuss issues with friends, teachers and family.

The importance of critical and analytical reading beyond the confines of an A-level syllabus cannot be stressed enough.

Interview

It is crucial that possible applicants are given tasks:
- That give them experience of dealing with subject-based questions and how they need to engage in the interview. (By engage, we mean answering questions that arise from the answers they gave to the original question from the interviewer).
- That make them think for themselves rather than regurgitate what they have been taught by a teacher.
- That make them realise they need to understand fully what each of them has written in his or her personal statement, a copy of which must be kept to refer to ahead of interviews. In addition, they must understand that not being able to talk in detail about what they have written is likely to be interpreted as a lack of motivation or commitment.
- That help them learn how admissions tutors will focus upon salient points in the statement as possible topics to bring up.
- That try to replicate the interview experience. Applicants should have a mock interview, preferably with someone who is knowledgeable on the subject and whom they do not know well. They should also watch videos produced by, for example, Oriel College Oxford, Oxford Learning Institute and Emmanuel College Cambridge to gain a clearer understanding of the interview process.

We feel very strongly that applicants, especially from non-selective state schools, will often have no experience of being interrogated on an academic issue. They may answer questions in class but they will not normally have had to face further questioning on their original answer. All applicants must be exposed to appropriate questioning related to their subject in a mock-interview scenario. A useful way of looking at an Oxbridge interview is as "an exam paper out loud."

Once applicants have an awareness of what the interview experience will be like, they should put their efforts into wider reading around their subject. This is much more important than doing repeated mock interviews. Extra-curricular activities that do not relate to the subject applied for will not be used in the selection process. No need to be a rounded student good at sport and music: this isn't what the tutors are looking for as it doesn't tell them much about a student's potential for studying, for example, biochemistry.

Subject

Candidates need to understand why they are applying for their chosen subject. Mainly the subject should relate to their abilities and interests, but it could also relate to their values (politics for example). Obsessive enthusiasm backed by evidence of serious interest is the only way forward here. One Oxford tutor has told us with "due humour" that in this context "geekiness is good!"

Students need to understand that they will mainly be asked subject-based questions, with the possible starting points being:
* something extracted from the personal statement;
* a piece of marked work (possibly in a different subject than that for which they are applying to study);
* something that has been covered in the A-level syllabus but that is then extended and developed. This type of questioning is intended to test how students can think for themselves and how they can apply their existing knowledge to new situations.

Tests

Potential applicants need to know that they may have to take additional tests either at school or at the interview and they need to have experience of being exposed to what is involved.

They may face a formal test:
* The Oxford or Cambridge thinking skills assessment (TSA) – for Cambridge this can cover subjects such as computing, engineering and sometimes PPS and land economy; for Oxford this covers PPE, economics and management, experimental psychology, psychology and philosophy and in the future geography.
* English literature admissions test (ELAT at Oxford).
* Biomedical admissions test (BMAT at both).
* Sixth Term Examination Paper (STEP at Cambridge for maths).
* LNAT – the national admissions test for law at Oxford and the Cambridge Law Admission Test.
* History aptitude test at Oxford (HAT).
* For maths, physics, computing and probably in the future engineering, students face a formal maths or physics test at Oxford.

Or they may face an informal test (an unseen poem, some text in a foreign language, a scientific problem, a piece of historical text) at both Oxford and Cambridge, depending on the subject applied for. Overall, Oxford seems to have more formal tests whereas Cambridge has more informal tests and also wants more in-depth information on AS-level performance.

Students need to familiarise themselves with the content and style of any formal tests and be informed of the relevant website details. We feel it is important that students are given the formal tests in a mock-exam situation and, where possible, that their answers are marked so they have a realistic idea of how they did. All the websites for the above tests have examples of past/sample papers. All the information on tests is collated at:

http://www.ox.ac.uk/admissions/undergraduate_courses/how_to_apply/tests/index.ht ml

http://www.cam.ac.uk/admissions/undergraduate/courses/ and also in Applicant Toolkit.

The really important preparation is for the candidate to be aware of the style and format of the questions, which don't look like A-level questions in many cases, and the time allowed for each element of the tests. The student should practise dealing with related unfamiliar texts, articles or problems even if they do not face a formal test. There may well be an informal test at interview.

Contextual issues and student background

All the above presumes the applicant has, of their own free will, decided they want to apply for an Oxford or Cambridge college. It does not try to deal with the wider issues of encouraging students to apply to Oxbridge. Nor does it address the perceived social injustices of the education system which Oxford and Cambridge universities are often accused of maintaining. Please do not confuse the applicant with the sociology of education issues that often come up in the media relating to Oxbridge application. These issues will be irrelevant to the applicant and will divert them from the GRIST framework.

Other issues such as college choice, understanding the Cambridge supervision system, the Oxford tutorial system and finding out contextual information that can be passed on to the Cambridge and Oxford colleges, should be covered with possible applicants. But we would argue that they are not as important as the above issues in the GRIST framework. See *Other points to consider* below.

Many organisations offer to help improve an applicant's chance of getting into Oxbridge. They often charge fees and you should be aware of the danger of over-preparation. We would argue that all they are doing is implementing elements of the GRIST framework, which can be done at a school or local authority level with the support of Oxford and Cambridge Universities themselves. We would also argue that Oxford and Cambridge Universities' methods of selections are as fair, or in fact fairer, than other common selection processes used by other universities, as they use a wider range of methods to make their final selection.

HOWEVER, one obvious weakness in the Oxbridge and Cambridge Universities' methods of selection is that there is not "equality of preparation". This clearly varies between schools and areas. It is therefore for schools, local authorities and Oxbridge themselves to help implement the GRIST framework and work towards "equality of preparation". To be fair, Oxford and Cambridge Universities do recognise this criticism and adjust their approaches accordingly.

What makes Oxford and Cambridge Universities different?
- The quality of the educational experience. Students will often be taught by the "leaders in their fields" and, in return, they will have to push themselves to

achieve very high levels of work. It should not be forgotten that there is, of course, academic excellence at other universities as well.

- More teaching is done individually. Students are expected to be self-starters and work independently.
- Whatever the degree, Oxbridge graduates have very good career prospects. A certain level of respect from employers is gained simply because of the university attended (though this effect diminishes over time).
- Colleges are normally friendly places, in pleasant surroundings. Accommodation provision is often very good. A close college community provides a friendly and welcoming home for students who are living away for the first time. Students soon get to know each other, and tutors get to know students individually, enabling them to respond to their individual academic needs. Oxbridge colleges still have a better level of funding than other universities, including generous bursary schemes such as the Oxford Opportunity Bursary.

What potential candidates need to know about the college system
- Oxford University and Cambridge University each have more than 20 colleges. Students should not be put off by some idiosyncratic pronunciations. Magdalene College, for example, is pronounced *maud-lin*.
- Lectures are taught by the university. English lectures, for example, will be taught at the university's English faculty. Tutorials (at Oxford) and supervisions (at Cambridge) involve being taught individually or in small groups at the student's own college. As the student specialises in later years of their course the tutorials will often be with tutors at other colleges. This is important because it means a student shouldn't feel they have to be a student at the college that has the "world expert" in their subject. If the student takes a course that this expert supervises, then the student is likely to have them as a tutor.
- Undergraduates live, eat and socialise at their colleges, in the main. Cambridge colleges, on the whole, will find accommodation for three years. Oxford colleges vary. Very few students are in private rented accommodation as undergraduates – they are usually "living out" in college-owned houses in their second year.
- It is unusual for two people from the same school to apply for the same subject at the same college.

Points for students to consider when choosing a college at Oxbridge
- Does the college offer accommodation for the duration of the course?
- Does the college have a fellow or director of studies in the relevant subject? Students should research the college that interests them most, but not become too attached. Applications may be pooled and an offer come from another college. About 25% of students receive an offer from a college that was not their first preference at Oxford.
- *Students cannot apply to both Oxford and Cambridge.*

13.2 Applying for medical school

As a result of more than 20 years' experience working with applicants for medicine and being on an admissions panel for a medical school, I have in my mind a common pattern for the people who *actually* make it to medical school (not the ones who *could* make it).
- They tend not to miss lessons, lectures or deadlines.

- They tend to have good time-management skills and can fit in their school commitments with their other activities.
- They tend to take lessons, lectures and advice from teachers seriously.
- They tend to take advantage of opportunities that are made available to them and often take the initiative themselves to contribute to the community of their school or sixth form.
- They acknowledge their academic weaknesses as much as their strengths.
- They work consistently from the moment that they start in year 12 and do not try to play catch-up in year 13.

Students entering year 12 and expressing an interest in a career in medicine should be encouraged to take a good look at themselves. Do they have the personal qualities listed above? Can they work on acquiring them?

For those with the ability, interest and attitude to apply for medicine, there are a number of specific issues to be aware of. These are:
- making sure they have chosen the right AS levels or equivalent subjects;
- getting relevant work experience;
- gaining as much knowledge as possible about medical careers;
- coming across well in their UCAS personal statement and at interview;
- preparing for the BMAT test and the UKCAT test.

N.B. Most applicants who make it to medical school have at least 3-4 A*s at GCSE and most have many more. If the student has grades below this, you may need to explore contextual reasons: perhaps they went to a very challenging secondary school, for example. If they are still very keen to apply for medical school with a weak GCSE foundation then you must emphasise that they must be looking at a massive improvement at AS level to have any hope of being considered.

There are some widening access schemes at various medical schools such as SGUL, KCL and Southampton. It is worth exploring the different criteria under which these schemes consider people.

Choosing the right AS levels
- *Essential AS levels:* Students who take chemistry, biology and either maths or physics will keep all the medical school options open. Students who take chemistry and biology will keep open the vast majority. Taking chemistry plus maths and/or physics will limit the student's range of choices.
- *Useful AS levels:* Critical thinking will help with section 3 of the BMAT test and the UKCAT test, but this should be taken only as a fifth AS level.
- *Students who take chemistry, biology and maths or physics:* These students have already met the entry criteria for medical school with their first three choices, so their fourth-choice AS level can (and should) be based on their strengths and interests. A few medical schools are not so keen on students offering chemistry, biology, maths *and* physics at AS level, as this shows a lack of breadth. Rather they should play to their strengths and choose something they are good at and which interests them.
- *Students who take chemistry and biology but do not want to do maths or physics:* These students could play safe and choose their third AS level from the following list: English, geography, history, modern or classical foreign languages or maybe another humanities or social science subject. Their fourth AS level could be based

on their strengths and interests and could include one of the social sciences (economics, government and politics, psychology or sociology) or theology/philosophy so they can cover ethics. This is an inexact science, compounded by the fact that all medical schools can have slightly different views. Generally, I would say play safe with the third choice but if you love art, for example, then do it as a fourth choice – go with your interests!

- *Students who want to take a fifth AS level:* This would normally be: critical thinking, further maths or a foreign language. But students should be careful not to overload themselves. Three A grades will look better than an A and four Bs.

Getting relevant work experience
- Any work experience should be in a role that gives the student a *realistic view* of medical life.
- Two or three different work experiences are better than just one.
- Medical schools tend to look favourably on work experience that students have organised for themselves.
- Long-term commitment (for example, spending half a day a week for a couple of months or more) is also viewed favourably.
- As well as work experience in hospitals and general practice, other possibilities might include, for example: volunteering in a nursing home; volunteering in a hospice for the terminally ill; volunteering for a children's group involved with disabilities or special needs; volunteering with other healthcare professionals.
- Students should be aware that *what they learn* from their work experience is the most important thing, not where they did it or the quality of it.

Here is an example showing how students can maximise the benefits from their work experience and build up useful material for personal statements and interviews.

Amina did some work experience in an old people's home in north London. Doesn't sound very glamorous, does it? However, there was much for her to learn.

- Amina found out what health problems affect the elderly particularly. She identified one, Alzheimer's disease, and then found a website dedicated to the subject, which gave her facts about dementia (many organisations which deal with specific health problems run websites providing information to the public).
- Amina related this information to areas of her A-level studies such as genetics, vascular systems and statistics.
- She also found out which health professionals deal particularly with the elderly. She discovered who did what, and saw how teams of professionals worked together.
- She also researched the importance of family to the elderly and tried to discover whether isolation from the family can have an adverse effect on health.

Finding out about medical careers
Any students interested in medicine should take a close look at the website of the British Medical Association (www.bma.org.uk). In particular, students should make sure they know about:
- the many different areas of medical work (surgeon, hospital consultant, general practitioner, medical researcher, medical lecturer, psychiatrist, geneticist, public

health physician, to name but a few) and the opportunities for work outside the NHS (armed forces, prisons, Home Office);
- the core skills and attributes of a doctor (these have been identified as competence, integrity, confidentiality, a caring nature, compassion, commitment, responsibility, advocacy, spirit of enquiry);
- the career path of a doctor, from medical degree through to hospital consultant or GP principal, and how long the training takes (nine to twelve years);
- the long hours and hard work involved.

Personal statements and interviews
UCAS personal statements are the initial way for students to sell themselves in the highly competitive atmosphere of applying for medical school – so it is worth getting them right. Moreover, applicants for medical school can expect to be interviewed by all their choices, and many questions in an interview will relate to the content of the student's personal statement.

Here are some points to consider both when writing a personal statement and when preparing for interview.
- Students will be expected to explain fully why they want be become a doctor and provide evidence to back up their claims. What evidence do they have that proves they are genuinely interested in scientific issues and the welfare of others?
- Students will be expected to have done some work experience in the fields of medicine or health. They must be able to explain what they learnt from this time.
- It is a good idea to know who the current Secretary of State for Health is and to have some idea about how the National Health Service is funded. Students should be aware of some current issues or difficulties facing doctors. Is there one that they could talk about in more depth?
- What disease or health problem interests them most – what steps have they taken to find out about it? Does it relate to anything they have learned at A level?
- Students will probably be asked what qualities they think make a good doctor. They should try to think of examples.

When preparing personal statements, it might be helpful for students to jot down their ideas under the following headings.
- **Three** reasons why I want to study medicine.
- What evidence do I have to support these reasons:
  o from A levels;
  o from work experience/part-time work/voluntary work;
  o from wider reading/research/media?
- Other things I have done, in the past/at the moment.
- Things I want to do in the future.
- What is my weakest point and what will I do about it?

At interview, it is worth remembering that admissions tutors are fed up with students saying things like, "I am enthusiastic, I can work in a team, I have good communication skills," without any evidence to support this. Interviewees need to think of *examples* that *prove* these qualities. For more preparation, students should look at:
The medicine sections in the *University Interviews Guide* (Gardner/ Hamnett), published by JFS School.

Medical School Interviews (Lee/Picard) published by iscmedical.

Preparing for the BMAT test

The BMAT test (bio-medical admissions test) is for applicants for medicine at Cambridge, Imperial, Oxford and UCL. It is taken at school as a public examination in November.

The test comprises:
- a 60-minute test of general aptitudes and skills (students will need to get acquainted with this type of test);
- a 30-minute test of science knowledge, based on GCSE science (students should revisit their GCSE science notes but deal with the questions at a more in-depth level – this is an incredibly hard test for most applicants!!!!);
- a 30-minute writing task (an AS in critical thinking would be useful; otherwise students can read *Thinking from A-Z* by Nigel Warburton or *Critical Thinking: An Introduction* by Alec Fisher).

Students can – and should – look at examples of the tests on the BMAT website, www.bmat.org.uk. These specimen papers give a good idea of what to expect, the level of questioning and how much preparation to do.

Finding out about the UKCAT test

Many medical schools use the UKCAT test. This aims to test mental ability in the areas of:
- Verbal Reasoning
- Quantitative Reasoning
- Abstract Reasoning
- Decision Analysis
- Non-Cognitive Analysis

There is no science paper and the tests are not curriculum based.
Visit: www.ukcat.ac.uk.

Medical schools intending to use the UKCAT test include: Aberdeen, Brighton and Sussex, Cardiff, Dundee, Durham, University of East Anglia, Edinburgh, Glasgow, Hull and York, Keele, King's College London, Leeds, Leicester, Manchester, Newcastle, Nottingham, Peninsula, Queen Mary, QUB, St Andrews, St George's, Sheffield and Southampton.

It is vitally important the test is practised using the downloadable online version so students can get used to the speed at which the questions have to be answered.

Finally, let's ask a doctor a few questions

I decided to put Professor Trisha Greenhalgh OBE on the spot with a few questions. She is a part-time GP and a columnist for the British Medical Journal. She developed the innovative Dick Whittington Project, which aimed to help students from non-traditional backgrounds, but with an aptitude for medicine, to get into medical school. This is what she said.

Why did you want to become a doctor? "Hard to answer, as I decided at the age of three. I was just fascinated with the human body, how it worked and how it sometimes failed. I wanted to be a part of that action."

Do you still like your job as a GP and why? "Yes. The best part of being a GP is supporting people who want to make their own decisions about how to manage their illness. Most illness these days is chronic (i.e. long term) not acute (i.e. sudden and short-term). We GPs spend most of our lives helping people with diabetes, high blood pressure, arthritis, kidney failure and so on live with their condition and stay independent and active. People these days generally don't want to 'put their trust in doctors' – they want to be in charge of their own lives. For example, an elderly lady who needs a hip replacement may decide she'd prefer to live with the pain than go through an operation. My job as a GP is to give her the information she needs to make the best decision for her, not to tell her what she should do."

In your view is there a type of person suited to medicine? "If you're not interested in people (especially old and sick people), forget it."

The media portrays the NHS as chaotic and underfunded. Why would someone want to work in an organisation that seems like this? "The NHS is not chaotic – but it is big and complex. It's the largest employer in the world (apart from the Russian Army and Indian Railways). Illness is a complex business – a person newly diagnosed with cancer will need around 20 different tests in five different hospital departments, plus a treatment package typically comprising one or two operations, 18 visits to a chemotherapy department, nine different drugs and a series of sessions with a psychologist or counsellor. But the chances of being cured of cancer today are many times better than they were 20 years ago. In other words, health care is complex because high-quality medicine is complex. If you can't stand this sort of heat, keep out of the kitchen!"

Does it really matter what medical school you go to? "No, not in terms of whether you're likely to get a job at the end. Personally I picked my medical school on the basis of (a) distance from my parents' house (far enough so they didn't visit too often), (b) opportunities for sport, and (c) teachers' advice (I was advised not to apply to Cambridge because I was from a working-class family and it was thought I wouldn't fit in there, so I applied and got in)."

If a student comes from a working-class background will they fit in? "See above. I'm not sure we have 'working class' any more in the old-fashioned sense. We certainly have rich people and poor people, and the rich ones will leave university with less debt. If you're poor, you must be prepared to invest in your own future by taking out a large loan. That's what I did, and I didn't regret it."

Many parents pay for extra tuition to help their children get the high A-level grades required. What if parents can't afford this? "By the time you're working at A-level standard tutors are less important than the work you put in yourself. From what I've seen, bright A-level students from poor backgrounds are the ones who make the most of 'free' opportunities – for example, they come up to the teacher at the end of every lesson and make them explain anything they didn't grasp. They attach themselves to pupils in the year above, and ask them more questions. And they find out about, and make use of, all sorts of free learning opportunities. Rich kids may have private tutors but it's not private tutors who get you into medical school – it's hard work, determination and planning."

13.3 Additional tests

With more and more applicants gaining the highest A-level grades, universities are finding it hard to sort the "very good" from the "good". Admissions tutors will take into account UCAS personal statements, but how can they be sure these are solely the work of the students (who may have been helped by their parents or schools)? School references, too, are so overwhelmingly positive that most applicants seem wonderful. Some universities or courses, therefore, are looking for some form of additional test to help them decide who will be able to cope with the rigours of their degrees.

For the HE adviser, keeping up with the range of tests being used is not easy. There are two central websites that try to keep an eye on things:
http://www.ucas.ac.uk/students/choosingcourses/admissions/
http://www.spa.ac.uk/admission-tests/tests-being-used.html

Many tests are administered by Cambridge Assessment:
TSA
STEP
BMAT
ELAT
http://www.admissionstests.cambridgeassessment.org.uk/adt/
N.B. Even though these tests are administered by Cambridge Assessment you could be either required or encouraged to take these tests by Bath, Bristol, Cambridge, Imperial, Oxford, UCL, RVC and Warwick universities.

Anyone considering Cambridge or Oxford will need to know if they will face a formal or informal test, and must visit:
http://www.ox.ac.uk/admissions/undergraduate_courses/how_to_apply/tests/index.ht
ml
http://www.cam.ac.uk/admissions/undergraduate/courses/ and see also Applicant Toolkit

Applicants considering law must visit:
www.lnat.ac.uk

Applicants for medicine and dentistry must visit:
www.ukcat.ac.uk

Increasingly other courses are using tests, for example:
- primary education degrees will use an English test;
- health professions may be asked to take an English test;
- architecture applicants may be given a design task.

It is vital that we make our students aware that they may well face a test, depending on to whom and for what they are applying. HE advisers face a patchwork of information sources to try to be on top of this issue.

13.4 Why do an art foundation course?

Many students who study art and design at A level will think about doing an art foundation course. But why is this necessary? The reason is that most sixth-form students take *art* A level, which is the study of painting, drawing and sculpture. Yet most university students in this field study *design* subjects, such as graphic, fashion, product or interior design. An art foundation course acts as a bridge between A levels and design degrees.

The facts about art foundation courses
- They are one-year long, full-time.
- Fees are not normally charged for students who are still 18 years old.
- Most courses make students work hard on their drawing skills.
- In the first term, students try out all the major types of design – graphic, fashion, product, interior and other types, depending on the course.
- In the second term they try to decide the area of art and design they would like to specialise in. They will begin to concentrate on this area so they have a specialist portfolio for the degree/foundation degree or HND course they want to apply for.
- It is very common for students to start an art foundation course believing they want to do a certain sort of design, such as fashion, and then, once they have tried everything out, to decide to do something different, such as illustration.
- It is a very intense year and it is not an easy option. Students should know by the end of it whether art and design is for them. If they decide *not* to do a degree in art and design, then they can apply for other courses on the strength of the A levels they already have.
- Most art and design degree/foundation degree and HND courses make the successful completion of an art foundation course an entrance requirement.
- Students do not apply for art foundation courses through UCAS. There may be a local admissions scheme, or students apply direct to colleges.
- Colleges hold open days and encourage students to visit before applying. Students should contact individual colleges for details.
- Students from BTEC National or Applied GCSE courses are sometimes considered for direct entry to higher education courses in art and design if their portfolios are strong enough. It is always advisable to contact the courses and institutions being considered directly.

UCAS, although it is not responsible for admissions to art foundation, keeps a list of available art foundation courses:
http://www.ucas.ac.uk/students/choosingcourses/specificsubjects/artanddesign/foundationcourses/

"Should I do a UCAS Apply as well?"
This is a common question from students interested in art foundation courses.
- For most people – those who definitely know they want to do an art or design degree – the answer will be "no". This is because it makes things too complicated when they want to apply for degree courses later on.
- If, however, they know they definitely want to do a degree which is *different* from art and design, then they can apply through UCAS for deferred entry and do the foundation course as a gap year.

13.5 Drama training

Students who wish to pursue a stage career can find essential information from:
- Conference of Drama Schools, www.drama.ac.uk; or
- Council for Dance Education and Training, www.cdet.org.uk

Would-be drama students should note that funding can be an issue.
- Most courses accredited by the National Council for Dramatic Training or NCDT (these are the ones that lead to professional acting, dance or stage management) are state funded through the HEFC and applicants will be treated the same as any other higher-education student.
- Some courses, however, are not state funded. Students who win places on these courses may be eligible for funding through other awards (such as a DADA) or scholarships, although competition for these will be fierce.
- Many drama schools are joining up with larger universities and will therefore come under HEFC arrangements. It is important that students contact the schools they are interested in to see what the funding situation is.

Students must be aware that only NCDT-accredited courses can guarantee membership of Equity (the acting trade union), which most people need to get acting work.

13.6 Music Conservatoire

There are two ways to apply for music courses. The route you take depends on the type of course you would like to study.
- For full-time undergraduate degree courses, you apply through the UCAS process and use the online application system Apply.
- If you'd like to study a practice-based music course, you apply through CUKAS, an admissions service for practice-based music courses taught at UK conservatoires.
- If you cannot make up your mind, why not apply through both systems? You can apply through both UCAS and CUKAS, then decide which course to take later in the year.

The CUKAS website allows an instrument search. For example, if I were a talented piccolo player I could apply to Royal Welsh College and Trinity Laban.

Visit: www.cukas.ac.uk

14. Student finance

The purpose of this section is not to provide detailed information about the current student finance situation (it will change constantly through the lifetime of this book and is in any case available from other sources) but to make HE advisers aware of the broad principles they need to follow when advising their students.

HOWEVER, bearing in mind the Browne Review in England of student and university finance, and the subsequent reforms due in the new Higher Education White Paper 2011, there has clearly been a seismic shift and due to interest in this area I have included in this section a paper by my colleague Peter Boursnell that factually tries to compare the new and the old systems of student finance in England.

There are separate systems of student finance in Northern Ireland, Scotland and Wales. We will have to wait and see how much they are influenced by the changes to student finance in England.

As HE advisers we will all have differing views on how student finance should be funded. However, with our students, it is our ethical role to explain the facts as they are, not how we would like them to be. We should neither sugar the pill nor put them off!

14.1 Introduction to student finance

As HE advisers, there are three main areas to consider:
* what the student finance arrangements are at any given time (see section below on current and new arrangements);
* how students apply;
* student budgeting.

What the student finance arrangements are
Students need to be aware of:
* fees;
* loans (both for fees and for maintenance);
* grants and national scholarship programme arrangement (for students from lower-income families);
* repayments;
* bursaries and scholarships given by individual universities;
* help for students with disabilities.

To get more information go to:
* www.direct.gov.uk/studentfinance This website will also take you to information for England, Scotland, Northern Ireland, Wales and countries abroad.
* www.ucas.com/students/studentfinance/ This is a useful section on grants and awards.
* www.practitioners.studentfinanceengland.co.uk This provides useful information for those advising students and also has some good resources.

Dance and Drama Awards (DADAs)
While many dance and drama courses are state funded, some 22 private dance and drama colleges have separate funding arrangements. Students who win places may be eligible for a DADA. To find out more about DADAs go to the information on www.direct.gov.uk (I just Google dance and drama awards).

National Health Service bursaries for health professional courses
To be eligible to apply for NHS financial support, you must be accepted for an NHS-funded place on a full or part-time course which leads to professional registration as a:
- doctor or dentist (you will be eligible for an NHS Bursary during the latter stages of your pre-registration training)
- chiropodist (including podiatrist), dietician, occupational therapist, orthoptist, physiotherapist, prosthetist, orthotist, radiographer, audiologist or a speech and language therapist
- dental hygienist or dental therapist
- nurse or midwife (degree course)
- nurse, midwife or operating department practitioner (diploma course)

You may be eligible for an NHS Bursary even if you have already had public funding for higher education. If you have previously had an NHS Bursary and wish to switch professions, you may also be eligible.
Visit: www.nhsbsa.nhs.uk *N.B. I have contacted Student Bursaries at NHSBSA and they have told me the NHS Bursary is under review with details due in April 2011.*

Social Work Bursaries
The social work bursary was introduced by the Department of Health as an incentive to train in social work. All eligible applicants will receive a non-income-assessed basic grant. The amount of the grant is dependant on where they study and whether they are studying full time or part time. The amount of the basic grant for undergraduate students is also dependant on whether they are subject to variable tuition fees. Postgraduate students may also apply for additional income-assessed elements.
Visit: www.nhsbsa.nhs.uk

How students apply
Students must be clear about:
- the application process;
- their residency status;
- deadlines.

There is a team of staff from Student Finance England who can help with enquiries when they arise, but HE advisers should allocate some time to looking at information on all the above websites, in particular the "practitioners" site.

Student budgeting
Students need to understand the concept of "money coming in and money going out", "debit and credit", "what they will be getting and what will they be paying out". Whatever terms we use, it is essential that they get the idea.

The following table is a simple way of getting students to think about these issues and could form the basis of a budgeting worksheet.

Income (annual)		Outgoings (weekly)	
Maintenance loan	£	Accommodation	£
Maintenance grant	£	Food	£
Parental contribution	£	Travel	£
Earnings	£	Socialising/entertainment	£
Sponsorship	£	Laundry	£
Bursary	£	Toiletries	£
TOTAL	**£**	Clothes	£
		Books and course equipment	£
		Photocopying and stationery	£
		Field trips	£
Divide total by 30 to get:		Anything else?	£
Weekly income	**£**	**TOTAL**	**£**

In my experience, whenever we get students to do an exercise like this, the difference between the income and the outgoings proves interesting and thought provoking! These days, any shortfall is usually covered by a student's interest-free overdraft from a bank.

Further reading
* *Student Money Matters* by Gwenda Thomas (published by Trotmans) – the best overview on student finance.

14.2 Student Loan Repayment Arrangements

Current arrangements and new arrangements from 2012 – a comparison
By Peter Boursnell, Brent Aimhigher (until July 2011)
peteboursnell@hotmail.com

This paper compares repayments on loans once the 2012 cohort have finished university in 2015. The figures are based on those announced by Government (yet to be passed by Parliament). All the case-study examples given are for graduates from universities that charge the full £9,000 tuition fees per year.

Note: Students deferring from 2011 to 2012 will have to apply for loans at the 2012 rates.

Headlines
* Under the current system, graduates start repaying their loan once they are earning above £15,000.
* Under the new system from 2012, graduates only start repaying their loans once they are earning above £21,000. (Note: The £21,000 threshold will increase in line with earnings from 2016 onwards.)
* As the average starting salary of graduates in England is between £18,00 and £19,000, this will mean a significant proportion of graduates won't have to repay anything for the first few years (and possibly longer) of their working life.

Repayment calculation

Current system: graduates repay their loan at the rate of 9% of what they earn above £15,000.

New system: graduates repay their loan at the rate of 9% of what they earn above £21,000.

Repayment examples

In September 2015, when most of the graduates under the new system will be starting work, these examples compare what they will be repaying per week compared to graduates under the old system. It is important to realise that repayment is based purely on income and is not dependent on the total amount of loan taken out.

A graduate earning £21,000
- Under the current system would pay back approximately £10 per week (regardless of the size of their loan)
- Under the new system would pay back **nothing** (regardless of the size of their loan)

A graduate earning £24,000
- Under the current system would pay back approximately £16 per week (regardless of the size of their loan)
- Under the new system would pay back approximately £5 (regardless of the size of their loan)

A graduate earning £30,000
- Under the current system would pay back approximately £26 per week (regardless of the size of their loan)
- Under the new system would pay back approximately £16 (regardless of the size of their loan)

A graduate earning £40,000
- Under the current system would pay back approximately £43 per week (regardless of the size of their loan)
- Under the new system would pay back approximately £33 (regardless of the size of their loan)

Interest on loan

- Interest on your loan will be charged at inflation plus 3% while you are studying, and up until the April after you leave university.
- From the April after you leave university if you are earning below £21,000, interest will be applied at the rate of inflation.
- Graduates earning between £21,000 and £41,000 will be charged interest on a sliding scale up to a maximum of inflation plus 3%.
- Graduates earning above £41,000 will be charged interest at the full rate of inflation plus 3%.
- A worrying variable will be the rate of inflation (RPI)!

The Government says that under the new arrangements:
- all graduates will pay less per month than they do under the current system;
- all outstanding repayments will be written off after 30 years;
- around a quarter of graduates, those with the lowest lifetime earnings, will pay less than under the current system.

The Browne Report suggested that only the top 40% of earners on average will pay back the full amount of their loan over the 30-year repayment period. This percentage was based on its recommendations and may be different under the Government's proposals.

Maintenance grants
From 2012, these will be slightly more generous than under the present system.

Case studies
The following case studies look at graduates from 2015 (under the current and the new fees arrangements) at various levels of income, and indicate exactly how their repayments are calculated and how repayments compare to their take-home pay.

Graduates on salary of £21,000	
Student starting university in 2011	Student starting university in 2012
Under the **current fees** arrangements	Under the **new fees** arrangements
Tuition Fees: £3,375 per year	Tuition Fees: £9,000 per year
Total loan for 3-year course: £10,125	Total loan for 3-year course: £27,000
Student finishes degree in June 2014 (takes a gap year, travelling the world)	Student finishes degree in June 2015
Student starts working in Sept 2015	Student starts working in Sept 2015
Both students on a starting salary of £21,000	
Student pays 9% of earnings above £15k = £10 per week (*approx*)	Student pays 9% of earnings above £21k = £0 per week (*nothing*)
Take-home pay after tax and NI would be £322 per week (*estimate*) £312 per week after loan payment (*estimate*)	Take-home pay after tax and NI would be £322 per week (*estimate*)
Note: the £10,125 does not include any maintenance loan. However, even with maintenance loan added, the amount repaid per week remains the same.	*Note: the £27,000 does not include any maintenance loan. However, even with maintenance loan added, the amount repaid per week remains the same.*

Graduates on salary of £24,000	
Student starting university in 2011	Student starting university in 2012
Under the **current fees** arrangements	Under the **new fees** arrangements
Tuition Fees: £3,375 per year	Tuition Fees: £9,000 per year
Total loan for 3-year course: £10,125	Total loan for 3-year course: £27,000
Student finishes degree in June 2014 (takes a gap year, travelling the world)	Student finishes degree in June 2015
Student starts working in Sept 2015	Student starts working in Sept 2015
Both students on a starting salary of £24,000	
Student pays 9% of earnings above £15k	Student pays 9% of earnings above £21k

= £16 per week (*approx*)	= £5 per week (*approx*)
Take-home pay after tax and NI would be £365 per week (*estimate*) £349 per week after loan payment (*estimate*)	Take-home pay after tax and NI would be £365 per week (*estimate*) £360 per week after loan payment (*estimate*)
Note: the £10,125 does not include any maintenance loan. However, even with maintenance loan added, the amount repaid per week remains the same.	*Note: the £27,000 does not include any maintenance loan. However, even with maintenance loan added, the amount repaid per week remains the same.*

Graduates on salary of £30,000	
Student starting university in 2011	Student starting university in 2012
Under the **current fees** arrangements	Under the **new fees** arrangements
Tuition Fees: £3,375 per year	Tuition Fees: £9,000 per year
Total loan for 3-year course: £10,125	Total loan for 3-year course: £27,000
Student finishes degree in June 2014 (takes a gap year, travelling the world)	Student finishes degree in June 2015
Student starts working in Sept 2015	Student starts working in Sept 2015
Both students on a starting salary of £30,000	
Student pays 9% of earnings above £15k = £26 per week (*approx*)	Student pays 9% of earnings above £21k = £16 per week (*approx*)
Take-home pay after tax and NI would be £448 per week (*estimate*) £422 per week after loan payment (*estimate*)	Take-home pay after tax and NI would be £448 per week (*estimate*) £432 per week after loan payment (*estimate*)
Note: the £10,125 does not include any maintenance loan. However, even with maintenance loan added, the amount repaid per week remains the same.	*Note: the £27,000 does not include any maintenance loan. However, even with maintenance loan added, the amount repaid per week remains the same.*

Graduates on salary of £40,000	
Student starting university in 2011	Student starting university in 2012
Under the **current fees** arrangements	Under the **new fees** arrangements
Tuition Fees: £3,375 per year	Tuition Fees: £9,000 per year
Total loan for 3-year course: £10,125	Total loan for 3-year course: £27,000
Student finishes degree in June 2014 (takes a gap year, travelling the world)	Student finishes degree in June 2015
Student starts working in Sept 2015	Student starts working in Sept 2015
Both students on a starting salary of £40,000	
Student pays 9% of earnings above £15k	Student pays 9% of earnings above £21k

= £43 per week (*approx*)	= £33 per week (*approx*)
Take-home pay after tax and NI would be £587 per week (*estimate*) £544 per week after loan payment (*estimate*)	Take-home pay after tax and NI would be £587 per week (*estimate*) £554 per week after loan payment (*estimate*)
Note: the £10,125 does not include any maintenance loan. However, even with maintenance loan added, the amount repaid per week remains the same.	*Note: the £27,000 does not include any maintenance loan. However, even with maintenance loan added, the amount repaid per week remains the same.*

Please note: These calculations are not official figures and have been estimated in good faith.

15. Graduate employment

The education bestowed on Flora Poste by her parents had been expensive, athletic and prolonged; and when they died within a few weeks of one another during the annual epidemic of the influenza or Spanish Plague which occurred in her twentieth year, she was discovered to possess every art and grace save that of earning her own living.
Stella Gibbons, Cold Comfort Farm 1932

15.1 What is graduate employment?

When I was training to become a careers officer in 1985, graduate employment was described to me as "a job that a graduate does", which looking back wasn't very helpful. For me the best definition of graduate employment came along in 2004. This is Elias and Purcell's Standard Occupational Classification (Higher Education). They have five major types of graduate occupation:

Traditional graduate occupations
The established professions for which, historically, the normal entry route has been via an undergraduate degree programme. Examples are barristers, doctors, engineers, higher-education and secondary-education teachers, and research scientists.

Modern graduate occupations
The newer professions, particularly in management, IT and creative vocational careers, are areas graduates have been entering since educational expansion in the 1960s. Examples are accountants, computer programmers, primary-school teachers and journalists.

New graduate occupations
Areas of employment, many in new or expanding occupations, where the route into the professional area has recently changed and is now via an undergraduate degree programme. Examples are marketing managers, physiotherapists and computer games designers.

Niche graduate occupations
Occupations where the majority of incumbents are not graduates, but within which there are stable or growing specialist niches that require higher-level skills and knowledge. Examples are leisure centre managers, hotel managers and retail managers.

Non-graduate occupations
All jobs that do not fall into the previous four categories are considered "non-graduate occupations". This does not automatically imply that it is not appropriate for a graduate to be doing them, or that a graduate cannot enjoy a fulfilling job. It means that, in the main, a degree is not required to enter these occupations.

This classification, in my opinion, deconstructs the graduate labour market rather well. Many people when advising on graduate employment will concentrate on traditional and modern graduate occupations, yet according to HECSU in 2007, while 25% of graduates will go into traditional and modern graduate occupations, 42% of graduates will go into new and niche graduate occupations (with 33% going into non-graduate occupations.)

15.2 Where are graduates employed?

As an HE adviser you can work at getting lots of information and facts to throw at those considering higher education. Here are a few, for example, on the graduate job market taken from www.prospects.ac.uk:

- There are 300,000+ new graduates each year yet there are only 80,000 formal training positions.
- Over 80% of graduates work in SMEs (small and medium enterprises) with fewer than 250 employees.
- Six out of ten new jobs are never advertised.

Our job is to interpret this information for them. In other words:

- Being a graduate does not get you a job by itself. It is only a licence to hunt.
- There may be other things you need to be concerned about, such as high A-level grades or relevant work experience, if you want to get a job with an AGR (Association of Graduate Recruiters)-type firm.
- You are not likely to be working for a big company.
- You need to network and do work experience.

Watch out for information that could be regarded as wishful thinking, such as The Times Top 100 Graduate Employers book. This is about where students would like to work, not where they are working!

It is definitely worth spending some time investigating the Association of Graduate Recruiters. They represent more than 800 of the UK's largest graduate recruiters in areas such as finance, construction, IT, retail, legal, logistics, energy and the public sector. They have a very high media profile and many reports in the media will be based on their work. They do not normally represent the SMEs who employ most graduates.

Over the years as an HE adviser you will have little influence on PEST effects – political, economic, sociological and technological changes – though it is important to try to be aware of them because they can have an effect on graduate employment, such as the off-shoring of jobs to other countries.

As you talk to 16-, 17- or 18-year-olds about graduate unemployment, be aware that we do not know what the graduate employment situation will be in four to six years time, so it is always best to talk about what will improve their chances in the future rather than how dreadful things are now.

Students left to their own devices can stick to considering graduate careers that are "known knowns": dentistry and journalism are popular examples. One student may want a well-paid profession in the science field and another a well-paid job in the arts field. For dentistry their belief would probably be confirmed, but journalism has been affected by new technology such as the internet and an oversupply of applicants to available jobs, holding wages down in many cases.

It is important to try to make students aware of other types of graduate occupation. I use the examples of environmental health practitioner and transport planners, but you could use many others.

15.3 How do you get graduate employment?

The impact of your degree choice
Students need to be aware that the subject they do will have an impact on the way the graduate employment market views them, and in my opinion students need to know this to help them deal with the graduate employment market.

I have developed five very broad categories to help us view different degrees. They have been developed through my experience rather than academic research, but I have found them useful in coping with a complex graduate employment market. The categories are not precise, and arguably some degrees could be in different categories, while they also presume that the student is doing a single-subject degree not a joint honours. However, when there are around 50,000 different course titles on UCAS course search, at least it is something to help us make the complex connections between degree choice and graduate employment more manageable.

Vocational Degree ("Ronseal" i.e. It does what it says on the tin!)
These are degrees that will try to train you up for a particular work area that either:
*   is governed by a professional body and you are able to work in the field (probably with further training/education) on leaving the course, such as pharmacy, quantity surveying and primary education.
*   requires training and experience, and while the degree may or may not lead to further professional training/education, you are normally able to enter that job market. The best example of this is probably hotel management.

It must be emphasised that with "Ronseal" degrees, going to a Russell Group/1994 Group university is not normally important – the only issue is how the degree is viewed by the industry it is connected to.

Of course many of these degrees have been affected by the global financial crisis and even these graduates may face difficulties in gaining employment, but the way to view them is "climate rather than weather". For example, due to funding restrictions in the NHS it might be difficult to get a place/job as a midwife. However, in the long-term many current midwives are retiring or working part time, and the birth rate in the UK is being sustained – so there will be a need for midwives!

When a "Ronseal" degree is being considered, it is most important that the career area is researched fully and work experience (where possible) is undertaken.

Vocational Degree (Professional Accreditation)
These are degrees which will set you on your way to qualifying in a professional area and the completion of your degree will give you exemptions from your qualifying exams, however there can be many other barriers and hoops to jump through to gain employment in the field. These include:
*   Law (many solicitors' firms offering traineeships may require very high A-level grades.)
*   Psychology (to become a clinical psychologist you will need a further three years' postgraduate education and places on these courses are hard to get.)
*   Broadcast journalism (while it could be argued that graduates gain many skills and are nearly work ready, the employment market for these graduates means there

will not be such a likelihood of work. Nevertheless, employment prospects were better before the global financial crisis than many cynics would think.)

- Business studies (these degrees can offer exemptions for professions such as accountancy, human resources and marketing. Gaining employment may depend on gaining relevant work experience, internships etc.)

Engineering degrees are probably best placed in this category – before the global financial crisis it could have been argued that civil engineering was a Vocational "Ronseal" Degree. However, I am putting engineering in this category because it does carry professional accreditation, and while approximately two-thirds of graduates go into engineering, a third do not. Also, while engineering graduates are extremely employable, the unemployment levels tend to be a little bit higher than for "Ronseal" degrees.

I could put science degrees in this category but arguably I could put them in the non-vocational category. While many graduates from science degrees will carry on into further study and some work in scientific research, it is clear from What Graduates Do that many do not. It might therefore be more helpful to us to guard against complacency and consider them as non-vocational so that we emphasise to these students that they really need to have a plan.

Acting degrees within the CDS (Conference of Drama Schools) would fall into this category as well, though with respect to future employment/unemployment prospects, stage management graduates tend to fare better in employment terms.

Within this category I would probably have another subcategory called Vocational Degree – Industry Acceptance. A major set of courses that would fall into this category would be design degrees. Employers, for example, in the graphic design field would be used to people having a design degree (which may be graphic design, but not necessarily. It could be another design degree). Design graduates have to accept that they may well be self-employed and/or entrepreneurs.

Vocational Degree (Mock)
Can I emphasise that while it may seem that I am about to be disparaging about a set of degrees, some of my own students go onto these degrees because they simply love the content of the course. I use this term Mock Vocational to try to understand degrees that may well have a vocational term in the title – such as forensic science, media studies or popular music – but the industry they are connected to never asked for them to be set up. For example, the Forensic Science Service as far as I can deduce never asked for forensic science degrees. They were happy with graduates in physics, chemistry, biology or biochemistry. Was the growth in these degrees related to the popularity of the CSI/Silent Witness television genre and the need to re-badge struggling science departments in universities?

Some are more relevant to employers than others. While some media degrees, for example, will have little direct use to a media-industry employer and will cover areas relating to sociology and media criticism (and therefore would fall into my non-vocational category), some can have a good reputation within the industry for teaching relevant skills e.g. Ravensbourne.

There can be other ways to "follow the dream"! I am a "follow your dreams" careers adviser. If somebody wants to make a living through popular music and they are obsessed by it, then go for it, "life is not a dress rehearsal". A student wanting to make dance music, however, does not need a university degree to do this. They could learn the software by reading a manual and doing it on their home computer in their bedroom. By doing a course in popular music they could meet like-minded people, learn business/entrepreneurial skills and get advice on their music making, but ultimately their music will be judged purely on whether there is a market for it, not on where or if the person went to university.

Non-vocational degree (with a plan)
Large numbers of students will do a degree based on a subject they love/like that does not have an obvious career connection – English, politics, history etc. Yet the vast majority of these students graduate and get jobs they are happy with. It always seems that around two-thirds of graduate vacancies ask for graduates from any degree subject. So these students will have plenty of career options, whatever subject they decide to study. The crucial issue seems to be that they have a plan, which could entail:

Gaining work experience
In one survey, nearly half of graduates from the arts and humanities obtained their current job through relevant work experience in a similar organisation. Work experience was perceived to be a vital.

"Work experience was perceived to be a crucial key to the labour market. Many felt that on exit from HE they were not 'work ready' because they lacked basic workplace experience, particularly those who graduated with non-vocational degrees."
Elias

Understanding how organisations recruit
Many AGR companies recruit graduates for fast-track training. This tends to happen, for example, in the fields of law, accountancy, investment banking and multinational business.
Methods of recruitment include:
- (sometimes) checking for *very high* A-level grades;
- (sometimes) considering the type of elite university the student graduated from;
- sending candidates to assessment centres;
- increasingly, expecting the applicant to have undertaken some sort of internship or work experience with the company.

These companies are often not bothered about the degree *subject*, as long as it is viewed as academic.

Undertaking postgraduate study
Traditionally, postgraduate courses were primarily for students training for careers such as secondary-school teachers, research scientists, journalists, solicitors and clinical psychologists. However, there has been a growth in the number of students taking a wide variety of postgraduate courses. Students need to know that an undergraduate degree may just be the start. Reasons for postgraduate study might include the following:
- "I really enjoy my subject."

- "I need to do a postgraduate course to pursue my chosen career."
- "It will make me stand out from the crowd and get me a better job."
- "I want to convert to a new career area." You could do a postgraduate conversion course in social work, speech therapy or surveying, for example, from any degree subject.
- "I don't know what to do and this will give me more time to decide." (This is *not* a good reason to undertake more study and incur more debt!)

If a postgraduate course relates to a well-researched plan and a clear end goal and it can be funded, then fine. But if it doesn't?

Working on your soft skills

Have you experience and evidence of:

- communicating with the public and workmates;
- working in a team;
- leadership;
- integrity and honesty.

Many employers will use these qualities to make their final decision on whether or not to give the student the job.

Non-vocational degree (without a plan)

These graduates are summed up in Tanya De Grunwald's book *Dude Where's My Career*, where she points out her position on graduating:

Visits to university careers service	0
Career brochures collected	0
Career presentations attended	0
Potential careers being considered	0
Jobs applied for	0

The sum total of many graduates' career planning: they put more effort into their holiday!

I feel many HE advisers can fall into a trap, whereby we will say, "Don't worry, 60% of graduate vacancies do not ask for a specific subject" and leave it at that. Instead, we need to emphasise that they still need a plan. If they leave employment issues until after graduating, they could well face what the French call *"trop de choix tue le choix"*: too much choice kills choice! They can become paralysed, unable to make a plan and overtaken in the graduate employment market by students who did have a plan. The earlier they can start planning the better. Many careers advisers in universities will agree that they should start planning in their first year.

When do we decide on graduate employment?

We have touched on this above, including the Stella Gibbons quote. The issue here is when do you make the decision: before you start your degree, during the degree or after the degree? In reality it's not that simple, and it has to be the student's choice, but they must know the implications of their actions. Sometimes students' actions can be affected by myths about graduate recruitment. HE advisers need to be aware of these myths and have the necessary information to explain them away. Here are examples of some common beliefs:

- "Just getting a degree will guarantee me a good job."

- "Employers always look for graduates with particular degree subjects."
- "I don't need to start looking for a job until after I've graduated."
- "All graduates want is a job with a high salary."
- "My job prospects will depend on what type of university I went to."
- "Graduates only work for big companies or major organisations."
- "Getting a degree is not worth the debt I will get into."

These issues are dealt with in an excellent article from 2004 that I feel is still very relevant, "Myths about graduate recruitment" in *What do graduates do? 2004*, which is available on the website www.prospects.ac.uk. This could still be Googled in January 2011.

It can be a good idea to give students some idea about the future of work. For example, they should consider the following:

- As life expectancy rises, people will have to work longer and retire older.
- Most of today's students will have at least two careers and seven jobs.
- Researchers claim that, whereas 30 years ago people had to learn one new skill a year, now it is one new skill a day – so today's students must be committed to lifelong learning.
- There could well be further growth in "hyphenated" careers – edu-tainment, e-learning, bio-informatics.

An interesting book on this subject is *Funky Business*, by Ridderstralle and Nordstrom. While I do not agree with everything the authors claim, the book does raise some very interesting points.

If students are looking especially for an AGR-type employer and want to start preparing for entering the graduate jobs market, a good starting point would be: *The Graduate Jobs Formula: how to land your dream job after graduation*, Paul Redmond, 2010, Trotmans.

Who is getting the graduate jobs?
Clearly there is a link between social background and who is getting certain graduate jobs:

- School
- Class
- Ethnicity
- Gender
- Postcode

Various research and reports constantly claim these issues have an effect on gaining graduate employment.

Good HE advice will involve telling people the truth based on research, and offering a positive way forward. For example, if a student wants to try to get employment with a highly selective AGR-type recruiter, you have to tell them the reality that issues like original A-level grades/university attended (which came first, the chicken or the egg) may matter. As Brown and Hesketh described in 2004:
"One case-study organisation received approximately 14,000 applications for 426 vacancies. Graduates applying from Oxford University had a 1 in 8 chance of success,

while the ratio for those applying from new universities was 1 in 235. The elite has been broadened beyond Oxbridge to include other universities in the Russell Group, but it is still an elite."

Positive ways forward could include:
* Helping students gain internships/contacts before going to university. See www.accessprofessions.com
* Making clear to students in good time the importance of understanding the grades and subjects they need to achieve entry to certain universities/employment.
* Making students aware of the vast range of careers open to them, not just the same old options such as medicine and law.

15.4 Why be graduate employed?

With the changes to student funding that were announced after the Browne Review in 2010, everybody was subjected to a promotional campaign on the benefits of being graduate employed. Many of these benefits I would agree with, such as those mentioned by Elias and Purcell:
* Labour market advantage
* Skills development
* Intellectual stimulation
* Social development

In the report *Beyond the financial benefits of a degree*, Mark Wilberforce emphasised:
* Graduates enjoy higher-quality jobs than non-graduates.
* Graduates enjoy better health outcomes, by being less likely to smoke, more likely to exercise and less prone to depression.
* Graduates' children also benefit from the educational success of their parents: graduates tend to have a greater involvement with their child's education.
* Graduates are more influential in the community, by being active citizens who are more likely to vote and participate in voluntary activities.
* Graduates show positive attitudes towards diversity and equal opportunities, such as on race and gender-equality issues.
* Graduates, with their higher levels of skill, are a source of wider innovation and economic growth.

To me this all seems entirely plausible! My problem is with the reporting of graduate earnings. According to two reports:
* Graduates' lifetime earnings would be £400,000 greater than those who ended their full-time education with A-levels – DFES 2001
* The *gross* additional lifetime earnings for individuals with an undergraduate qualification is approximately £160,000, or between 20 and 25% more, than for those with two or more A-levels –PWC/UUK 2006

I thought the DFES 2001 report was rubbish then and I think it rubbish now. How can you compare a historical group that was based on approximately 8% of the population going to university with a group now of 40% of the population going to university?

More interestingly the PWC/UUK report breaks earnings down into degree areas:

Gross additional lifetime earnings (wage premiums) by degree subject compared to two or more GCE A levels (pooled Labour Force Survey 2000-2005)

Medicine	£340,315
Engineering	£243,730
Maths/Computer sciences	£241,749
Physical/Environmental science	£237,935
Architecture	£195,297
Business and finance	£184,694
Social sciences	£169,267
Subjects allied to medicine	£166,017
Average degree	**£160,061**
Library and information studies	£130,021
Technology	£119,484
Education	£114,935
Biosciences	£111,269
European languages	£96,281
Other languages	£92,346
Agricultural sciences	£81,935
Linguistics	£71,920
Humanities	£51,549
Arts	£34,494

While this information is very interesting, there is no point just basing advice on earnings. We as HE advisers have to help our students make decisions based on their interests, abilities, values and attitudes.

Finally, to sum up:
- Apart from a few exceptions, a degree alone is not enough – purely a licence to hunt.
- There is increased emphasis on skills and experience.
- 60% (approx) of graduate jobs do not specify a degree discipline.
- Formal graduate-training schemes are only 10-15% of opportunities.
- There is increased uptake of postgraduate study.
- 70% of formal placements lead to a job.
- 80% of jobs are not formally advertised.
- Be aware of PEST (political, economic, sociological and technological) effects.

Part Four: Higher-education advice for other age groups – year 9s, year 11s and adults

16. Higher-education issues for year-9 students

As the situation currently stands for year 9s, it is worth remembering that:

* this will probably be the first time these students have ever had to make any important decisions which could affect their futures;
* all schools are governed by the national curriculum, which states that certain GCSE subjects are compulsory – that is, mathematics, English language and literature, science;
* year-9 students have some choice over the rest of their GCSEs, which will come from the fields of: humanities; design and technology; social sciences; performing arts; languages.

Since the publication of the first edition of this book in 2006 when we were expecting the introduction of The Diploma in England, many schools have been through a process of change, which meant wholesale changes in timetabling and partnerships with other local schools. We are now unsure of the position of The Diploma and schools are now dealing with the introduction of the English Baccalaureate.

16.1 What is the English Baccalaureate?

It is a measurement of any pupil who secures good (A*-C) GCSE passes in all of the following:
English
Maths
The sciences: the following qualifications are recognised as good passes:
* GCSE A*-C passes in core science together with additional science.
* GCSE A*-C passes in at least two subjects (physics, biology or chemistry) if the pupil has taken triple science. Pupils will not need to have passed all three, but will need to have entered all three single sciences.
* GCSE A*A*-CC passes in science double award.

Pupils therefore need a minimum of two good GCSE passes in sciences to achieve the English Baccalaureate.
A modern or ancient foreign language: this includes community languages.
A humanity: history or geography – currently only history, ancient history and geography count in the category of humanities as part of the English Baccalaureate. (N.B. Faith schools are lobbying Government for religious studies to be counted as one of the humanities.)

The White Paper says: "This combination of GCSEs at grades A*-C will entitle the student to a certificate recording their achievement." This information is correct as of February 2011. Reference: The Key: The service for school leaders.

The English Baccalaureate and its relationship with university entrance

This is my own opinion, but I think it is very important to stress that the English Baccalaureate seems clearly to be a device through its use in league tables to *encourage schools* to *encourage pupils* to take history or geography, a language and more science (maths, English and a lesser amount of science are covered by the national curriculum). Universities individually decide their own entrance requirements, they are not set for them by the Government! HE advisers need to be wary of people trying to connect the English Baccalaureate to university entrance. They are not necessarily connected!

On the one hand the English Baccalaureate is a positive thing in that it will keep so many options open when it comes to AS choices, including more of the facilitating subjects at AS level (facilitating meaning subjects which are commonly asked for as a university course requirement). On the other hand we could be looking at a large dose of wishful thinking, if we think a pupil should do a foreign language when they would have been happier with a non-English Baccalaureate subject. In the main they will be perfectly fine applying for even the most selective universities with good GCSE performances in English, maths, science and some other subjects, whatever those subjects may be. The only "known known" here is that if they do not do history, geography or a language they probably will not be majoring in one of these subjects at university.

16.2 What year-9 students need to know

- Most pupils normally do between seven and eleven GCSEs.
- Whatever their choice of GCSEs, it is unlikely to make any difference to the career options available to them in the future. There are just a few careers where it is important to choose the right GCSEs. For example, design careers will be more difficult to get into for students who do not take GCSEs in art or design; likewise, becoming a geography teacher will be difficult to get into if they do not take geography GCSE.
- None of the newer GCSEs (such as media studies) is essential for any career.
- Students should make their GCSE choices according to their strengths, interests and abilities. Their career ideas may well change between year 9 and year 13, but their strengths, interests and abilities are more likely to remain the same.
- Students should not choose a subject in order to be with a best friend. Again, their best friend may change, but their strengths, interests and abilities are likely to remain the same.
- Students should not be tempted to choose a subject simply because of an inspirational teacher. If the subject does not match their strengths, interests and abilities, they may flounder.
- There has been an increase in the number of students choosing various NVQ level 2 courses at year 9. Students need to know that this could have implications in terms of the range of A levels that will be open to them – and therefore degrees as well. However, this does not mean that such students will not be able to go to university. The university may still be looking for C grades in GCSE maths and English.
- Students must be aware that the set they are in can affect the level of GCSE they will take. If they are in a lower science set, for example, they will probably take

the foundation science GCSE paper, which is *not* a preparation for science A levels. This also applies to other subjects.

- Students should be encouraged to take their decision making seriously. Choosing GCSEs is good practice for later decisions about A levels and other post-16 courses, sixth forms, universities and careers.

17. Making post-16 choices

17.1 Advising year-11 students

There are many ways in which year-11 students might decide the subjects or course they will study in sixth form or at a further education college. Some may already have a career idea and know which courses they need to do. Others may simply choose the courses or course they think will be the easiest, which may not be advisable!

It would be unrealistic to expect all 15- or 16-year-olds to know exactly what they would like to do in the future. However, they are about to make some significant choices that will have an important impact on their future options. Before getting into the detail of choosing particular subjects, therefore, HE advisers should encourage students to take a moment to think about some wider issues. Students should take a look at their future and ask themselves, **"What do I want from my future career?"**

Do they want:
- something useful and interesting to do?
- enough money to stop worrying?
- a feeling that they are improving, not stuck?
- plenty of challenges?
- future goals they can aim for?

If they are still unclear about the future, then they should think about:
- what really interests them (school subjects, hobbies, part-time jobs, work experience);
- where their abilities lie (communication skills, school subjects, manual dexterity);
- their values and attitudes (do they want to earn lots of money, do they want to help people, do they *not* want to work long hours?)

Of course, students must consult with parents, teachers and advisers. But they must also be aware that the responsibility for deciding what they want to do in the future lies with them and no one else.

In the following sections relating to post-16 choices we concentrate on A levels, BTEC National and the International Baccalaureate simply because of the numbers of people doing these qualifications. There are other qualifications such as the Advanced Diploma, the Cambridge Pre-U and NVQ level 3 in apprenticeships leading to university. We have concentrated on the first three because, especially with A levels and BTEC National, so many people do them.
N.B. CACHE is mentioned in the A-Z of course descriptions.

It is the HE adviser's responsibility to understand what these courses involve, the differences in their learning styles and their possible outcomes, as this may help with guidance on how the student can make decisions on what options to choose.

HE advisers can become bogged down in a myriad of issues when advising year-11 students on post-16 choices, yet in the main there are really only three "known knowns":

- That if you know what you want to study at university there may be a subject or subjects that you have to study at sixth form.
- That if you do not know what you want to study when you are making your post-16 choices you will leave more options open if you choose some facilitating subjects (subjects that are commonly asked for in university entrance requirements – English, maths, biology, chemistry, physics, modern or classical languages, history and geography. Art and music can also often be required by related degrees).
- That some universities have a non-preferred/preferred list of A levels for the institution or for a course.

These three principles provide the basis for the Informed Choices document on post-16 choices produced by the Russell Group in collaboration with the Institute of Career Guidance. It is available on the Russell Group website www.russellgroup.ac.uk in the Policies section.

Adapted from Informed Choices www.russellgroup.ac.uk

17.2 The student's five-point plan for making post-16 choices

1. Know what you want to study? Check out the entry requirements

If you have a university course you are keen on, have you checked the relevant university website or UCAS course search to find out whether this course requires certain subjects at advanced level?

2. Not sure yet? Keep your options open!

If you are not sure about what course you want to study at university, have you tried to choose at least two facilitating subjects (maths, English, physics, biology, chemistry, geography, history, languages)? To get a rough idea of the options the different facilitating subjects will give you in applying to university, you can look at the UCAS website or university websites.

3. GCSEs and other qualifications matter …

Make sure you understand the GCSE or other requirements for entry to a competitive university. Are you on track to achieve the grades to progress onto the course/courses you want to do at A level or equivalent, and the university course you may choose to do?

4. Think balance

Do you have a balance of subject choices that reflect your abilities, strengths and interests?

Have you considered how certain subject combinations relate to university courses?

5. Make sure you know WHY

If you want to take a subject you have not studied before, can you talk for a minute on what this subject is about? Try and unpick why you wish to study this subject. It's not enough to say: "It's interesting", "I think I'll like it" or, "It will be fun".

Many of the questions that come up on post-16 choices are dealt with in Informed Choices, which I played a large part in writing. But please be aware that this content is related to Russell Group universities. It doesn't speak for the whole university sector. Do also look at AHEAD, published by the Specialist Schools and Academies Trust (SSAT). To gain a general idea of which AS levels to choose, look in this book at *Appendix A: An A-Z of university subjects with essential information for students.*

18. A levels

18.1 How are A levels organised?

There are many combinations and permutations for studying AS and A2 levels, but students should be aware that the example below is *the norm*, and that this is what universities require.

- In year 12 students will normally choose four subjects at AS level (AS stands for "Advanced Subsidiary"):

Subject 1   Subject 2   Subject 3   Subject 4

- In year 13 students will normally reduce this to three A2 level subjects:

Subject 1   Subject 2   Subject 3

In each subject, you will normally take two units at AS level, followed by two harder units at A2 level. Sciences, maths, music and applied A levels are exceptions, with six units overall. In the example above (which is the most common programme followed by sixth formers) the fourth subject is "banked" as an AS level at the end of year 12.

Remember that there are many other combinations and permutations for studying AS and A2 levels, but the example above is the norm and this is what most universities require. Some students are taking AS levels in year 11 – they should still take a programme of study in the sixth form that will lead to them following three A2 levels in year 13!

18.2 What kinds of subjects are on offer?

When thinking about choices, it is helpful to organise the subjects available into groups.

The sciences	Biology Chemistry Further maths Maths Physics	• It is possible to do all five of these subjects in certain circumstances. However, many sixth formers who are good at science/maths are now taking three of the above, plus an AS level in something completely different.
The arts and humanities	English literature English language and literature Geography History Classical civilisation History of art Philosophy Religious studies	• Many sixth formers choose all four of their subjects from this group. There is no law against this, especially for those who like writing lots of essays! • It would be good to take an AS subject in something completely different (for example, a science) but only if the student feels he or she has a strength in a particular subject.
Languages	French Spanish	• Taking two languages would normally be the maximum. However, two languages would

	German Italian Latin Ancient Greek	definitely be held in a positive light.
Creative/talent-based subjects	Art Dance Music Music technology Photography	• As a general rule, students should pick only one subject from this group. Those who wish to choose two should take advice. • All are challenging, academic subjects.
Social sciences	Economics Law Politics Psychology Sociology	• It would normally be advisable to pick no more than two subjects from this group as they are all (perhaps with the exception of sociology) new subjects not studied at GCSE.
Vocational subjects	Childcare CACHE Accountancy Business studies Information technology	• Students should not take accountancy *and* business studies. Likewise, they should not choose economics *and* business studies.
Subjects that are a mix of these groupings	Media studies Theatre studies Physical education	• Involves social sciences/arts and humanities. • Involves arts and humanities/creative. • Involves sciences/social sciences/talent-based.
Critical thinking	• This is different from all other subjects at AS level. It is about learning how to reason, and how to write in a coherent, logical way. • Critical thinking is usually studied as a fifth AS level. Students often have to achieve high grades at GCSE to show they can cope with the workload.	

18.3 How students can maximise their A-level grades

It is really important that HE advisers get across to year-11 students that the people who tend to get the high grades at A level are the ones who work consistently from the start of year 12.

Remember the following (do not confuse this with the UCAS Tariff) and bear in mind that the calculations below assume a 600-point A level – many are now 400-point awards. The principle is the same:
• The maximum score you can achieve in an A level (your overall qualification) is 600
• The maximum score you can achieve in an AS level (year 12) is 300
• The maximum score you can achieve for A2 (year 13) is 300
• The AS level is easier than the A2, yet they carry equal weighting towards your final mark, which is then turned into a grade.
This presumes you are doing a 6-unit A level.

Think about it. The better you do at AS level when the questions are easier means that you are under less pressure to get higher scores when you are doing A2.

138

Look at the table below:

A-level grades: for 4-unit subjects
(*2 units at AS & 2 units at A2*)
(all subjects except sciences, maths & music)
To find out your grade, compare the total of your unit scores with the minimum scores below.

Grade	maximum	A	B	C	D	E
AS	200	160	140	120	100	80
A2	200	160	140	120	100	80
Overall grade	400	320	280	240	200	160

A-level grades: for a 6-unit A level
To find out your grade, compare the total of your unit scores with the minimum scores below.

Grade	maximum	A	B	C	D	E
AS	300	240	210	180	150	120
A2	300	240	210	180	150	120
Overall grade	600	480	420	360	300	240

Let's look at some case studies (for a 6-unit and a 4-unit A level):

Student A	6 Unit	4 Unit	Student B	6 Unit	4 Unit
AS	285 (A)	190 (A)	AS	218 (B)	145 (B)
A2	205 (C)	137 (C)	A2	246 (A)	164 (A)
Overall grade	490 (A)	327 (A)	Overall grade	464 (B)	309 (B)

Student B did better at A2 than Student A but Student A is the one who is going to get the high grade.

19. BTEC Nationals

By Liz King, Haringey Sixth Form Centre
liz.king@haringey6.ac.uk

In 2010 more than 140, 000 students who had studied BTEC National qualifications were successful in gaining a place at university. This is a large cohort of students, 30% of total acceptances, who will benefit from specialist advice when making their choice of which BTEC subject to study and when preparing their university applications.

BTEC qualifications have been available for more than 25 years and they now comprise a suite of qualifications from entry level up to university level. Focusing on work-related learning, BTECs mix the knowledge needed by employers with underpinning theory.

Within each level there are a number of qualifications of different sizes available. At Level 3 there are four different sizes of BTEC qualification (collectively known as BTEC Nationals). The most common is the BTEC Level 3 Extended Diploma (formerly the BTEC National Diploma). This is made up of 18 units and is equivalent to three A levels. There are corresponding qualifications equivalent to two A levels (BTEC Level 3 Diploma – formerly the BTEC National Certificate), one A level (BTEC Level 3 Subsidiary Diploma – formerly the BTEC National Award) and a new qualification equivalent to an AS (BTEC Level 3 Certificate).

BTEC qualifications were renamed for courses starting study in September 2010 and the table below shows the relationship between the old names (NQF) and the new names (QCF).

BTEC Level 3 Nationals

Old Qualification Title	Qualification Title from September 2010	Credits	Equivalent to
BTEC Level 3 National Diploma	BTEC Level 3 Extended Diploma	180	3 GCE A levels
BTEC Level 3 National Certificate	BTEC Level 3 Diploma	120	2 GCE A levels
BTEC Level 3 National Award	BTEC Level 3 Subsidiary Diploma	60	1 GCE A level
	BTEC Level 3 Certificate	30	1 GCE AS level

19.1 How BTEC grades are awarded

When advising students it is useful to understand how BTEC grades are awarded.

The coursework assignment for each unit is designed by each individual centre. The assignments are designed so that students can provide evidence against a range of criteria at pass, merit and distinction level. To get a Merit grade for a unit, a student needs to complete all the pass and all the merit criteria to a good standard. Similarly, to get a Distinction a student should meet all the pass, merit and distinction criteria.

This system rewards conscientious students who are prepared to work steadily throughout the year. It is always clear to students how well they are doing and what they need to improve to get higher grades. Evidence can include practical work, written coursework, oral presentations and evaluations.

The overall grade for the qualification is calculated using a formula. Each unit (18 in the case of the Extended Diploma) is graded Pass, Merit or Distinction. These grades are converted to points (not to be confused with UCAS points – a common student misconception) and the total is given an overall grade. Some of the grades can appear counter intuitive. For example a student who passes every unit with a merit might be expected to get an overall grade of Merit Merit Merit (for an Extended Diploma), but actually they would gain a Distinction Merit Merit. Worked examples of how students achieve different grades are given in this Credit and Grading Notes for BTEC Level 3 in IT document:
http://www.edexcel.com/migrationdocuments/BTEC%20Nationals%20from%202010/Nationals-IT-supplementary-credit-and-grading-notes.pdf

BTEC Level 3 qualifications are included within the UCAS Tariff and can be used as university entry qualifications, both on their own and mixed with other qualifications such as A levels, CoPE and Ifs. The new Distinction* grade has been included in the UCAS Tariff tables as given:

BTEC qualifications (QCF) (Suite of qualifications known as Nationals)
http://www.ucas.com/students/ucas_tariff/tarifftables

Grade				Tariff points
Extended Diploma	Diploma	Subsidiary Diploma	Certificate	
D*D*D*				420
D*D*D				400
D*DD				380
DDD				360
DDM				320
DMM	D*D*			280
	D*D			260
MMM	DD			240
MMP	DM			200
MPP	MM			160
		D*		140

PPP	MP	D		120
	PP	M		80
			D*	70
			D	60
		P	M	40
			P	20

19.2 University entry requirements

BTEC Nationals are made up of a mixture between core and optional units. Normally there are only four or five core units in an 18-unit BTEC Level 3 Extended Diploma, the other 13 or 14 being taken from a wide range of options. This means that the same qualification taken in different institutions can contain widely different combinations of units. It is essential to ensure all the units are listed on the UCAS application to help universities understand what topics an individual student has covered.
Some universities, especially Russell Group and 1994 Group universities, name specific units that must be passed with particular grades. For example the Royal Veterinary College (http://www.rvc.ac.uk/Undergraduate/BVetMed/EntryReqs.cfm) has the following entry requirements for its Veterinary Medicine course:

The National Level 3 Extended Diploma must be in **Animal Management** with DDD (Distinctions) overall, including Distinctions in **all** of the following units: Understand the principles of Animal Nutrition Understand the Principles and Carry Out the Practice of Biochemistry and Microbiology Understand the Principles of Inheritance and Genetic Manipulation Fundamentals of Science Chemistry for Biology Technicians **OR** Understand the Principles of Chemistry for Biological and Medical Science	See additional GCSE requirements.
BTEC National Diploma in Applied Science	
Applicants with BTEC ND in Applied Science may be considered on a case-by-case basis, if predicted DDD (Distinction, Distinction, Distinction). We may specify certain modules to be taken; therefore students taking the BTEC ND Applied Science are encouraged to contact the Admissions Office at enquiries@rvc.ac.uk with details of their chosen modules for further advice.	

In 2009, 2,540 BTEC students were accepted by Russell Group universities and a further 3,659 BTEC students were accepted by 1994 Group universities. It is uncertain at the time of writing how universities will incorporate the new Distinction* grade within offers, although early indications suggest that courses looking for AAA at A level will be looking for Distinction* Distinction* Distinction*.

The major barrier to students progressing to competitive university courses can be their GCSE profile. Many students studying BTEC Nationals don't have five GCSEs grade A*-C, and often don't have both GCSE English and maths at grade C. Some universities, including Million+ institutions, are using the five-GCSE matriculation requirement as a way of coping with the problem of over-subscribed courses. As some students doing BTEC Nationals may only have three or four GCSEs grade A*-C, it is worth being upfront with them about the options that may be closed to them if they choose to go straight to Level 3. Depending on their circumstances, some students would be better advised to take an extra year to study Level 2 (BTEC First or GCSE) qualifications before moving on to Level 3.

It is encouraging to note that a number of students each year progress into higher education having worked their way up from Level 1, through the BTEC suite of qualifications, to Level 3. As an alternative pathway for students who have missed out on getting qualifications in secondary school, BTEC is a proven and achievable route to success.

19.3 Applying outside a student's subject area

BTEC Nationals are very flexible qualifications. While there are many obvious links between the subject studied for BTEC National and courses available at university, students can make very successful applications for quite different courses. Examples of successful applications have included:

BTEC National Diploma Music Technology – BA Philosophy
BTEC National Diploma Media – BSc Nursing
BTEC National Diploma Performing Arts – BA Psychology
BTEC National Diploma Business – LLB Law
BTEC National Diploma Public Services – BA Sociology
BTEC National Certificate Sport – BA Accounting and Finance
BTEC National Diploma ICT– BA Social Work

All the above examples are of students who have gone on to study at 1994 Group universities.

Applicants who are successful in applying outside their subject area often have a number of common strategies. The first is to get relevant work experience or voluntary work. The second is to research thoroughly their intended subject, by reading widely around the subject and attending any lectures, workshops, summer schools or open-day talks. Finally, they compose a strong personal statement that highlights their passion for the subject, carefully makes links between their current studies and their chosen course and demonstrates that they have a real understanding of the demands of the subject.

If students are applying for academic courses, it is really helpful if they can write positively about the theories they have learned about on their BTEC course. One powerful, and successful, personal statement for sociology at Royal Holloway, University of London, from a BTEC Public Services student spoke eloquently about the theoretical perspectives of crime and detailed the specific sociological studies that had been studied as part of the BTEC course.

None of this is rocket science; these are the same techniques employed by students from all backgrounds who make successful applications to competitive courses. But by allowing their passion for their chosen subject to shine through BTEC students can persuade admissions tutors to offer them a place on a non-traditional course or more academic course.

Many teachers, students and parents can have a limited view of what students who study BTEC Nationals can go on to do at university. To challenge this, it is possible to use data from UCAS Adviser Track/Progression Reports to highlight the diverse courses that students do apply to and are successful at getting offers from. Collating this information into a useable form can take time but, once assembled, it can be used at sixth-form open evenings for new students, at enrolment, induction and during the UCAS process to reassure anxious students and parents that BTEC Nationals are qualifications that open doors in the future.

19.4 Top tips for applying to university

- Encourage students to be ambitious.
- Widen their expectations as to the subjects they could study at university.
- Research course entry requirements carefully as many courses don't state their BTEC entry requirements and general GCSE requirements clearly. If in doubt, phone the university.
- Get tutors to highlight the academic and theoretical nature of the BTEC courses, especially when writing references for competitive courses.
- Highlight early on the need for students to work to a high standard from the start of the course and not rely on going back to upgrade work in the second year. An application that shows lots of Distinctions and Merits achieved in the first year is far more persuasive than one that relies totally on predicted grades.
- Challenge university decisions that seem unfair, as staff sometimes make errors in their decisions because they don't fully understand BTEC qualifications; they can be persuaded to change their offer.
- Never underestimate what BTEC students can go on to achieve.

20. IB – University attitudes to the International Baccalaureate

By Penny Longman, Careers and Higher Education Adviser,
Bexley Grammar School and Christ the King St Mary's Sixth Form College
pennylongman1@gmail.com

The International Baccalaureate was started in 1968 in Geneva, and as the name suggests, is an international qualification, taught in numerous countries. In the UK for many years it was offered primarily in independent schools, but over the past five to ten years it has become increasingly popular in the state sector. Amidst repeated claims of A-level grade inflation, with universities insisting they had significant difficulty differentiating between the most able applicants, Tony Blair promised support in November 2006 to enable at least one school or sixth-form college in every local authority to offer students the choice of studying the IB, and funding was made available for this. Of the 83 schools registering an interest in offering the IB in the three years to September 2010, 70 of them were state schools.

However, whilst the restructuring of A levels (including the introduction of the A*) announced at the same time has taken place, Government support for the IB appeared gradually to fade in favour of 14-19 Diplomas. The high profile of the Diplomas now seems in turn to be being replaced by a push towards a broad spread of "academic" subjects with the concept of the "English Baccalaureate" of five A*-C in GCSE covering English, maths, science, a foreign language and history/geography.

If schools decide to adapt their GCSE offer to maximise success in the English Baccalaureate this may encourage increased interest in the IB, which would provide a natural progression. At a time when the landscape of UK qualifications seems to be constantly changing, the IB also has the potential advantage, as an international qualification, of being outside the jurisdiction of such curriculum changes.

IB structure
The IB is highly valued by universities but parents and students are likely to know less about it than about A levels, so it is helpful for advisers to be familiar with the structure of the qualification, and with university attitudes towards it. This is particularly important when giving impartial advice to students considering the IB as a post-16 option where they are not currently in a school that offers the qualification, and may therefore not have easy access to detailed information about it.

IB students study six subjects taken from different subject groups, giving them a broad and balanced curriculum (see http://www.ibo.org/diploma/curriculum/ for a full explanation). Three of the subjects are taken at higher level, and three at standard. It is compulsory to take English, maths, a science, a foreign language and a humanities subject ("individuals and societies") and the sixth choice can either be a creative one such as visual arts or music, or can instead be a second option from the foreign language, science, or "individuals and societies" groups. This means students can specialise in a particular area whilst maintaining breadth of study. The foreign language can be taken *ab initio,* counting as one of the three standard-level choices, so students without a foreign language GCSE can still access the IB.

In addition, all students complete an extended essay on a subject of their choice, stretching their independent study skills, and their critical thinking and philosophical understanding are developed through studying Theory of Knowledge (TOK).

All IB students also complete at least 150 hours of CAS (creativity, action, service) which means they are automatically combining their academic study with a variety of constructive activities, through which they gain numerous skills such as leadership, time management and social skills (and plenty to talk about in a personal statement).

The diploma is marked out of a maximum of 45 points; 7 points can be achieved in each of the 6 subjects (regardless of whether they are higher or standard), with a maximum score of 3 from the "core" element (extended essay and TOK).

The IB and UCAS
In 2007, after lengthy deliberations by an expert group, the IB was included in the UCAS Tariff, but the weighting given to it has proved problematic (even though it was slightly revised for 2010 entry onwards, see http://www.ucas.com/students/ucas_tariff/tarifftables/). Initially, there was no provision for students who did not gain the full diploma, even though they may have done well in up to five subjects. These students are awarded the IB Certificate rather than Diploma, and rather than an overall UCAS points score, the revised tariff awards them up to 130 points for each higher-level subject and up to 70 for each standard-level one, with additional points still available for the "core" element. This should provide some reassurance to students hesitant about embarking on the Diploma in case one subject lets them down.

Universities are consistently positive about the abilities, attitude and study skills of students who have studied the IB. However, the offers made to IB students bear little relation to the UCAS Tariff when compared to offers made to A-level students for comparable courses.

This has implications for offering guidance to students choosing between the two routes:
* If students choose the IB on the understanding that it yields high UCAS Tariff points they are likely to be disappointed when applying to universities. The "selective" universities that they may be seeking to apply to do not make offers in terms of the UCAS Tariff.
* On the other hand, if students look at the UCAS Tariff and then at the IB points universities actually require, and compare those with the A-level grades required, they may well conclude that A levels provide an "easier" route into prestigious universities than the IB and be discouraged from choosing it. Such conclusions are misleading.

It is more helpful to compare whether similar ability students seem to achieve the points/grades required by similarly competitive courses, regardless of whether they took A levels or the IB. As Careers and HE Adviser in a state school offering a choice of IB and A levels, I have looked carefully at attainment and destinations. Obviously each student's progress and achievement is unique, with all sorts of variables that cannot be reduced simply to a set of statistics, but results over the past

146

few years suggest that similar ability students' success rate in gaining entry to comparably competitive courses is fairly equally spread across the two routes.

The IB or A level? How university offers compare
I have found it helpful to draw up a rough translation between the offers made to IB and A-level students over the past few years. Students need to be aware that only a rough comparison is possible, as there continues to be some variation between universities and even between departments within the same university. However, this rough guide gives IB students some context when researching university courses and entry requirements, and also alerts them to any anomalies, where individual universities/ departments seem out of line with the general picture. (For example, until 2009 Exeter University offers to IB students were extremely favourable, although this situation changed during the 2009 entry cycle, and their requirements are now much more in line with other institutions.)

In general, a course that requires AAA at A level is likely to ask for 36-38 points at IB (38 if it is a very competitive AAA course, which may be moving towards A*AA). For 2011 entry, with competition for places more intense than ever, a requirement of 38-39 points is not unusual for a course which requires A*AA or higher. Courses requiring AAB usually ask for 34 to 36 from IB students. For ABB the IB offer is likely to be 32 to 34 points. A BBB course is likely to require about 30-32 IB points or occasionally 33.

"Translation" tends to become more inconsistent the lower the entry requirements. Where universities make offers in UCAS Tariff points, they frequently still make IB students offers in terms of IB points, usually starting at 24 (the minimum required for achieving the diploma) and going up to about 28-30.

The IB and prestigious universities
IB offers from Oxford and Cambridge tend to range from 38 to 42 points. Staff teaching both A levels and IB confirm that the offer comparisons given above are generally fair, because an A grade at A level is similar to a 6 in IB higher level (a high A or A* is more like a 7), so 36-38 points in the IB can reasonably be compared to straight As at A level, 32 to straight Bs etc.

Therefore these offers do not mean it is harder to get into a prestigious university having studied the IB. The terms of an offer may sometimes seem more challenging, particularly for a highly selective course, but the university may be more likely to make an offer in the first place because of the scope for differentiation between able candidates. They do not even mean it is harder to get into Oxford and Cambridge, although their offers appear so high. It is hard to quantify the advantage that may have been gained from the nature of the IB course when it comes to an Oxbridge application, including the opportunity to discuss the extended essay in interview.

Neither is it possible to conclude that it is easier to get into a prestigious university having studied the IB, although universities are consistent in their appreciation of IB students.

IB maths
When advising students making post-16 choices it is also helpful to make them aware of university requirements regarding IB maths. The IB offers three choices for maths: higher level, standard level and maths studies. Maths studies is the most accessible to students who are not particularly mathematically orientated, and is a good choice if they are not planning to take a university course requiring maths. For maths-related courses the more selective universities will require higher-level maths, which requires considerable mathematical aptitude. This applies to economics courses at the most selective universities and many engineering courses, as well as to maths degrees, and it is important for students to take this into account when choosing their IB subjects.

When the IB is not ideal
The IB offers a broad course that caters for the spread of abilities of most students but there are groups of students for whom this general curriculum is not ideal:
- Students with a strong artistic flair, for example, are restricted to one "creative arts" choice out of six IB subjects, and may flourish more with an arts-orientated choice of A levels.
- Similarly, students with a very mathematical or scientific orientation may be better advised to take double maths, physics and chemistry at A level rather than the closest IB equivalent of higher maths, physics, chemistry and standard English, foreign language and humanities subject.

Requirements in detail
Over the last two or three years universities have begun to publish more detail about their IB requirements and it is worth being aware of some of this detail when advising students. Whilst IB offers are given in terms of a total points score (out of 45), many universities also require certain points scores in the three higher-level subjects. When choosing the IB, students need to look carefully at university requirements for higher-level subjects, especially if they already have a university course in mind. Although there is no direct correlation between higher-level IB subjects and A2, or standard level and AS, a parallel seems to be drawn by some universities. So an offer of 34 may for example include a requirement of 18 points at higher level, and individual points scores in higher-level subjects are sometimes specified. This may seem contrary to the concept of the IB as a whole curriculum rather than a collection of separate subjects, but is common practice in universities, and probably reflects the fact that they wish to ensure students have achieved a certain level in subjects related to their university studies.

Results time
IB results are published in early July each year, and students achieving the terms of their offers will have their places confirmed at this point. Students who are "near misses" will usually have to wait until A-level results are released before their universities can make a decision on whether to confirm their place. This does mean they have time to plan carefully in case they should need to enter clearing, and can be ready to contact universities right at the start, should they need to. There is possibly slightly more flexibility shown by universities towards IB "near misses", even in the current squeeze, but anecdotally that flexibility seems more likely if they have achieved the individual or higher-level points scores required, than if they have missed those, but gained or even exceeded the overall points score.

Conclusion

There is no easy route into highly selective university courses. It is essential that students choose the route, and combination of subjects, that will inspire them to achieve their best. Finding out exactly what is required by universities of IB students can take slightly more research than for A levels, but the information is available and students may need to be encouraged to look at it carefully and interpret it realistically. Without proper advice and guidance students considering the IB may be deterred from taking a course that would be ideal for them. Similarly, students already studying the IB may need additional expert advice and guidance to support them in making university choices that are both aspirational and realistic.

21. An A-Z of post-16 subjects with descriptions of course content

The aim of this section is not to give entirely accurate descriptions for every post-16 course that exists (there are far too many), rather to give an overview of the different subjects. This is because in reality many students are considering subjects they know very little about, so therefore need general, not detailed, descriptions.

Accounting *The practice of keeping and checking the financial accounts of a business (that is, its income and expenditure), and of preparing reports on a business's assets, liabilities, etc.*

A course in accounting covers areas such as:
* the system of accounting (subsidiary books and ledger accounts, recording VAT, verifying accounts, trading and profit-and-loss accounts, balance sheets, using computers in accounting);
* how such systems are used in the published accounts of limited companies;
* the processes involved in reaching a final figure for the income of a company, or the "determination of income" (final accounts and balance sheets, capital and revenue income and expenditure, depreciation, disposal of fixed assets, stock valuation);
* the use of accounting in management and decision making (ratio analysis, costing, break-even analysis, budgetary controls).

Students need good number skills. They will also be expected to read about and research topics, make presentations and write essays and reports.

Art (A level) *Painting, drawing, sculpture, etc.*

Work is based on a series of projects, using a range of 2D and 3D media. Students develop skills in a variety of different media, according to the requirements of each project. They will be expected to record the development of each project through the keeping of a sketchbook or journal.

The study of art is usually split across three areas, and students are expected to complete projects in each. These are:
* thematic enquiry (exploring media and ideas in a sequential manner);
* expressive study (looking at the expressive use of the formal elements of art and using these appropriately in the interpretation of the student's own ideas);
* an externally set assignment (students have to prepare ideas in response to a question paper and will then have, say, eight hours to complete a final piece of work).

Art and design (AGCE/National) *The practical development of creative skills.*

This vocational course will specifically develop creative skills and knowledge in:
* fine art;
* sculpture;

- graphic design;
- photography;
- jewellery;
- 3D design;
- CAD;
- product design.

Art history *The study of the painting, sculpture and architecture of the Western world, from classical times to the modern era.*

Students learn how European art has grown and changed over the centuries and investigate certain periods of art in depth. Areas for study might include art from:
- the classical world;
- the medieval world;
- the Renaissance;
- Europe after the Reformation;
- Europe after the French Revolution;
- post-impressionism and the birth of modern art.

Students will also have the opportunity to study the work of individual artists in depth.

Art history students develop skills in analysing visual images by looking at both the style and content of works of art. They are encouraged to develop their opinions, and to express them through written essays and during class discussions.

Biology *The study of living things, their structures, functionings, evolution, etc.*

AS level biology expands students' knowledge of topics such as: transport; digestion; reproduction; ecology. They are also likely to investigate the developing areas of molecular biology and gene technology.

Work will take a variety of forms and involve a range of skills, such as:
- making clear notes from lectures and reference texts, researching topics and writing essays from the resulting information;
- interpreting data in different forms, for example graphs, histograms, pie charts;
- evaluating scientific information;
- applying biological principles to new problems and situations;
- practical work, including microscope work, dissection and physiological experiments;
- maintaining written records of all practical work;
- use of maths, including statistics, calculating percentages, ratios, etc;
- use of ICT.

Business studies (A level/AGCE/National) *The study of how businesses are organised and operate.*

A course in business studies will cover a number of areas:

- financial management (accounting, budgeting, classifying costs, break-even analysis);
- production (efficiency, controlling operations, quality control);
- people management (management structure and organisation, motivation and leadership);
- marketing (market research and analysis, marketing strategy, advertising and promotion);
- business structures (partnerships and companies, internal organisation into departments, starting a small business);
- objectives and strategy (how they are set);
- external influences on a business (the economy, the government, the law, etc.).

Students should have an interest in how a business operates and they may be considering a career in business. They will need good number, writing and ICT skills. The course is likely to include the preparation and interpretation of business data, so an ability to understand tables, graphs and charts would be useful.

CACHE Diploma in Childhood Studies *The knowledge, skills and experience to work in a childcare setting.*

Students take units covering:
- work with young children;
- the developing child;
- health and community care;
- play, curriculum and early learning;
- work with babies in the first year of life;
- the provision of services and the protection of children;
- anti-discriminatory and anti-bias practice;
- working with parents.

Students should note that this course generally takes up the whole timetable and is not taken with any other AS level.

Chemistry *The study of the composition, properties and reactions of substances.*

AS-level chemistry is split into three areas:
- organic chemistry (looking at all the compounds of carbon, including plastics);
- inorganic chemistry (looking at the chemical elements and all their compounds *except* those containing carbon);
- physical chemistry (looking at the way the physical properties of substances influence their chemical structures, properties and reactions).

Some AS-level courses emphasise the practical application of chemistry and explore the most up-to-date areas of chemical research and development, such as the use of chemistry in genetic engineering. All courses emphasise practical laboratory work and students are likely to have to take a practical examination to test their laboratory skills. Other work may include written answers to sample examination questions and independent research.

Classical civilisation *The study of ancient Greek and Roman culture, specifically through literature, art and archaeology.*

Areas for study might include:
*   tragedy (for example, works by Greek dramatists Aeschylus and Sophocles);
*   satire (for example, works by Roman satirists Horace and Petronius);
*   Greek comedy;
*   classical archaeology (i.e. looking at Greek and Roman remains to find out about ancient culture and society);
*   the epic poems and histories (for example, Homer's *Iliad* and *Odyssey*);
*   art and architecture;
*   Roman Britain.

Students have to read and discuss set texts in a critical manner. They may also visit museums, art galleries, theatres and archaeological sites and be expected to produce reports on these visits. There will be essay writing as well as group discussions, debates and presentations, for which they will be expected to carry out independent research.

Classical Greek *The study of the language and literature of classical Greece, from the earliest recorded writings (around 800BC) to about 300BC.*

The course will involve:
*   studying the grammar and vocabulary of classical Greek in order to develop sufficient linguistic skills to be able to read moderately challenging Greek texts;
*   studying set texts taken from classical Greek literature (for example, the works of Homer, Euripides, Plato, Aristophanes and Sophocles). The set texts are studied not only as works of literature but also as a means to understanding the culture, politics and society of classical Greece.

The language element of the course will involve translating unseen pieces of Greek prose into English. The literature element will involve answering questions on passages from the set texts, translations from the set texts, and essays. Excellent language skills required.

Construction and the built environment (AGCE/National) *The knowledge and practical skills needed to work in the fields of architecture, surveying, construction, civil engineering, town planning and property development.*

Students are likely to cover, for example:
*   the development of the built environment;
*   building science and materials;
*   town planning;
*   the processes involved in surveying;
*   financial issues relevant to the built environment;
*   legal issues relevant to the built environment;

- civil engineering technology;
- architectural design and drawing;
- computer-aided design.

As well as classroom activities, this course is likely to involve site visits and practical projects, including ICT-based work.

Critical thinking *The development of the thinking skills necessary in order to arrive at a judgement based on sound reasons.*

Students learn to:
- identify and evaluate the different elements of an argument;
- judge the reliability of sources of information;
- know when clarification is needed;
- present their own arguments in a clear, logical and coherent way.

Written work involves, for example, preparing a critical evaluation of a given argument or writing a reasoned case using evidence provided.

Dance *The practical and theoretical study of dance.*

Dance courses usually involve:
- choreography and performance;
- analysis and recording of work;
- understanding and appreciation of dance in terms of content and context.

Students need to have performing/technical dance skills and choreographic skills. The course will also involve reading and essay writing.

Design and technology *Three separate and distinct AS levels (DT: product design; DT: graphics; DT: fashion) all of which investigate how items are designed and manufactured, following the process from initial sketches to finished product.*

All three AS levels involve a major coursework element and students are expected to design and make products using a variety of materials, and put together a full design folder showing all stages of the process. They are expected to make clear notes and diagrams from videos, demonstrations and textbooks to help with their projects.

Students also:
- study and understand the design process as used by professional designers;
- learn to evaluate existing products;
- develop graphical skills, such as sketching, various kinds of technical drawing, computer graphics and the use of CADCAM (computer-aided design and manufacture);
- study materials, their properties and uses;
- study manufacturing processes and industrial practices;
- study the relationships between design, society and the environment;
- write essays from assembled information.

Courses often include visits to design studios, manufacturers and retail outlets.

Drama and theatre studies *The practical theatre skills of acting and design, as well as the study of how to devise and stage a piece of theatre.*

On a practical level, students are likely to be involved in:
- putting on a production of a play, working towards a performance when their acting or design skills will be assessed.

On a theoretical level, there are two areas of study:
- the analysis and comparison of contrasting texts, in order to discover how plays are structured;
- the investigation of the contexts in which plays are performed (for example, how plays can be interpreted in performance, or the history of a play's performance over the years).

Students need skills in performance or design, and any experience of or aptitude for devising (such as writing plays) would be helpful. Drama students also need skills in reading, research and essay writing.

Economics *The study of the commercial activities of society (i.e. the production and consumption of goods and services) through the understanding of various economic concepts and theories.*

Specifically, the course involves learning about markets (how they work and why they fail) and about the management of a country's economy. To do this, students are expected to:
- develop an understanding of various economic concepts and theories;
- investigate current economic issues, problems and institutions;
- apply economic theories in a range of contexts, appreciating both their value and limitations in explaining real-life situations;
- analyse the strengths and weaknesses of the market economy and the role of government within it.

Economics students need good critical and analytical skills. They must also have a strong interest in economic affairs and a desire to explore why and how the study of economics contributes to an understanding of the modern world.

Engineering (AGCE/National) *The application of scientific principles to the design, construction and maintenance of machinery and building work.*

Engineering courses involve a number of compulsory and optional units. The kinds of subjects covered include, for example:
- mathematics and its application in engineering;
- applied science in engineering;
- mechanical principles and applications;
- electrical and electronic principles and applications;
- engineering materials, processes and production techniques;
- engineering drawing;
- engine technology;
- fault diagnosis, maintenance and servicing;

- robotics.

Students need a good maths brain, a practical mind and the ability to think laterally.

English language and literature *The study of a range of literary and non-literary texts.*

The course might include work on, for example:
- the spoken word (unprepared commentary, drama);
- writing for specified purposes and audiences;
- using different writing styles for different audiences and purposes;
- short-story writing;
- further reading and analysis of literary texts;
- investigating different types of non-fiction.

Students are expected to produce both analytical work and creative work.

English literature *The understanding and appreciation of literary texts.*

Students study a range of literary texts (drama, poetry and prose) from different periods and explore the connections between them. As well as looking at form, structure and language, students are expected to focus increasingly on how a text is influenced by social, cultural and historical forces.

Lessons will mostly take the form of class discussions of texts, but students will also be shown how to produce structured and detailed written work based on their own interpretations. There will also be a certain amount of research. Note that students are expected to read independently beyond the coursework and set texts.

Film studies *The critical analysis of films and the study of film movements.*

The course might include:
- the critical analysis of short sequences from films;
- the study of cinema topics or film movements (for example, 1960s British cinema, Italian neo-realism);
- the study of individual films (for example, Mike Leigh's *Secrets and Lies*);
- research into the work of a particular film-maker;
- investigation into the meanings, messages and values conveyed through film;
- practical exercises in film journalism.

A good knowledge of a wide range of films is essential. The course is likely to involve a great deal of reading, so good research and writing skills are required.

Further mathematics *A course of very advanced pure maths and applied maths (mechanics, decision maths and statistics).*

- Pure maths: advanced topics in algebra, calculus, trigonometry, geometry and vectors and numerical methods. These might involve concepts such as scalar and cross product of vectors with application to three-dimensional space,

different co-ordinate systems, and solutions of a range of differential equations, hyperbolic functions, matrices and mathematical induction.
- Mechanics: relative motion, collisions, more complex motion in one dimension, stability, application of vectors in mechanics, variable mass, moments of inertia of a rigid body and rotation of a rigid body.
- Decision maths: algorithms, algorithms on graphs, the route inspection problem, critical path analysis, linear programming, matchings and flows in networks.
- Statistics: the binomial and Poisson distributions, continuous random variables, continuous distributions, samples and hypothesis tests.

Obviously, extremely good maths skills are needed! The advantage of further maths is that the small size of the class and the calibre of the pupils are likely to create an atmosphere conducive to lively discussion and personal interaction with the teacher.

Geography *The study of the natural features of the earth's surface (landforms, climate, soil, etc.) and man's response to them.*

The course is likely to be split into three areas:
- landforms and their management (for example, river and coastal environments, the impact of flooding and dam-building, coastal defence strategies);
- human environments (for example, the differences between rural and urban environments and the demands on each);
- an environmental investigation based on field work (this might involve a residential field trip in year 12 of about five days).

The course will involve different types of work and a variety of skills, such as:
- research from videos, CD-ROMs, texts, journals, newspapers, the internet;
- data collection and presentation;
- critical thinking, problem solving and decision making;
- group discussions and presentations;
- statistical analysis;
- ICT skills.

As well as the residential field trip, students are likely to go on several day trips to different locations and attend lectures and conferences.

Government and political studies *The science of government (i.e. how states are formed, directed and administered) with particular reference to the institutions and political traditions of the UK.*

The course would look at, for example:
- the relationship between people and politics (i.e. the nature of democracy, political parties and their ideologies, the role of pressure groups);
- the system of government in the UK (i.e. the constitution, the electoral system, the role of Parliament, the power of the Prime Minister);
- current political issues and ways in which the system of government in the UK is changing.

Students are required to take part in class discussions, debates and presentations as well as to carry out independent research and write essays.

Health and social care (AGCE/National) *The study of the physical and social factors that lead to health, and of the principles behind health-care provision and management.*

There are four main areas of study:
- core aspects of health and social care (for example, equal opportunities and clients' rights, communication, physical aspects of health, human growth and development, services provision, research;
- early years health and social care (for example, child development, educating for health);
- physical and medical factors relating to health and social care (for example, the role of exercise, behavioural psychology, mental health awareness, nutrition, complementary therapies, anatomy and physiology);
- health-care provision and policy (for example, health and social care management, family and social trends, provision for older people, provision for disabled people).

Students need to be very interested in the health- and social-care sectors and the issues that affect them. The course will involve independent reading and research, and practical work.

History *The discipline of interpreting past events involving human beings.*

The specific topics studied for AS-level history will depend very much on the examination board chosen by individual schools and colleges. Many courses, however, focus on:
- 20th century European history (for example, the rise of fascism in Germany, revolution in Russia);
- 19th and 20th century British history (for example, the rise of the British Labour Party 1850-1918, the changing role of women, the relationship between the State and the poor 1830-1939).

Whatever the topics, students are expected to:
- work with original and secondary documents;
- carry out research using a variety of sources;
- develop skills in evaluation and essay writing;
- select and use information accurately;
- present a logical argument and be aware of different interpretations.

As well as exams involving structured essay questions and source-based questions, students might also have to produce a coursework assignment of around 2,000 words.

Information and communication technology (ICT) *The study of how technology can be used to gather, process and store information.*

A course in ICT might include:
- looking at the way information is used within organisations and society, including the legal and practical implications;
- studying how information is gathered, processed and stored using a variety of software and hardware applications, and how it can be managed and manipulated;
- learning to use software for problem solving, usually by completing a practical project.

AGCE courses put extra emphasis on how ICT is used within organisations and businesses, covering topics such as:
- database design;
- spreadsheet design;
- ICT and business accounts;
- developing websites.

Courses tend to be task-based, with students learning problem solving and decision making through practical projects. There is also likely to be group work, case studies and independent study. Students will develop an understanding of the opportunities provided by ICT as well as practical skills in a wide range of applications.

Note: ICT is *not* a computer programming course.

Latin *The study of the language and literature of the ancient Romans, particularly from the first century BC when Latin achieved its classical form.*

The course will involve:
- studying the grammar and vocabulary of Latin in order to be able to understand reasonably uncomplicated Latin texts;
- studying set texts from classical literature in both prose form (for example, the writings of Cicero) and verse (such as Virgil's *Aeneid* and the poems of Catullus);
- acquiring some understanding of the culture, politics and social life of ancient Rome.

The language element of the course will involve translating from unseen Latin texts and comprehension tests based on unseen Latin passages. The literature element will involve answering questions based on passages from the set texts.

Law *An understanding of the English legal system (both civil and criminal law) and the formulation and presentation of legal arguments.*

Law courses cover issues such as:
- the concept of liability (legal obligation or responsibility);
- law making;
- dispute solving.

Students will also study specific areas of the law such as:
- criminal law;
- freedoms (civil liberties);

- contracts;
- consumer protection;
- tort (an area of the law relating to civil injury and actions for damages).

Students are required to carry out independent reading, participate in class discussions, prepare set topics for discussion and write set pieces of work. They will probably take part in practical exercises such as mock trials, interviews and negotiations. They may have to practise answering situation-based questions under a time constraint. Good communication skills (both oral and written) are essential, as well as analytical and critical-thinking skills.

Leisure and recreation (AGCE/National) *Knowledge and understanding of how leisure organisations are run, from sports clubs to theme parks.*

Students investigate all areas of the sports and leisure industries, including sports clubs, health clubs, fitness centres, leisure centres, outdoor activity centres and theme parks. Topics include:
- safety;
- marketing;
- customer services;
- business systems;
- human resources;
- financial planning;
- coaching provision;
- sports sponsorship;
- health and fitness;
- countryside recreation;
- children's play;
- sports officiating.

Mathematics *The sciences (such as algebra, geometry and calculus) concerned with the study of number, quantity, shape and space.*

There are two types of maths AS level. One is studied in year 12 and may lead on to A level in year 13. The other, called "Use of Maths", is an AS level only and is studied over years 12 *and* 13.

An AS-level maths course will involve units of both pure maths and applied maths. For the applied maths, students will probably have a choice of statistics, mechanics or decision maths. The topics covered would probably include:
- pure maths – algebra, graphs, trigonometry, calculus, numerical methods, co-ordinate geometry, exponentials, logarithms;
- statistics – probability, representation and summary of data, correlation and regression;
- mechanics – kinematics, vectors, work and energy, collisions;
- decision maths – ideas underpinning decision making in applied business scenarios.

Media studies *The study and analysis of the media (television, radio, films, newspapers, magazines) – what they are and how they work, the processes and technologies involved, and their effect on their audiences.*

Note: a "medium" is any means or agency for communicating information and news to the public.

Media studies is both a practical and academic subject.
The practical – Students will probably be required to put together a project in the form of, for example, a TV or radio production or a newspaper or magazine article, working individually or in groups. Each student may be expected to write an accompanying commentary on the project (of about 2,000 words).
The academic – Students learn about:
- the concepts and languages of the various media and how words and images are used to represent ideas (this is achieved through close analysis and comparison of actual examples from the media);
- media institutions, production processes and technologies;
- the ways audiences receive and consume information from the media.

Students need to have good analytical and writing skills. They will also need to be able to work independently and in groups and to show initiative. Note that the practical work may involve giving up time out of school hours.

Modern foreign languages (French, German, Italian and Spanish) *Learning to understand and communicate in another language, in both spoken and written forms.*

The main aims of an AS-level course in a modern language are:
- to enable students to communicate confidently, on a personal and practical level, in a foreign language;
- to develop students' knowledge and understanding of another culture.

Courses are usually topic-based and focus on contemporary political, economic and social issues. For example, topics might include: human relationships; daily life; the environment; work; leisure; international affairs.

The work will have four components:
- *listening* to radio, television, songs, plays, poems, interviews and discussions in the foreign language;
- *reading* novels or extracts from novels (usually 20th century ones), newspapers, magazine articles, surveys and official documents;
- *speaking* in pairs, in groups or on tape, discussing, debating, playing roles, seeking information, sustaining a conversation;
- *writing* at varying lengths and in various registers, including summaries, letters, essays and creative pieces.

Students are expected to read extensively in the language they are studying and lessons may well be conducted mainly in the foreign language.

Music *Performing and composing, as well as music appraisal.*

An AS-level music course will cover the key areas of:
* performance (both solo and ensemble recitals, in a variety of musical styles, achieved through regular rehearsals and coaching sessions);
* composition (learning how to handle harmonies, developing your own compositional style);
* listening (studying how music works by analysing technical details and cultural context).

Music courses are usually diverse in content, covering classical music, world music, pop music and jazz.

Music technology *The study of how music is composed and recorded, particularly using computer technology.*

On the practical side, music technology involves, for example:
* recording live music;
* using digital recording techniques;
* composing using computer sequencers;
* creating a performance from a score on a computer.

On the analytical side, the course might involve:
* listening to music from all ages, but particularly pop music and film music;
* analysing pop music using the language of music theory and technology;
* studying the history of music technology.

The ability to play an instrument and read music is essential. Much of the work is carried out on computers so good ICT skills are required.

Performing arts (AGCE/National) *The knowledge and skills required for a career in the performing arts, both on stage (dancing, acting, music) and behind the scenes (administration, marketing, production, design).*

This course will cover a variety of subject areas, all designed to give students an insight into the performing arts sector. For example:
* performance skills (contemporary dance techniques, acting techniques, musicianship, work for audition);
* creating work for performance (choreography, turning text into performance, music composition);
* technical skills (sound design, lighting design, stage and costume design, music technology, recording techniques);
* administration (working in performing arts, venue administration, stage management);
* background (investigating the performing arts industry, historical and contemporary contexts).

As well as classroom work, students are expected to visit arts-related organisations and carry out independent research into the sector.

Philosophy *An introduction to philosophical themes and major philosophers. The central issue of philosophy is whether or not we can rationally justify our beliefs* *and opinions, particularly in the areas of reality (metaphysics), knowledge (epistemology), moral judgement (ethics) and language (semantics).*

Philosophy students investigate subjects such as:
- the theory of knowledge (how can we know about anything? How can we prove beyond doubt that the objects around us really exist?);
- moral philosophy (how can we know if something is a "good" or "bad" act?);
- other philosophical themes such as the philosophy of the mind, political philosophy and the philosophy of science;
- the works of major philosophers, for example Descartes's *Meditations*, Sartre's *Being and Nothingness* and Nietzsche's *Beyond Good and Evil*.

An interest in the kinds of issues outlined above and a reflective temperament are required here! Students will need a talent for putting forward and analysing arguments. They will be expected to carry out independent research, write essays and contribute to class discussions and debates.

Photography *The creative use of photography, film, video and digital imaging.*

Photography is studied as a branch of art and design and the emphasis is on *creative* expression and enquiry (i.e. the production, selection and manipulation of images to produce different meanings). More than half the course is likely to involve practical projects and students are able to build up portfolios for art college. Students become familiar with:
- camera use;
- the darkroom;
- the studio;
- ICT methods.

There is also a certain amount of analytical work including:
- the understanding of images;
- critical analysis of the work of others;
- photographic history;
- planning and development of projects.

Before committing to a course in photography, it is a good idea to have experimented taking a lot of photographs already (some sixth forms may require evidence of this before accepting students for photography courses). Much of the practical work will be carried out outside the classroom so students will need to show good levels of independence and initiative.

Physical education *The analysis of sports skills and sporting performance; the application of this knowledge to improve performance.*

Students are required to take part in practical sports sessions and will be assessed on their personal performance, but much of the teaching will probably take place in the classroom and deal with the varied *theoretical* content of the course. This includes:
- anatomy (the physical structure of the body), physiology (the functioning of the body) and psychology (the study of behaviour);
- the application of the knowledge of anatomy, physiology and psychology in order to improve sports performance;

- improving performance through critical analysis (for example, a student might be asked to show how he or she has improved his/her personal performance in a number of sports, through selecting, applying and developing particular skills);
- investigation into current issues in physical education.

Students will need to have reached a good level of personal performance in at least two sports. Students who have not taken PE at GCSE level may need to familiarise themselves with the subjects of anatomy and physiology.

Physics *The study of the properties of matter and energy, based on maths.*

The study of physics develops both practical and theoretical skills. On the theoretical side, students will:
- increase their understanding of physical concepts;
- learn to apply physical concepts to unfamiliar situations;
- learn to use maths effectively;
- look at the impact of physics on society and its role in developing new technologies.

On the practical side students will:
- use a wide range of scientific apparatus;
- learn to take very accurate readings;
- learn to extract information from a variety of sources, including graphs, practical data, textbooks and journals.

Examples of topics that might be studied at AS level include: mechanics; radioactivity; electricity; thermal energy; astrophysics; solid materials; nuclear and particle physics; medical physics; electronics.

Courses are designed to build on concepts that students have already learnt at GCSE, but the AS level is likely to be much more demanding. Students must be prepared to work hard and think hard!

Psychology *The study of human behaviour.*

The course will aim to develop understanding of psychological principles and concepts, including:
- social psychology (social influences, ethics, relationships, pro- and anti-social behaviour);
- physiological psychology (stress and coping with stress);
- cognitive psychology (memory, perception, attention, language and thought);
- developmental psychology (early socialisation of children, cognitive development, intelligence, development of gender);
- individual differences (abnormality, eating disorders, atypical development, psychopathology);
- research methods;
- approaches in psychology (the major schools of thought).

Students need to be able to understand and evaluate psychological theories and evidence, and present their knowledge in essays and answers to structured questions.

Religious studies *The study of religious ethics and philosophy.*

Religious studies courses are open to students of any religious persuasion or of no religious persuasion at all. Students are assessed on the merits of their arguments about the issues raised, not on their personal beliefs.

Courses are likely to cover two main areas:
- religious ethics (the set of moral principles and values held by a religious group);
- philosophy of religion (the arguments used by religious groups to explain their beliefs).

The type of work will probably include:
- research from books, television, videos, newspapers and journals;
- group discussions and debates;
- seminars;
- conferences including input from speakers representing different ethical and philosophical positions.

Science (AGCE/National) *The practical application of science, in commerce, industry or research.*

This course is for students who wish to pursue specific careers in science (for example, laboratory work). It covers a range of subjects, such as:
- investigating science at work;
- monitoring and controlling (for example, chemical processes, the transfer of energy, the activity of the human body);
- carrying out scientific investigations (sampling, testing, analysing materials);
- imaging and sensing;
- making and using materials for a purpose (for example, polymers);
- using digital electronics;
- maintaining health through biophysics or nutrition;
- mathematics for scientists.

The course will involve plenty of laboratory work, calculations and practical tasks.

Sociology *An understanding of contemporary society, including its structures and social processes.*

A course in sociology should help students to reflect on their own experience of the social world in which they live, as well as to develop knowledge and understanding of sociological theory. For example, students will:
- investigate certain topics from a sociological viewpoint, such as families, health, the media, education, politics, religion or crime;
- study different sociological theories and methods;
- write a research proposal and carry out a research project.

Sociology students have to become skilled at data analysis. As well as writing essays, students are likely to participate in classroom debates, group work activities, research projects and presentations.

Travel and tourism (AGCE/National) *Investigation into all aspects of the travel and tourism industries, both worldwide and in the UK.*

Topics include, for example:
* tourism development;
* UK tour operations;
* travel agency operations;
* travel service providers;
* tourism information services;
* worldwide travel destinations;
* tourist and visitor attractions;
* adventure tourism activities;
* business and executive travel;
* UK passenger transport.

The course also covers the business side of the industry, dealing with, for example: marketing; customer services; human resources; business systems; financial management; legal issues relating to travel and tourism.

Detailed information about any of these AS subjects can be found on the websites of the exam boards: www.ocr.org.uk, www.aqa.org.uk and www.edexcel.org.uk

22. Higher-education advice for adults

Many higher-education issues are the same for adults (normally deemed to be students aged 21 years or over) as for school or college leavers. However, there are a few important differences, outlined here.

If the person is in employment
There needs to be a realistic discussion about what the student's new financial situation will be when he or she is in higher education. Questions an adviser should ask include:
* Will you be keeping your employment?
* Will you study part time or full time?
* If a mortgage has to be paid, will sufficient funds be available?
* Would it be a good idea to see an independent financial adviser? Or in England, a Next Step adviser may be able to talk through this issue.

Students may also want to check with the university/college about other financial support such as the Additional Fee Support Scheme or the Access to Learning Fund.

Those who go into full-time study may be eligible for a student loan (which has to be repaid). They may be eligible for a maintenance grant if their household income is below a certain amount, or a special support grant if they get or qualify for income support or housing benefit. They are likely to qualify for the special support grant if they are a single parent or their partner (if they have one) is also a student or if they have certain disabilities (in 2011). They do not have to pay back grants.

If the person is unemployed
As a full-time student, they are eligible to apply for student finance to fund their course. This therefore means that only certain groups of full-time students in higher education may remain or be eligible for certain income-related benefits. Every case will be assessed on an individual basis, especially if the income they could get via student finance might be too high for them to remain on benefits. More information can be obtained from Jobcentre Plus and their local authority.

There needs to be some thorough research into what benefits the student would keep and what he or she might lose. Would the student be able to keep housing benefit? Would it be a good idea to see a benefits adviser (if available)? However, in 2011 in England, part-time students can remain on income support, income-related Employment and Support Allowance (ESA), Council Tax Benefit, income-based Jobseekers Allowance and New Deal Allowance. They may be eligible for support as stated above.

They can get more information from the Direct Gov website (www.direct.gov.uk) about benefits, funding, eligibility and entitlement. They can even use the student finance calculator to estimate the funds they may be eligible for. Information for funding for nursing, social work and other healthcare professions can be obtained from the NHS Business Service Authority: http://www.nhsbsa.nhs.uk/Students

Is the course going to lead to anything?

The person needs to be clear about what the course is likely to lead to. A 40-year-old starting a degree in social work will have excellent job prospects. A 40-year-old doing a degree in media studies will find it much harder to gain employment in this field. It is very important to help the student find out what the graduate employment outcomes are for the course that they are considering. Looking at www.unistats.com tells us the percentage of mature students on a course, and it also tells us the overall graduate destinations of the students on a course. It doesn't, in 2011, tell us what the graduate destinations of the mature students on the course are.

Access courses

Access to HE courses are designed to prepare students for higher education by drawing on their existing experience gained through employment, travel, or caring for a family. Students learn how to make notes, write essays, carry out research, develop ideas and gain experience of the assessment methods used on a degree course. They also learn core subjects usually linked to the degree or diploma they wish to study. Substantial amount of home study is also expected to successfully meet the demands of the course. For more information about Access to HE courses and where to find a local college, contact the Open College Network, who are the awarding body for access qualifications. They can be contacted at www.nocn.org.uk/learners or alternatively visit www.accesstohe.ac.uk

Access programmes enable students to gain credits through coursework and examinations, leading to an access diploma or certificate, which is a nationally recognised qualification for entry to a degree course. Occasionally, I come across admissions tutors for highly selective courses who ask for something more than just the access course – perhaps an A level or some extra evidence of wider reading.

Part-time diplomas/degrees

Many universities offer these, allowing students to work, sometimes in their previous full-time job. They will often take one or two years longer than the full-time degree. Some financial help is available to part-time students. They are not eligible for a student loan for 2011/2012 on a part-time course.

If their income and that of their partner, if they have one, is below a certain amount, they may be eligible for:
- A fee grant to help with the cost of tuition fees and
- A course grant to help with other study costs such as books, materials and travel.
The help they get will depend on how "intensive" their course is, their household income and personal circumstances. They do not have to pay back grants.

However, new part-time students starting their courses in the 2012/13 academic year in England will benefit from new loans for tuition, provided Parliament approves the relevant legislation.

Open University

The Open University (OU) is the United Kingdom's only university dedicated to distance learning. For most courses, students do not need to have previous qualifications. Nearly all OU students study part time and about 70% of undergraduate students are in full-time employment. Around 44% of students start their courses without the entry qualifications they would need at a conventional university. More information can be found on the website www.open.ac.uk

Confidence

HE advisers need to be aware that for many adults – perhaps they are women returners, a newly released ex-prisoner or someone who has been doing a job he has hated for years – the prospect of entering higher education may seem daunting (more daunting, of course, than for a sixth-form student whose entry to higher education is probably taken as read). Extra time and care may be needed to reassure them and answer their concerns. I have found the Morrisby Profile to be especially useful in these situations. Other career profile tools such as Adult Directions at www.cascaid.co.uk or the Skills Health Check on the Next Step website (www.nextstep.direct.gov.uk) can be useful.

Dependent children

If the person has dependent children, their care will have to be taken into consideration. Further education colleges running access courses and universities may well have crèche facilities. Parents also need to know about current benefits (in 2011) such as childcare grants, parents' learning allowance and child tax credit. More information is available through www.direct.gov.uk/studentfinance

Refugees and overseas students in higher education

Excellent information on this subject is available through UKCISA, who protect the interests of international students in the UK: www.ukcisa.org.uk

Also visit the Refugee Council website www.refugeecouncil.org.uk

In my experience, the two big issues for this category of student are the meeting of residency requirements (in order to be considered as a home student) and the value of any qualifications gained outside the UK. Students with overseas qualifications can be referred to NARIC (National Recognition Information Centre), which provides a number of different services, such as: providing a letter of comparability; a translation waiver scheme; a career path report; a fast-track service. Information is available from www.naric.org.uk

Many thanks to Moji Muse for her help in updating this section:
mojimuse@gmail.com

Appendix A: An A-Z of university subjects with essential information for students

This alphabetical reference section is for students who have an idea about the subject they would like to study at degree level, but now need further information. For each subject, it points out the issues that students need to be aware of and includes website addresses for finding out more. Apologies that subject requirements are based on AS levels – go to course search on www.ucas.com or university online prospectuses for entry requirements that involve other qualifications.

Accountancy	*Helpful information:*
	• Put simply, accountancy is concerned with the management of money. In fact, it offers career prospects in a variety of different areas. There is scope, for example, for people interested in the intricacies of accounting procedures; or in high finance; or in getting into general management; or in becoming entrepreneurs.
	• Many graduates going into accountancy will have a degree in some other subject. Therefore, most firms recruiting students for traineeships (leading to chartered status) will be more concerned with original A-level grades, level of degree pass and performance at an assessment centre. A degree in accountancy, however, will mean some exemptions from professional exams.
	• It might also be worth considering a general business and management degree. This would allow the student to specialise in accountancy and finance, and would also mean professional exemptions.
	Essential AS levels: None.
	Useful AS levels: Possibly maths and economics.
	Websites:
	• The Institute of Chartered Accountants in England and Wales, www.icaew.co.uk
	• The Association of Chartered Certified Accountants, www.accaglobal.com
	• The Chartered Institute of Management Accountants, www.cimaglobal.com
	• The Chartered Institute of Public Finance and Accountancy, www.cipfa.org.uk
	Retail banking
	IFS School of Finance: ifslearning.ac.uk
	Building Societies Association: www.bsa.org.uk
	Investment and Corporate Banking
	London Investment Banking Association: www.liba.org.uk
	Insurance
	The Chartered Insurance Institute: www.cii.co.uk
	Financial Services Skills Council: www.fssc.org.uk

Actuarial science	*Helpful information:*
	• Actuaries calculate insurance and pension risks using statistical techniques.
	• Students need to be very good at maths and very interested in financial issues. They will also need staying power: there will be more years of professional training after graduation.
	• It is a good idea to try to meet an actuary and talk to them about what the job involves.
	Essential AS levels: Maths.
	Useful AS levels: Further maths, economics and business studies (but not both).
	Websites: Visit www.actuaries.org.uk
Advertising	*Helpful information:*
	• Advertising agencies arrange, produce and consign advertisements on behalf of companies and organisations who appoint them to handle their "account".
	• A degree in advertising will not guarantee a job with an advertising agency.
	• Advertising is not often studied as a specific degree – it is more commonly included as part of a marketing or business and management degree.
	• Art directors with advertising agencies will normally have followed the art and design route, rather than studying the business side.
	Essential AS levels: None.
	Useful AS levels: Art and design (for would-be art directors); business studies (AS/AGCE/BTEC National) may improve your knowledge of marketing, of which advertising is a part.
	Websites:
	• CAM Foundation, www.camfoundation.com
	• Institute of Practitioners in Advertising, www.ipa.co.uk
Aeronautical engineering	*Helpful information:*
	• Students must make sure they know whether the courses they are applying for will lead them to become a chartered engineer or an incorporated engineer under UK-SPEC regulations.
	• Related careers include: aircraft design and construction; space and satellite research; maintenance of airline fleets.
	• Students will need to be able to explain *why* they are applying for an aeronautical engineering degree, as opposed to any other engineering degree. They should look at the world around them. Do they see examples of aerospace that fascinate them? Why are they fascinating? How do they look? How were they made? What elements of maths and physics were used?
	• Be aware of programmes such as "a year in industry". Visit www.yini.org.uk.
	Essential AS levels: Maths, physics.
	Useful AS levels: Further maths, DT, ICT.
	Websites:

	• The Royal Aeronautical Society: www.raes.org.uk • Also try www.aerosociety.com/careers
American studies	_Helpful information:_ • This could be the course for students who want to study some literature, some history and some politics, and who would like to study at a foreign university. • Courses vary. Some offer the chance to study film, music or visual arts. Others are more like a traditional English or history degree. It is essential to know which are which. • Students applying for American studies should include in their personal statements any examples of American literature and history that have fascinated them. • This degree could open up some popular career areas (though graduates may have to do extra training, a postgraduate course or a conversion course). For example: accountancy; advertising; armed forces; banking; barrister; chartered secretary; civil aviation; civil service; health services management; human resources management; information technology; information science; insurance; journalism; leisure and recreation management; management; management consultancy; marketing; police; personal adviser (careers officer); public relations; publishing; restaurant management; retail management; social work; solicitor; surveying; teaching; TEFL teaching; television, film and radio. _Essential AS levels:_ Requirements vary but English and history are often asked for. _Useful AS levels:_ Politics. _Websites:_ Visit www.americansc.org.uk
Anthropology	_Helpful information:_ • Students must be very clear that they understand what anthropology is. It is the study of human behaviour, beliefs, institutions and the various societies in which people live. It could cover a wide range of subjects, such as culture, ethnology, folk traditions, religion, magic, sorcery and ecology. • It is important to find out whether a student is interested in the social or biological aspects of anthropology, or both. • University admissions tutors are looking for evidence of interest (books read, museums visited, overseas trips). If a student has travelled abroad, can he or she compare other societies with our own? • www.prospects.ac.uk career suggestions: social researcher; aid/development worker; charity officer; local government officer; community arts worker; market researcher. • This degree could open up some popular career areas (though graduates may have to do extra training, a postgraduate course or a conversion course). For example: accountancy; advertising; armed forces; banking; barrister; chartered secretary; civil aviation; civil service; health services management; human

	resources management; information technology; information science; insurance; journalism; leisure and recreation management; management; management consultancy; marketing; police; personal adviser (careers officer); public relations; publishing; restaurant management; retail management; social work; solicitor; surveying; teaching; TEFL teaching; television, film and radio. ***Essential AS levels:*** None. ***Useful AS levels:*** A small number of courses prefer a science AS level such as biology or sociology. ***Websites:*** Visit http://www.intute.ac.uk/anthropology/
Archaeology	***Helpful information:*** • Students really must try and get some experience of excavations and digs (visit www.britarch.ac.uk). • They should read as much about archaeology as possible and think about how archaeology helps us to understand history. • Generally, archaeology does not require such high grades as a history degree. • www.prospects.ac.uk career suggestions: archaeologist; historic buildings inspector/conservation officer; museum/gallery curator; museum education officer. • An archaeology degree could open up some popular career areas (though graduates may have to do extra training, a postgraduate course or a conversion course). For example: accountancy; advertising; armed forces; banking; barrister; chartered secretary; civil aviation; civil service; health services management; human resources management; information technology; information science; insurance; journalism; leisure and recreation management; management, management consultancy; marketing; police; personal adviser (careers officer); public relations; publishing; restaurant management; retail management; social work; solicitor; surveying; teaching; TEFL teaching; television, film and radio. ***Essential AS levels:*** None. ***Websites:*** • Visit www.archaeology.co.uk • Or try www.english-heritage.org.uk
Architecture	***Helpful information:*** • Architecture is a multi-disciplinary profession requiring a combination of artistic, technological and sociological expertise. The challenge of architecture is to produce, within a given budget, an aesthetically pleasing design which will stand up to wear and tear and is the kind of building people would like to live or work in. • Students *must* have a portfolio of drawings that includes: their own ideas for buildings; drawings of existing buildings. This is essential. Other artwork could be included as an addition. • They *must* be able to write about their ideas, concentrating on

	the three elements of design: the look, the cost and the making. For example, can they describe their favourite building and say why they like it?
	• They *must* show an interest in the history of architecture (for example, classical Greek and Roman, Gothic, organic and international styles) and in the work and influence of important architects from different historical periods (for example, Vitruvius, William of Sens, Frank Lloyd Wright and Le Corbusier). There are many books on this but a good starting point is *The Story of Architecture* by Jonathan Glancey.
	• They will need to have confirmed their commitment to a career in architecture through work experience.
	• Students should be made aware of the length of training – five years, plus two years in professional practice, before qualification!
	Essential AS levels: For a small number of degree courses, maths and/or physics and art (some ask for an arts/science mix).
	Useful AS levels: Art, maths and physics.
	Websites:
	• The Royal Institute of British Architects, www.architecture.com
	• For more ideas, try www.greatbuildings.com
Art and design	***Helpful information:***
	• There are five main areas of specialisation: fine art; graphic design; product/industrial design; interior design; textiles/fashion design.
	• Mostly, artistic sixth-form students take art A level, which is the study of painting, drawing and sculpture. Yet most university students in this field study design subjects (graphic, fashion, product, interior). Most courses therefore require students to take a diploma in art foundation studies. This acts as a bridge between A levels (or AGCE) and design degrees.
	• Art foundation courses are usually full time and last for one year. Fees are not normally charged if the student is still eighteen years old.
	• A foundation course has three stages – exploratory, pathway and confirmation. In the first term students try out all the major areas of design. In the second term they try to decide which area they would like to specialise in. They then begin to concentrate on this area so that they have a specialist portfolio ready for the degree or HND course they wish to apply for.
	• Students are expected to work hard on their drawing skills.
	• A small number of degrees now include an added art foundation course at the start.
	• Students considering a career in art and design should be aware that they may take longer than other graduates to become established in their chosen career path and that they have a strong chance of being self employed, so they will need to be self starting and independent.
	Most entrants to art and design degrees will have done a one-year

	art foundation course after their A levels. Some AGCE/Diploma art and design students gain entry to higher education courses without doing a foundation course. ***Essential AS levels:*** Art A level or art and design AGCE (these allow students to build up the portfolio they need to get onto an art foundation course – otherwise they will have to create a portfolio completely by themselves), possibly DT. BTEC National students will usually be able to get straight onto a degree without having done a foundation course. ***Useful AS levels:*** DT, photography, history of art. ***Websites:*** • Design Council, www.designcouncil.org.uk.
Banking	***Helpful information:*** • While it is possible to take a degree in this field, employers in banking have no particular preference for any specific degree subject (although a numerate discipline, or a subject such as economics, law or business studies, could be useful). Employers will therefore be very interested in A-level grades, level of degree pass and performance in assessment tests. • There are two main areas of banking: retail/personal banking and building societies; investment and corporate banking. ***Essential AS levels:*** None. ***Useful AS levels:*** Possibly maths, business studies and economics (do not do these two together). ***Websites:*** For retail/personal banking and building societies • IFS school of finance, www.ifslearning.ac.uk • Building Societies Association, www.bsa.org.uk For investment and corporate banking • Association for financial markets in Europe, www.afme.eu Financial Services Skills Council: www.fssc.org.uk
Biochemistry	***Helpful information:*** • Biochemistry is the study of biology at a molecular level. Students will have covered topics in biology and chemistry A level that will be relevant to the study of biochemistry. • Most developments in medicine and agriculture will involve biochemistry. • A significant minority of graduates will go on to postgraduate study. • Course content in the first two years can be very similar to other degrees, such as biomedical sciences, pharmacology and microbiology. ***Essential AS levels:*** Always chemistry. Some degrees will say you must also have biology, while some stipulate chemistry plus *one* of maths, physics or biology. Taking AS levels in chemistry, biology and maths or physics will keep all biochemistry courses open.

	Websites: Visit www.biochemistry.org • Cogent is the sector skills council for the chemicals and pharmaceuticals, oil and gas, petroleum and polymer industries. Visit www.cogent-ssc.org
Biology	**Helpful information:** • Courses involve botany, human biology, zoology, micro-organisms and biochemistry. Topics that students have already studied for their biology and chemistry A levels will be relevant. • Degree courses can involve much independent research, so examples of an interest in biology outside of school will be useful. Also, if a student is applying for a more specialist course (for example, botany) can he or she explain why? • A significant minority of graduates will go on to postgraduate study. **Essential AS levels:** Biology and chemistry. **Useful AS levels:** Maths or physics. **Websites:** Visit www.iob.org
Building (building services engineering, building surveying, construction management)	**Helpful information:** • Students should have a clear idea about why they want to enter this career field and evidence to support this (for example, relevant work experience or talks with building professionals). • They should think about building projects that interest them – local, national or international. • Related careers include construction management, project management, site management. **Essential AS levels:** For many courses in this field, maths and/or physics. **Websites:** Visit www.ciob.org.uk www.cskills.org www.rics.org
Business studies	**Helpful information:** • These courses always include the study of: economics; human resources; marketing; accounting; finance; and, usually, quantitative methods (statistics) and ICT. • The four-year sandwich business studies degree (UCAS code N100) is now a very established course. Students should not presume that courses at modern universities are inferior – the ex-polytechnics (who developed this course) now have many years' expertise. • There is a plethora of different course names (business studies, business and management, business management, business administration, commerce and so on) – but it's all the same thing. • Some courses allow students to specialise in a particular field (for example, marketing) by the end of the course. Others stay general to the end.

<table>
<tr>
<td></td>
<td>

• Universities will be interested in students' personal qualities and what they have learned from any work experience or part-time work. Any evidence of working in a team would be particularly useful.

Essential AS levels: None.

Useful AS levels: Possibly maths, economics, and business studies (try to avoid doing the last two together). An AGCE or AS level in business studies would confirm a student's interest. Be aware that many courses require GCSEs in maths and English language at grade C or above.

Websites:

• Visit Chartered Management Institute: www.managers.org.uk
• Other websites to visit include: the Financial Services Skills Council www.fssc.org.uk
• People 1st, the sector skills council for the hospitality, leisure, travel and tourism industries. People 1st covers: contract food service providers, events, gambling, holiday parks, hospitality services, hostels, hotels, membership clubs, pubs, bars and nightclubs, restaurants, self-catering accommodation, tourist services, travel services and visitor attractions. www.people1st.co.uk
• Skillsmart, the sector skills council for the retail sector www.skillsmartretail.com
• SkillsActive is the sector skills council for the active leisure and learning industry embracing sport and fitness, outdoors and adventure, playwork, camping and caravanning. www.skillsactive.com

</td>
</tr>
<tr>
<td>

Chemical engineering

</td>
<td>

Helpful information:

• Students must make sure they know whether the courses they are applying for will lead them to become a chartered engineer or an incorporated engineer through UK-SPEC.
• Chemical engineering involves designing and developing lab ideas into the manufacturing process – chemicals, medicines, plastics, fuels.
• Students will need to be able to explain why they are applying for a chemical engineering degree, as opposed to a more general engineering degree. They should look at the world around them. Do they see examples of chemical engineering that fascinate them? Why are they fascinating? How do they look? How were they made? What elements of chemistry, maths and physics were used?
• Be aware of programmes such as "a year in industry". Visit www.yini.org.uk

Essential AS levels: Chemistry and maths, and sometimes also physics.

Websites:

• The Institution of Chemical Engineers: www.icheme.org

</td>
</tr>
</table>

Chemistry	*Helpful information:* • Chemistry has been suffering a lack of applicants, so entry requirements may be flexible. It is also possible to specialise in chemistry through a natural sciences course. • Applicants should think about the topics that have interested them in their A-level chemistry studies. Any extra reading of scientific journals or knowledge about science issues in the news (using specific examples) looks impressive. Students should try to find out about the practical applications of chemistry, such as food science or the pharmaceutical industry. • A significant minority of graduates will go on to postgraduate study. *Essential AS levels:* Chemistry and usually maths or physics. Some courses require chemistry, maths and physics, while some prefer chemistry, maths and biology. *Websites:* Visit www.rsc.org • Cogent is the sector skills council for the chemicals and pharmaceuticals, oil and gas, petroleum and polymer industries. Visit www.cogent-ssc.org
Civil engineering	*Helpful information:* • This involves the design, planning, construction and maintenance of infrastructure and large-scale structures. • Students must make sure they know whether the courses they are applying for will lead them to become a chartered engineer or an incorporated engineer through UK-SPEC. • Students should be able to explain why they are applying for a civil engineering degree, as opposed to a more general engineering degree. They should look at the world around them. Do they see examples of civil engineering that fascinate them? Why are they fascinating? How do they look? How were they made? What elements of maths and physics were used? • Be aware of programmes such as "a year in industry". Visit www.yini.org.uk • Visit the websites of the professional bodies listed here. *Essential AS levels:* Maths and physics. *Useful AS levels:* Further maths, DT. *Websites:* Visit www.ice.org.uk
Classical studies	*Helpful information:* • For a classics degree, students will normally be required to have an A level in Latin or ancient Greek. For classical studies or classical civilisation, however, most A levels would be considered. If not ancient Greek or Latin, some flair for languages will definitely help. • The course covers literature, drama, history, politics and philosophy. It is suitable for students who enjoy reading books and thinking about the ideas behind them. • Applicants should think of examples that prove their interest. They should try to visit museums with relevant collections and

	ancient sites (in Rome or Greece if possible!) • www.prospects.ac.uk career suggestions: archivist; museum education officer; advertising copywriter; public relations officer; historic buildings/conservation officer. • This degree could open up some popular career areas (though graduates may have to do extra training, a postgraduate course or a conversion course). For example: accountancy; advertising; armed forces; banking; barrister; chartered secretary; civil aviation; civil service; health services management; human resources management; information technology; information science; insurance; journalism; leisure and recreation management; management; management consultancy; marketing; police; personal adviser (careers officer); public relations; publishing; restaurant management; retail management; social work; solicitor; surveying; teaching; TEFL teaching; television, film and radio. ***Essential AS levels:*** For classics courses, Latin or ancient Greek. Classical studies and classical civilisations courses will consider most subjects. ***Useful AS levels:*** A modern foreign language, English literature and history. ***Websites:*** • Visit www.classicspage.com • Also, www.british-museum.ac.uk
Computing	***Helpful information:*** • Computing degrees vary in their content and there is a wide range of courses on offer. Students must make sure they know exactly what they have applied for, and make this explicit in their personal statement. • Some courses will be very concerned about students' maths ability. For others this will be less of an issue. Some courses may be interested in students with good design ideas. • Related careers could include: network specialists; software programmers; multimedia specialists; hardware engineers. • Applicants should try to think about all the experience they have had with computers and programming, inside and outside of school, and any work experience that may have involved computer systems. What did they learn from this? Did they have any ideas for improvement? ***Essential AS levels:*** For some courses, maths. For a very small number of courses, further maths would be helpful. ***Useful AS levels:*** Maths, physics, philosophy and ICT. ***Websites:*** Visit www.bcs.org.uk www.e-skills.com
Dentistry	***Helpful information:*** • Dentists preserve and extract teeth, design and fit dentures, improve irregular teeth. They can perform some types of surgery above the neck.

	• Applicants will need to be able to explain *why* they want be become a dentist and provide evidence to back up their claims. • Admissions tutors will be interested in any work experience in dentistry, especially if the student can explain what they learned from it. • Admissions tutors will also want to know that applicants have a high level of manual dexterity. Students should try to think of things they have done that *prove* their manual dexterity. • It is helpful to show an interest by being aware of some current issues or difficulties facing dentists. Perhaps there is one that the student could talk about in more depth at interview. • Students can only apply for four courses in dentistry through UCAS. ***Essential AS levels:*** Chemistry and biology would be acceptable for most courses, but a few still prefer chemistry, biology and maths or physics. • Most dental schools will require you to take the UKCAT: www.ukcat.ac.uk • Visit the websites of the British Dental Association (www.bda.org) and the General Dental Council (www.gdc-uk.org) • The British Dental Hygienists Association, www.bdha.org.uk
Dietetics	***Helpful information:*** • The dietician's skill is to translate the science of nutrition into understandable and practical information about food and health. • Students will need to be able to explain fully why they want to enter this career and provide evidence to back up their claims. If they have done any relevant work experience, they will be expected to explain what they learned from it. It is helpful to think about what qualities are needed for a career in dietetics (with examples). • Students can show their interest by being aware of some current issues or difficulties associated with this career. Perhaps there is one that they could talk about in more depth. • A list of registered degrees with accreditation for working in the NHS are on the BDA website. ***Essential AS levels:*** Chemistry and biology. ***Websites:*** • The British Dietetic Association, www.bda.uk.com
Drama	***Helpful information:*** • Anyone wishing to enter a career in professional acting must check out the essential information on the website of the Conference of Drama Schools (www.drama.ac.uk). An abridged version of *The Conference of Drama Schools Official UK Guide to Drama Training* is available by download from the website. • Applicants must be clear about which courses train their students to work as professional actors and which courses are

<table>
<tr><td></td><td>

more concerned with the criticism and analysis of the theatre. Professional courses involve acting, singing and dancing.

- Students should think about what plays and playwrights they like and why. Those applying for acting courses must be clear about what they have learned from roles they have played so far. Those applying for technical courses should think about the problems they encountered in the productions they have been involved with, and how they dealt with them.
- Professional courses will involve auditions. Students should seek advice from teachers or tutors with recent and successful experience of helping people prepare for audition.
- Yes, 80% of actors may be unemployed at any one time. However, there can be shortages of stage management professionals. Moreover, an acting course can be good preparation for many other careers (though it may be necessary to do extra training, a postgraduate course or a conversion course). For example; accountancy; advertising; armed forces; banking; barrister; chartered secretary; civil aviation; civil service; health services management; human resources management; information technology; information science; insurance; journalism; leisure and recreation management; management; management consultancy; marketing; police; personal adviser (careers officer); public relations; publishing; restaurant management; retail management; social work; solicitor; surveying; teaching; TEFL teaching; television, film and radio.
- For an honest idea of the industry see www.equity.org.uk
- Each initial audition will cost around £35 to £45. There is no charge if you are called back for further auditions.
- The sector skills councils for acting are: Creative and Cultural www.ccskills.org.uk and Skillset www.skillset.org

Essential AS levels: Some courses require English literature. A few courses require English and theatre studies.
Useful AS levels: English literature, English literature and language, theatre studies.
Websites: Visit www.drama.ac.uk

</td></tr>
<tr><td>

Economics

</td><td>

Helpful information:
- A large number of economics graduates will enter business, commerce and finance-related occupations.
- It is important for applicants to show they have a genuine interest in economics – not just an interest in working for an investment bank!
- Students should keep abreast of economic issues in the news. If they are studying economics at A level, can they say what topics they have enjoyed and why?
- If they are not studying economics at A level, they must be prepared to do some extra reading on economics issues. Also, they should think about the A levels they *are* taking to see if they have any cross-curricular links with economics.

</td></tr>
</table>

181

	Essential AS levels: Some courses require maths. *Useful AS levels:* Maths and economics. *Websites:* Visit www.res.org.uk
Electrical/electronic engineering	*Helpful information:* • Students must make sure they know whether the courses they are applying for will lead them to become a chartered engineer or an incorporated engineer through UK-SPEC requirements. • Students must be able to explain why they are applying for a degree in electrical or electronic engineering, as opposed to a more general engineering degree. They should look at the world around them. Do they see examples of electrical or electronic engineering that fascinate them? Why are they fascinating? How do they look? How were they made? What elements of maths and physics were used? • Be aware of programmes such as "a year in industry". Visit www.yini.org.uk *Essential AS levels:* Maths and physics. *Useful AS levels:* Further maths, DT, ICT. *Websites:* • Institution of Electrical Engineers, www.iee.org
Engineering	*Helpful information:* • The purpose of engineering is the design and manufacture of the "hardware" of life. Engineers have a hand in the creation of everything in use everywhere. • Students must make sure they know whether the courses they are applying for will lead them to become a chartered or an incorporated engineer. • Students must be able to explain why they are applying for a general engineering degree, as opposed to a more specialised engineering degree. They should look at the world around them. Do they see examples of engineering that fascinate them? Why are they fascinating? How do they look? How were they made? What elements of maths and physics were used? • Be aware of programmes such as "a year in industry". Visit www.yini.org.uk *Essential AS levels:* Maths and physics. *Useful AS levels:* Further maths, DT, chemistry *Websites:* • Royal Academy of Engineering, www.raeng.org.uk
English	*Helpful information:* • Students need to be genuinely enthusiastic about poems, plays and novels, from classical civilisations to the present day. Wider reading, beyond the A-level syllabus, is absolutely essential. • In the personal statement, students should write about their favourite authors, poets and dramatists and explain why they like them. At interview, the texts chosen for discussion will be

	those mentioned on UCAS Apply.
	• It is also helpful to think about issues relating to literature in a wider context, such as the difference between studying a text in depth or reading it for pleasure, and its links with history and religion.
	• Most degrees are literature based. Students should *not* go on about creative writing and journalism!
	• www.prospects.ac.uk career suggestions: teaching; journalism; lexicographer; information officer.
	• This degree could open up some popular career areas (though graduates may have to do extra training, a postgraduate course or a conversion course). For example: accountancy; advertising; armed forces; banking; barrister; chartered secretary; civil aviation; civil service; health services management; human resources management; information technology; information science; insurance; journalism; leisure and recreation management; management; management consultancy; marketing; police; personal adviser (careers officer); public relations; publishing; restaurant management; retail management; social work; solicitor; surveying; teaching; TEFL teaching; television, film and radio.
	Essential AS levels: English literature or English literature and language.
	Useful AS levels: History, religious studies, a modern foreign language, philosophy.
Environmental health	***Helpful information:***
	• Environmental health officers work mainly for local authorities, in the areas of food health, public health, occupational health, housing and environmental protection.
	• This is a degree for people who like applying science in a very practical way.
	• There are many degree courses with "environment" in the title. For a career in environmental *health*, the degree should be CIEH accredited.
	Essential AS levels: Any two from biology, chemistry, maths and physics. Some courses prefer biology and chemistry. Some courses may consider students without a science A level but will ask for higher entry requirements.
	Websites:
	• The Chartered Institute of Environmental Health, www.cieh.org
Environmental science/studies	***Helpful information:***
	• Applicants must be able to prove that they have taken in as much as possible of the world around them – from knowledge of their own immediate locality to awareness of world issues.
	• In personal statements and interviews, students must be able to discuss in detail the field visits they have been on and include examples from their A-level syllabus. It is also helpful to mention any magazines they have read or TV programmes they

	have watched – but they must be prepared for more in-depth discussion at interview. • These courses contain many practical elements – they are about doing, not just thinking. So students should try to think of examples where they have actually done and completed something, rather than just thought about it. • www.prospects.ac.uk career suggestions: countryside manager; environmental consultant; environmental education officer; nature conservation officer; recycling officer; waste management officer. • This degree could open up some popular career areas (though graduates may have to do extra training, a postgraduate course or a conversion course). For example: accountancy; advertising; armed forces; banking; barrister; chartered secretary; civil aviation; civil service; health services management; human resources management; information technology; information science; insurance; journalism; leisure and recreation management; management; management consultancy; marketing; police; personal adviser (careers officer); public relations; publishing; restaurant management; retail management; social work; solicitor; surveying; teaching; TEFL teaching; television, film and radio. ***Essential AS levels:*** Many courses will ask for two from biology, chemistry, maths, physics and geography. ***Websites:*** Visit www.geography.org.uk Institution of environmental sciences http://www.ies-uk.org.uk/ Land based and environmental industries www.lantra.co.uk
European studies	***Helpful information:*** • Applicants need to prove (with evidence) that they are comfortable with grammar, comprehension, reading and translation. • Students should emphasise the A-level work they have done, visits abroad, and a knowledge of the literature, history, politics, geography and culture of the country they are interested in. • It is helpful to read newspapers, magazines and websites in the appropriate language. • www.prospects.ac.uk career suggestions, as well as teaching, translating and interpreting: accounting, diplomatic service, logistics, event organiser. • This degree could open up some popular career areas (though graduates may have to do extra training, a postgraduate course or a conversion course). For example: accountancy; advertising; armed forces; banking; barrister; chartered secretary; civil aviation; civil service; health services management; human resources management; information technology; information science; insurance; journalism; leisure and recreation management; management; management consultancy; marketing; police; personal adviser (careers officer); public relations; publishing; restaurant management; retail

	management; social work; solicitor; surveying; teaching; TEFL teaching; television, film and radio. ***Essential AS levels:*** A modern foreign language. ***Websites:*** • The Institute of Linguists, www.iol.org.uk • www.languageswork.org.uk
Fashion and clothing	***Helpful information:*** • Everyone knows about fashion designers, but what about pattern cutters, garment technologists, buyers, merchandisers and retail management? There are now many courses that concentrate on the "business" of fashion, such as: fashion merchandising management; fashion marketing; fashion promotion; fashion management. • If you want to become a fashion designer, however, you should do an art foundation course (see **Art and design**). ***Useful AS levels:*** Art, DT, AGCE/BTEC National art and design, AGCE business studies. ***Websites:*** • Visit www.canucutit.co.uk • Also www.skillset.org
French	***Helpful information:*** • Applicants need to prove (with evidence) that they are comfortable with grammar, comprehension, reading and translation. • Students should emphasise the A-level work they have done, visits abroad, and a knowledge of French literature, history, politics, geography and culture. • It is helpful to read newspapers, magazines and websites in French. • www.prospects.ac.uk career suggestions, as well as teaching, translating and interpreting: accounting, diplomatic service, logistics, event organiser. • This degree could open up some popular career areas (though graduates may have to do extra training, a postgraduate course or a conversion course). For example: accountancy; advertising; armed forces; banking; barrister; chartered secretary; civil aviation; civil service; health services management; human resources management; information technology; information science; insurance; journalism; leisure and recreation management; management; management consultancy; marketing; police; personal adviser (careers officer); public relations; publishing; restaurant management; retail management; social work; solicitor; surveying; teaching; TEFL teaching; television, film and radio. ***Essential AS levels:*** French. ***Useful AS levels:*** Another modern foreign language. ***Websites:*** • The Institute of Linguists, www.iol.org.uk

	• www.languageswork.org.uk
Geography	***Helpful information:*** • Applicants must be able to prove that they have taken in as much as possible of the world around them – from knowledge of their own immediate locality to awareness of world issues. • In personal statements and interviews, students must be able to discuss the field visits they have been on and include examples from their A-level syllabus. It is also helpful to mention magazine articles or TV programmes they have seen – but they must be prepared for more in-depth discussion at interview. • These courses contain many practical elements – they are about doing, not just thinking. So students should try to think of examples where they have actually done and completed something, rather than just thought about it. • www.prospects.ac.uk career suggestions: cartographer; geographical information systems officer; planning and development surveyor; town planner. • This degree could open up some popular career areas (though graduates may have to do extra training, a postgraduate course or a conversion course). For example: accountancy; advertising; armed forces; banking; barrister; chartered secretary; civil aviation; civil service; health services management; human resources management; information technology; information science; insurance; journalism; leisure and recreation management; management; management consultancy; marketing; police; personal adviser (careers officer); public relations; publishing; restaurant management; retail management; social work; solicitor; surveying; teaching; TEFL teaching; television, film and radio. ***Essential AS levels:*** Most degrees require geography. ***Useful AS levels:*** Some BSc degrees also prefer one of biology, chemistry, maths or physics. ***Websites:*** Visit www.geography.org.uk
Geology/earth sciences	***Helpful information:*** • Geoscience includes all the sciences (geology, geophysics, geochemistry) that study the structure, evolution and dynamics of the earth and its natural resources. It investigates the processes that have shaped the earth through its 4,600 million-year history and uses the rock record to unravel that history. • Geoscience is very much concerned with the real world beyond the laboratory and has direct relevance to the needs of society. It involves exploring and production, geological surveys, land use and environmental issues. • Applicants must be able to prove that they have taken in as much as possible of the world around them – from knowledge of their own immediate locality to awareness of world issues. • In personal statements and interviews, students must be able to discuss the field visits they have been on and include examples

	from their A-level syllabuses. It is also helpful to mention any magazine articles or TV programmes they have seen – but they must be prepared for more in-depth discussion at interview. • These courses contain many practical elements – they are about doing, not just thinking. So students should try to think of examples where they have actually done and completed something, rather than just thought about it. • www.prospects.ac.uk career suggestions: wellsite geologist; hydrogeologist; geological mapper; minerals surveyor. • This degree could open up some popular career areas (though graduates may have to do extra training, a postgraduate course or a conversion course). For example: accountancy; advertising; armed forces; banking; barrister; chartered secretary; civil aviation; civil service; health services management; human resources management; information technology; information science; insurance; journalism; leisure and recreation management; management; management consultancy; marketing; police; personal adviser (careers officer); public relations; publishing; restaurant management; retail management; social work; solicitor; surveying; teaching; TEFL teaching; television, film and radio. ***Essential AS levels:*** Usually two from maths, physics, chemistry and biology. ***Useful AS levels:*** Geography and geology. ***Websites:*** • Visit www.geography.org.uk • Also try www.geolsoc.org.uk
German	***Helpful information:*** • Applicants need to prove (with evidence) that they are comfortable with grammar, comprehension, reading and translation. • Students should emphasise the A level work they have done, visits abroad, and a knowledge of German literature, history, politics, geography and culture. • It is helpful to read newspapers, magazines and websites in German. • www.prospects.ac.uk career suggestions, as well as teaching, translating and interpreting: accounting, diplomatic service, logistics, event organiser. • This degree could open up some popular career areas (though graduates may have to do extra training, a postgraduate course or a conversion course). For example: accountancy; advertising; armed forces; banking; barrister; chartered secretary; civil aviation; civil service; health services management; human resources management; information technology; information science; insurance; journalism; leisure and recreation management; management; management consultancy; marketing; police; personal adviser (careers officer); public relations; publishing; restaurant management; retail

	management; social work; solicitor; surveying; teaching; TEFL teaching; television, film and radio. ***Essential AS levels:*** German. ***Useful AS levels:*** Another modern foreign language. ***Websites:*** • The Institute of Linguists, www.iol.org.uk • www.languageswork.org.uk
History	***Helpful information:*** • Applicants need to get across their passion for history – with evidence to support this. For example, they need to show they are genuinely interested in periods of history other than those they are studying at A level. • It is a good idea to think about the links between history and the other subjects they are studying (for example, English literature). Also, students should try to think of examples where they have learned independently and not just relied on their teachers. • www.prospects.ac.uk career suggestions: teaching; archivist; education administrator; careers information officer; records manager. • This degree could open up some popular career areas (though graduates may have to do extra training, a postgraduate course or a conversion course). For example: accountancy; advertising; armed forces; banking; barrister; chartered secretary; civil aviation; civil service; health services management; human resources management; information technology; information science; insurance; journalism; leisure and recreation management; management; management consultancy; marketing; police; personal adviser (careers officer); public relations; publishing; restaurant management; retail management; social work; solicitor; surveying; teaching; TEFL teaching; television, film and radio. ***Essential AS levels:*** Most degrees require history. ***Useful AS levels:*** Economics, English literature, philosophy, politics, sociology and theology/religious studies. ***Websites:*** Visit www.history.org.uk
History of art	***Helpful information:*** • Students who have not studied history of art before need to visit galleries and museums. In interviews, applicants will be expected to talk about the works of art they have seen and what they felt about them. Can they say who is their favourite artist? What is their favourite period of art? • Students must be familiar with the main European schools of painting. • www.prospects.ac.uk career suggestions: heritage officer; museum/gallery curator; fine arts auctioneer/valuer; commercial art gallery manager; arts administrator; antique dealer. • This degree could open up some popular career areas (though

	graduates may have to do extra training, a postgraduate course or a conversion course). For example: accountancy; advertising; armed forces; banking; barrister; chartered secretary; civil aviation; civil service; health services management; human resources management; information technology; information science; insurance; journalism; leisure and recreation management; management; management consultancy; marketing; police; personal adviser (careers officer); public relations; publishing; restaurant management; retail management; social work; solicitor; surveying; teaching; TEFL teaching; television, film and radio. ***Essential AS levels:*** None. ***Useful AS levels:*** Art, English literature, history, theology/religious studies, French, German, Spanish and Italian. ***Websites:*** Visit www.artchive.com
Hotel and catering	***Helpful information:*** • These courses can lead to a variety of jobs in the hotel and catering trades: hotel manager, professional chef, receptionist and restaurant manager. They can also be a springboard to many other leisure-based industries. • Many hospitality/hotel management courses are similar to business studies courses in that they cover economics, marketing, finance and human resources. However, case studies will relate to the hospitality industry, and students will also study hotel and catering operations. More and more courses are incorporating culinary arts. • Courses normally involve hospitality work placements at home or abroad. ***Essential AS levels:*** None. ***Websites:*** • People 1st, www.people1st.co.uk • Institute of Hospitality, www.instituteofhospitality.org
Information science	***Helpful information:*** • The information specialist has to deal with a range of sources far beyond books and other printed material. Information professionals and librarians are always needed to manage information and may work in education, health, business and government. • You can do an accredited degree or a postgraduate conversion course. ***Essential AS levels:*** None. ***Websites:*** • Chartered Institute of Library and Information Professionals, www.cilip.org.uk
Italian	***Helpful information:*** • It is not essential to have studied Italian already. However, applicants need to be taking a foreign language A level and to

	be able to prove (with evidence) that they are comfortable with grammar, comprehension, reading and translation. • Students should emphasise the A level work they have done (in Italian or another modern foreign language). Visits abroad and a knowledge of Italian literature, history, politics, geography and culture are useful. • It is helpful to read newspapers, magazines and websites in Italian. • www.prospects.ac.uk career suggestions, as well as teaching, translating and interpreting: accounting, diplomatic service, logistics, event organiser. • This degree could open up some popular career areas (though graduates may have to do extra training, a postgraduate course or a conversion course). For example: accountancy; advertising; armed forces; banking; barrister; chartered secretary; civil aviation; civil service; health services management; human resources management; information technology; information science; insurance; journalism; leisure and recreation management; management; management consultancy; marketing; police; personal adviser (careers officer); public relations; publishing; restaurant management; retail management; social work; solicitor; surveying; teaching; TEFL teaching; television, film and radio. ***Essential AS levels:*** Italian or another language such as French, German or Spanish. ***Useful AS levels:*** Another modern foreign language. ***Websites:*** • The Institute of Linguists, www.iol.org.uk • www.languageswork.org.uk
Journalism	***Helpful information:*** • Traditionally, taking an undergraduate course in journalism has never been the main route into this career. Normally, entrants would have done a degree in some other subject and then taken an accredited postgraduate course. • There are now hundreds of undergraduate courses. Some – but not all – have been accredited by the National Council for the Training of Journalists, the Periodicals Training Council and the Broadcast Journalism Training Council. It is essential to visit the websites below for detailed information. • Students considering a career in journalism should try to do things under their own initiative – student newspapers, community websites – to prove their interest and aptitude. ***Essential AS levels:*** None. N.B. English and media studies AS levels are not essential! However, applicants should be taking at least one essay/report-writing subject. ***Websites:*** • National Council for the Training of Journalists (newspapers and magazines), www.nctj.com • Periodicals Training Council (magazines), www.ppa.co.uk

	• Broadcast Journalism Training Council (television and radio), www.bjtc.org.uk • www.skillset.org
Law	***Helpful information:*** • Barristers act as advocates in court on behalf of the prosecution or defence. They can be instructed by solicitors and other professionals. They will normally be self-employed. • Solicitors give legal advice and information on a vast variety of personal and business matters. They will brief barristers and, increasingly, will plead in court. • Around half of all barristers and solicitors have not studied law as an undergraduate degree. In fact, many employers in the law field are more concerned about candidates having very high A-level grades and a good degree pass. Some are more interested in what university the applicant went to, rather than what subject they did. • Larger solicitors' firms offering traineeships may ask applicants to attend an assessment centre. Would-be lawyers may also have to do a period of paralegal work in order to gain a traineeship – especially if their original A-level grades were not high. Many employers expect students to have undertaken an internship with them. • Students applying for undergraduate degrees should show an interest in studying law as an intellectual discipline (for example, ethics), not just as a means to becoming a solicitor or barrister. They should read the law sections in the broadsheet newspapers and follow legal arguments in the press (would they be able to talk at interview about specific examples?) • Students need to find out more about the law by: visiting some law courts; doing relevant work experience (can they say what they learned from it?); reading books such as *Learning the Law* by Glanville Williams and *Understanding the Law* by Geoffrey Rivlin. • Some universities use an additional test for law applicants – the LNAT. Students need to find out more by visiting www.lnat.ac.uk ***Essential AS levels:*** None. ***Useful AS levels:*** Critical thinking (useful for the LNAT). There are really no essential AS levels for becoming a barrister or solicitor, though it might be safer to choose some facilitating subjects. Choosing one essay/report-writing subject would be sensible. ***Websites:*** • Barristers – General Council of the Bar of England and Wales, www.barcouncil.org.uk • Solicitors – The Law Society, www.lawsociety.org.uk • Legal executives – The Institute of Legal Executives, www.ilex.org.uk • Licensed conveyancers – The Council for Licensed

	Conveyancers, www.conveyancer.org.uk
Management	*Helpful information:* • Management is a vast and confusing field, with a vague terminology. It is not so much one structured career as an activity – making the best use of human resources, money, material and equipment in order to achieve a given objective. • The subjects that are always studied for these degrees are: economics; human resources; marketing; accounting; finance; and, usually, quantitative methods (statistics) and ICT. Some courses allow you to specialise in a particular field (for example, marketing) by the end of the course. Others stay general to the end. • Management courses tend to be roughly the same as business studies courses. The difference is that management courses are run by the traditional universities and therefore often demand higher A-level grades. Students should not automatically presume that management courses are better than the business studies courses offered by the former polytechnics. Management courses tend not to have a sandwich year, which many would argue is a disadvantage compared to business studies courses. • Applicants need to think about why they are interested in the topics covered by a management course. They should think about their personal qualities and what they have learned from any work experience or part-time work. Any evidence of working in a team would be particularly useful. *Essential AS levels:* None. *Useful AS levels:* Possibly maths, economics and business studies (but not the last two together). *Websites:* • Visit Chartered Management Institute: www.managers.org.uk • Other websites to visit include: the Financial Services Skills Council www.fssc.org.uk • People 1st, the sector skills council for the hospitality, leisure, travel and tourism industries. People 1st covers: contract food service providers, events, gambling, holiday parks, hospitality services, hostels, hotels, membership clubs, pubs, bars and nightclubs, restaurants, self-catering accommodation, tourist services, travel services and visitor attractions. www.people1st.co.uk • Skillsmart, the sector skills council for the retail sector www.skillsmartretail.com • SkillsActive is the sector skills council for the active leisure and learning industry embracing sport and fitness, outdoors and adventure, playwork, camping and caravanning. www.skillsactive.com
Marketing	*Helpful information:* • Marketing is the promotion of goods and services to the public

	and businesses. It is an umbrella term that covers advertising, direct marketing and public relations as well as marketing. • It is important to understand the different types of marketing: "above the line" means paid-for advertising in the media; "below the line" means non-media advertising or promotion. • Many marketing courses are similar to business studies in that they cover economics, marketing, finance and human resources. However, case studies will relate to the marketing industry and students will also study marketing operations. • Courses can provide a springboard into many marketing-related industries. ***Essential AS levels:*** None. ***Websites:*** • The Chartered Institute of Marketing, www.cim.co.uk • The Institute of Direct Marketing, www.theidm.com • www.camfoundation.com
Materials science (including biomedical materials science)	***Helpful information:*** • Materials science is a fascinating multi-disciplinary course that involves biology, chemistry, engineering, maths and physics. It is a wide-ranging science, covering metals and non-metals. • It is very closely related to biomedical materials science and metallurgy. • It can lead to a wide variety of jobs, such as: metallurgist; textile technologist; polymer scientist. ***Essential AS levels:*** Normally two from chemistry, maths, physics and biology. ***Websites:*** Visit www.materials.org.uk
Mathematics	***Helpful information:*** • Admissions tutors will be mainly interested in students' strength in maths. However, students also need to appear enthusiastic. They can prove their love of maths through, for example, wider reading, entering competitions or joining maths clubs. It is also helpful to mention other interests related to maths, such as IT, chess or philosophy. • Applicants should try to include evidence of maths that they have learned by themselves, or maths problems they have solved through determination. • Students should be able to explain how they would like to use their maths degree in their future career. • One book definitely worth reading is *How to solve it* by Polya. • www.prospects.ac.uk career suggestions: statistician; operational researcher; meteorologist; actuary; financial risk analyst. • This degree could open up some popular career areas (though graduates may have to do extra training, a postgraduate course or a conversion course). For example: accountancy; advertising; armed forces; banking; barrister; chartered secretary; civil aviation; civil service; health services management; human

	resources management; information technology; information science; insurance; journalism; leisure and recreation management; management; management consultancy; marketing; police; personal adviser (careers officer); public relations; publishing; restaurant management; retail management; social work; solicitor; surveying; teaching; TEFL teaching; television, film and radio. ***Essential AS levels:*** Maths and sometimes further maths. ***Useful AS levels:*** Physics. ***Websites:*** • Visit www.ima.org.uk • Also www.mathscareers.org.uk
Mechanical engineering	***Helpful information:*** • Students must make sure they know whether the courses they are applying for will lead them to become a chartered engineer or an incorporated engineer through UK-SPEC requirements. • Mechanical engineering is specifically concerned with the design, development, installation, operation and maintenance of just about anything that has moving parts. If an object is man-made, mechanical engineering skills will have been involved at some stage during its development and manufacture. • Applicants will need to be able to explain why they are applying for a mechanical engineering degree, as opposed to a more general engineering degree. They need to look at the world around them. Do they see examples of mechanical engineering that fascinate them? Why are they fascinating? How do they look? How were they made? What elements of maths and physics were used? • Be aware of programmes such as "a year in industry". Visit www.yini.org.uk ***Essential AS levels:*** Maths and physics. ***Useful AS levels:*** Further maths, DT, ICT. ***Websites:*** • The Institute of Mechanical Engineers, www.imeche.org
Media studies (including communication studies)	***Helpful information:*** • Students must be very clear about the sort of media course they are applying for. Some are more theoretical, others more practical. Of the more practical courses, does the student know exactly what it will train him or her to do? Also, these courses by themselves will not normally guarantee a job in the media. So, do the student's reasons for applying *correspond with* the content of the course? • Many media courses will expect to see some sort of work experience or examples of taking initiative (for example, writing a sixth-form newsletter or contributing to a website). • Students should try to think of examples (with evidence) of occasions when they have worked in a team. This is very important in media industries.

	Essential AS levels: A few courses ask for English or media studies. ***Useful AS levels:*** English, media studies, sociology and psychology. ***Websites:*** • Visit www.skillset.org • Also www.ft2.org.uk
Medicine	***Helpful information:*** • The different areas of medicine are: general practice; hospital service; public health; occupational health; research; teaching. • Students can only apply for four medicine courses through UCAS. Some medical schools will ask applicants to take the BMAT test (for more information visit www.bmat.org.uk) or the UKCAT test (www.ukcat.ac.uk). • Applicants will be interviewed and many of the questions will relate to the content of their personal statement. • Students must be able to explain fully why they want become a doctor and provide evidence to back up their claims. What evidence do they have that proves they are genuinely interested in scientific issues and the welfare of others? • It is a good idea to have done some work experience in the fields of medicine or health. What did they learn from it? • Here are some other ideas that might impress admissions tutors: being aware of some current issues or difficulties facing doctors (is there one that they could write about in more depth?); thinking about what qualities make a good doctor (especially if the student has these qualities and can prove it); finding out more about one or two medical issues outside the syllabus (for example, about the roles of health professionals, or social factors which influence health and disease); thinking about which disease interests them most and why. ***Essential AS levels:*** Doing chemistry, biology and either maths or physics will keep all the medical school options open. Doing chemistry and biology will keep open the vast majority. Doing chemistry and maths or physics will limit the range of choices much more. Critical thinking AS level done as a 5th subject will help with parts of the UKCAT and BMAT tests. ***Websites:*** • British Medical Association, www.bma.org.uk • For information on medical schools, visit www.medschools.ac.uk
Music	***Helpful information:*** • Courses may cover: performing; composing; teaching; sound engineering; instrument technology. • Students must be clear about the type of course they are applying for and why. While there are still a large number of traditional courses, there has been a growth in popular and commercial music courses. Even among traditional courses,

	some put more emphasis on musicology while others emphasise performance.
	• Students who are very interested in performance must be sure they can explain why they do *not* want to go to a *conservatoire*.
	• At interview, questions will be based on the interests expressed in the student's personal statement. If the student has mentioned a particular composer, he or she should expect questions on that composer's use of instruments, harmony, counterpoint, time signatures and other compositional techniques, as well as historical setting, influences, etc.
	• Students need to have a wide grounding in music history, beyond what they have studied for music A level. As well as their areas of particular interest, they must have an overview of the Renaissance (1400-1600), baroque (1600-1750), classical (1750-1800), romantic (1800-1900) and modern (1900 onwards) periods.
	• www.prospects.ac.uk career suggestions: teaching; private music teacher; music therapy; community arts worker; sound technician.
	• This degree could open up some popular career areas (though graduates may have to do extra training, a postgraduate course or a conversion course). For example: accountancy; advertising; armed forces; banking; barrister; chartered secretary; civil aviation; civil service; health services management; human resources management; information technology; information science; insurance; journalism; leisure and recreation management; management; management consultancy; marketing; police; personal adviser (careers officer); public relations; publishing; restaurant management; retail management; social work; solicitor; surveying; teaching; TEFL teaching; television, film and radio.
	Essential AS levels: For most traditional courses, music and Grade VII/VIII.
	Websites:
	• Visit www.abrsm.org
	• The Incorporated Society of Musicians, www.ism.org
	• The British Phonographic Industry, www.bpi.co.uk
	• www.musicalchairs.info
Nursing	***Helpful information:***
	• These courses cover: hospital and community nurses; health visitors; midwives.
	• Applicants will need to be able to explain fully why they want to enter nursing and provide evidence to back up their claims. What qualities are needed for nursing? Does the student possess these qualities?
	• If students have done some work experience related to nursing, they will be expected to explain what they learned from it.
	• It is a good idea to be aware of some current issues or difficulties associated with nursing. Is there one that they could

	talk about in more depth? *Essential AS levels:* Some courses ask for biology or another science. *Websites:* • NHS Careers, www.nhscareers.nhs.uk • Royal College of Nursing, www.rcn.org.uk • Royal College of Midwives, www.rcm.org.uk
Occupational therapy	*Helpful information:* • Occupational therapy is about helping people with physical and mental disorders live as full a life as possible by overcoming as much as possible the effects of their disability. These courses are also sometimes called rehabilitation therapy. • Applicants will need to be able to explain fully why they want to go into occupational therapy and provide evidence to back up their claims. What qualities are needed for this career? Does the student possess these qualities? • If students have done some work experience related to occupational therapy, they will be expected to explain what they learned from it. • It is a good idea to be aware of some current issues or difficulties associated with occupational therapy. Is there one they could talk about in more depth? *Essential AS levels:* Some courses ask for biology. Some will also consider psychology, physical education, sociology or another science. It is not always necessary to have a science A level. *Websites:* • The College of Occupational Therapy, www.cot.co.uk
Optical work (optometry and orthoptics)	*Helpful information:* • Optometrists (previously known as ophthalmic opticians) are trained professionals who examine eyes, test sight, give advice on visual problems, and prescribe and dispense spectacles or contact lenses. They also recommend other treatments or visual aids where appropriate. Optometrists are trained to recognise eye diseases, referring such cases as necessary, and can also use or supply various eye drugs. • Orthoptists are concerned with the diagnosis and treatment of ocular motility and problems relating to vision. • Applicants will need to be able to explain fully why they want to become an optometrist or orthoptist and provide evidence to back up their claims. What qualities are needed for these occupations? Does the student possess these qualities? • If students have done work experience related to optometry, they will be expected to explain what they learned from it. • It is a good idea to be aware of some current issues or difficulties associated with optometry and orthoptics. Is there one they could talk about in more depth? *Essential AS levels:* For optometry, any two from biology, chemistry, maths or physics (some courses prefer biology as one of

	the choices). For orthoptics, just biology can be acceptable. *Websites:* • The College of Optometrists, www.college-optometrists.org • British Orthoptic Society, www.orthoptics.org.uk
Pharmacy and pharmacology	*Helpful information:* • Pharmacists are qualified to dispense drugs and are most familiar to us in high-street community pharmacies. However, there are also pharmacists working in primary care, in hospitals and in the pharmaceutical industry. • Pharmacology is the study of drugs. A pharmacology degree provides many different career opportunities but does not qualify a person to dispense drugs. • Applicants will need to be able to explain fully why they want to become a pharmacist and provide evidence to back up their claims. What qualities do pharmacists need? Does the student possess these qualities? • If students have done some work experience related to pharmacy, they will be expected to explain what they learned from it. • It is a good idea to be aware of some current issues or difficulties associated with pharmacy. Is there one that they could talk about in more depth? *Essential AS levels:* Doing chemistry, plus one from biology, maths and physics, will keep virtually all course options open. Some courses prefer chemistry, biology and maths. Doing chemistry and biology will make many course options available. *Websites:* • Royal Pharmaceutical Society of Great Britain www.rpharms.com • British Pharmacological Society, www.bps.ac.uk
Philosophy	*Helpful information:* • A good starting point for students interested in philosophy is to read *Philosophy: The Basics* by Nigel Warburton. Then try Bertrand Russell's *Problems of Philosophy*. • Applicants must be able to explain why they want to study philosophy. They should be able to describe how their current studies relate to philosophy (philosophy is at the root of most academic subjects). • www.prospects.ac.uk career suggestions: higher education lecturer, civil service fast streamer, secondary school teacher. • This degree could open up some popular career areas (though graduates may have to do extra training, a postgraduate course or a conversion course). For example: accountancy; advertising; armed forces; banking; barrister; chartered secretary; civil aviation; civil service; health services management; human resources management; information technology; information science; insurance; journalism; leisure and recreation management; management; management consultancy;

	marketing; police; personal adviser (careers officer); public relations; publishing; restaurant management; retail management; social work; solicitor; surveying; teaching; TEFL teaching; television, film and radio. ***Essential AS levels:*** None. ***Useful AS levels:*** Maths, classical civilisations, philosophy and religious education/theology. ***Websites:*** Visit www.royalinstitutephilosophy.org
Photography	***Helpful information:*** • It is possible to get into a career in photography either through a higher-education course or through other routes such as being a photographer's assistant. • Digital imaging is changing the industry rapidly. • Admissions tutors will expect to see a portfolio and will want students to be able to talk about their work. ***Useful AS levels:*** Art, AGCE art and design, DT, BTEC National photography, photography. ***Websites:*** • The Association of Photographers, www.the-aop.org • The British Institute of Professional Photography, www.bipp.com • www.skillset.org
Physics	***Helpful information:*** • A physics degree involves the study of matter and energy, and will also cover chemical physics, biophysics, engineering, materials science and astronomy. • Students need to think about what area of physics interests them most. Would they like to specialise in this area? Which areas of their physics and maths A levels have they enjoyed the most? • It is a good idea for students to think of examples, from their wider reading or from the media, that relate to what they have learned at A level. ***Essential AS levels:*** Maths and physics. ***Useful AS levels:*** Further maths, chemistry. ***Websites:*** • The Institute of Physics, www.iop.org
Physiotherapy	***Helpful information:*** • Physiotherapists use exercises and movement, electrotherapy, manipulation and massage to treat the injured, disabled, sick and convalescents of all ages for a large variety of conditions. It is strongly related to occupational therapy. • Applicants will need to be able to explain fully why they want to become a physiotherapist and provide evidence to back up their claims. What qualities do physiotherapists need? Does the student possess these qualities? • If students have done work experience related to physiotherapy, they will be expected to explain what they learned from it.

	• It is a good idea to be aware of some current issues or difficulties associated with physiotherapy. Is there one that they could talk about in more depth? ***Essential AS levels:*** Most courses will consider applicants with just biology. However, some ask for a second science – chemistry, maths or physics. ***Websites:*** • Chartered Society of Physiotherapy, www.csp.org.uk
Politics	***Helpful information:*** • Students must have some knowledge of political philosophies, political history and the workings of government. Those who are not taking politics A level must acquire this through their own reading. • Students should follow current affairs, in order to show they are aware of the political world around them. • It is a good idea to find out more about the politics of a country other than the UK. • For all the above, students should use specific examples to illustrate their points. • www.prospects.ac.uk career suggestions: public affairs consultant; politician's assistant; government research officer; social researcher; civil service fast streamer. • This degree could open up some popular career areas (though graduates may have to do extra training, a postgraduate course or a conversion course). For example: accountancy; advertising; armed forces; banking; barrister; chartered secretary; civil aviation; civil service; health services management; human resources management; information technology; information science; insurance; journalism; leisure and recreation management; management; management consultancy; marketing; police; personal adviser (careers officer); public relations; publishing; restaurant management; retail management; social work; solicitor; surveying; teaching; TEFL teaching; television, film and radio. ***Essential AS levels:*** None. ***Useful AS levels:*** Politics, history, philosophy, law. ***Websites:*** Visit www.psa.ac.uk
Psychology	***Helpful information:*** • There are many different areas: clinical psychology; educational psychology; occupational psychology; criminal and legal psychology. • Students should be aware that psychology degree courses do not involve helping people with their problems! Courses cover subjects such as personality types, testing intelligence, perception, memory and developmental psychology. • Students who want to become professional psychologists must make sure that the course they have chosen has been accredited by the British Psychological Society.

	• Applicants should think of examples from their current studies (even if they are not doing psychology A level) that in some way relate to psychology. • The main reasons for rejection are a lack of reading about psychology and not understanding what is involved in a psychology degree course. Students should definitely read an introductory book about psychology. They should try to get across in their personal statement that they know what a psychology degree entails. ***Essential AS levels:*** A few courses ask for one of biology, chemistry, maths or physics, but most have no specific requirements. ***Useful AS levels:*** Biology, maths, psychology and sociology. ***Websites:*** • The British Psychological Society, www.bps.org.uk
Public relations	***Helpful information:*** • Public relations is about reputation – the result of what you do, what you say and what others say about you. Public relations is the discipline that looks after reputation, with the aim of earning understanding and support, and of influencing opinion and behaviour. It is the planned and sustained effort to establish and maintain goodwill and mutual understanding between an organisation and its public. • Many graduates of public relations courses go on to work in the industry. However, many graduates in a wide range of other disciplines also go on to careers in public relations. So the main reason for doing this degree should be the student's interest in the content of the course, because it will not in itself guarantee a job in PR. • Students should be aware that it is possible to study public relations as part of a marketing degree. ***Essential AS levels:*** None. ***Websites:*** • The Institute of Public Relations, www.cipr.co.uk • Public Relations Consultants Association, www.prca.org.uk
Radiography	***Helpful information:*** • Diagnostic radiographers use X-rays, ultrasound or magnetic resonance imaging to produce images of the body. Therapeutic radiographers work as part of the cancer treatment team. • Applicants will need to be able to explain fully why they want to become a radiographer and provide evidence to back up their claims. What qualities do radiographers need? Does the student possess these qualities? • If students have done some work experience related to radiography, they will be asked to explain what they learned from it. • It is a good idea to be aware of some current issues or difficulties associated with radiography. Is there one that they

	could talk about in more depth? ***Essential AS levels:*** Normally at least one of the sciences – biology, chemistry, maths or physics – is required. ***Websites:*** • Society of Radiographers, www.sor.org
Religious studies/theology	***Helpful information:*** • There is no need to be religious to study many of these degrees. In fact, students who are very conservative in their beliefs may not enjoy the majority of courses in this field. • Those who are not studying RE at A level will still find it easy to gain examples from other arts A levels to use as evidence of their interest. Students should think about RE-related aspects of their studies in history, English literature, philosophy, languages or theatre studies. • It is a good idea to try to gain some knowledge of a broad range of religions – and provide evidence of this. • www.prospects.ac.uk career suggestions: higher education lecturer; minister of religion; charity officer; youth worker; advice worker. • This degree could open up some popular career areas (though graduates may have to do extra training, a postgraduate course or a conversion course). For example: accountancy; advertising; armed forces; banking; barrister; chartered secretary; civil aviation; civil service; health services management; human resources management; information technology; information science; insurance; journalism; leisure and recreation management; management; management consultancy; marketing; police; personal adviser (careers officer); public relations; publishing; restaurant management; retail management; social work; solicitor; surveying; teaching; TEFL teaching; television, film and radio. ***Essential AS levels:*** None. ***Useful AS levels:*** Religious studies/theology, philosophy, English literature, history. ***Websites:*** Visit www.multifaithcentre.org
Retail management	***Helpful information:*** • Many retail management courses are similar to business studies courses in that they cover economics, marketing, finance and human resources. However, case studies will relate to the retail industry and students will also study retail management operations. Courses normally involve retail work placements. • These courses can provide a springboard to many different retail jobs (store managers, buyers, merchandisers) in various retail-based industries. • However, many retailers who run graduate training schemes will consider graduates from a wide range of other disciplines. Generally, those who are successful in gaining a place will have done part-time work in the retail industry as students.

	Essential AS levels: None. ***Websites:*** • Skillsmart, the sector skills council for the retail sector www.skillsmartretail.com • British Retail Consortium, www.brc.org.uk • Look at the websites of large retailers such as John Lewis or Arcadia Group Limited.
Social work	***Helpful information:*** • This degree leads to jobs such as: field social worker; education welfare officer; probation officer; residential care worker. • Students will need to show an understanding of social and community work at a basic level – it would be a good idea to read *Introduction to Social Work* by Coulshed and Orm. They will also be expected to show an understanding of, and an ability to define the meaning of, discrimination. What does it mean? How does it manifest itself? How can it be challenged? • Students will need to have demonstrated a commitment to this career through work experience (paid or voluntary sectors). • All candidates have to be police checked (but a criminal conviction does not mean automatic exclusion). • Read *Anti-Discriminatory Practice* by Neil Thompson, published by Palgrave Macmillan. ***Essential AS levels:*** None. ***Useful AS levels:*** AGCE/BTEC National in health and social care, sociology, law, psychology. ***Websites:*** • General Social Care Council, www.gscc.org.uk • Also visit www.socialworkcareers.co.uk
Sociology	***Helpful information:*** • Students who are not taking sociology A level should do some introductory reading on the key themes of: social theory; social change; social identities and structures. • In their personal statement, students should use examples from their A levels or their wider reading to get across their interest in sociology. • It is a good idea to keep abreast of current affairs and issues that affect society, past, present and future. • www.prospects.ac.uk career suggestions: social researcher; community development worker; probation officer; further education college lecturer; housing manager. • This degree could open up some popular career areas (though graduates may have to do extra training, a postgraduate course or a conversion course). For example: accountancy; advertising; armed forces; banking; barrister; chartered secretary; civil aviation; civil service; health services management; human resources management; information technology; information science; insurance; journalism; leisure and recreation management; management; management consultancy;

	marketing; police; personal adviser (careers officer); public relations; publishing; restaurant management; retail management; social work; solicitor; surveying; teaching; TEFL teaching; television, film and radio. ***Essential AS levels:*** None. ***Useful AS levels:*** Sociology, psychology, geography and media studies. ***Websites:*** Visit www.britsoc.org.uk
Spanish	***Helpful information:*** • Applicants need to prove (with evidence) that they are comfortable with grammar, comprehension, reading and translation. • Students should emphasise the A-level work they have done, visits abroad, and a knowledge of Spanish literature, history, politics, geography and culture. • It is helpful to read newspapers, magazines and websites in Spanish. • www.prospects.ac.uk career suggestions, as well as teaching, translating and interpreting: accounting, diplomatic service, logistics, event organiser. • This degree could open up some popular career areas (though graduates may have to do extra training, a postgraduate course or a conversion course). For example: accountancy; advertising; armed forces; banking; barrister; chartered secretary; civil aviation; civil service; health services management; human resources management; information technology; information science; insurance; journalism; leisure and recreation management; management; management consultancy; marketing; police; personal adviser (careers officer); public relations; publishing; restaurant management; retail management; social work; solicitor; surveying; teaching; TEFL teaching; television, film and radio. ***Essential AS levels:*** Spanish (some courses will also consider French, German or Italian). ***Websites:*** • The Institute of Linguists, www.iol.org.uk • www.languageswork.org.uk
Speech and language therapists	***Helpful information:*** • Speech and language therapists assess and treat all kinds of voice, speech and language defects. • Applicants will need to be able to explain fully why they want to go into speech therapy and provide evidence to back up their claims. What qualities do speech therapists need? Does the student possess these qualities? • If students have done some work experience related to speech therapy, they will be expected to explain what they learned from it. • It is a good idea to be aware of some current issues or

	difficulties associated with speech therapy. Is there one that they could talk about in more depth? ***Essential AS levels:*** Some degrees want a science such as biology, chemistry or physics. Some specify biology, but some will consider candidates without a science AS level. ***Useful AS levels:*** A modern foreign language (for example, French, German, Spanish, Italian), English language (and literature), psychology. ***Websites:*** • Royal College of Speech and Language Therapists, www.rcslt.org
Sport	***Helpful information:*** • Sport graduates may go on to become professional players, or they may go into teaching, coaching, instruction or sports administration. • Students must be clear about the type of course they are applying for. Sport courses tend to cover physiology, psychology, sports performance, coaching and the business and administration of sport. A leisure management course will be more like a business studies course. A sports journalism course is a journalism course. A sports therapy course is closer to a physiotherapy course. • Admissions tutors will be interested in applicants' sporting history to date (they need to make sure this comes across in their personal statement). However, being a talented sportsperson is not enough in itself to get a student onto a course. ***Essential AS levels:*** Many courses want to see one of biology, chemistry, maths or physics. ***Useful AS levels:*** Physical education, psychology. ***Websites:*** • Sport England, www.sportengland.org • www.sportandrecreation.org.uk
Surveying	***Helpful information:*** • Surveying is the measurement, management, development and valuation of anything and everything – whether it is natural or man-made. • There are different types of surveying. The main ones are: general practice surveying (valuation, estate agency, auctioneering and property development); quantity surveying (building accountants); building surveying; land surveying; mineral surveying. • Admissions tutors will be concerned with why students want to enter this career field and what they have done to find out about it, for example through work experience. ***Essential AS levels:*** None. ***Useful AS levels:*** For some types of surveying (for example, building surveying) maths and physics could be helpful. For estate

	management (general practice surveying) most A level combinations will be considered. ***Websites:*** • Royal Institute of Chartered Surveyors, www.rics.org
Teacher training (primary/secondary)	***Helpful information:*** • Students must be clear in their minds that they really do want to do a teacher training degree, rather than study a different subject and then take the postgraduate route into teaching (PGCE). • Students must have had some sort of work experience or observational experience in a school appropriate to the age range they are applying for. And they must do more than just describe their experience. What did they learn from it? What difficulties did the teachers face? What did they enjoy about the job? What initiatives were being implemented? Did they think there was too much testing? • They must also decide whether there is an academic discipline they want to specialise in. If there is, they must say why. If not, they must say why not. ***Essential AS levels:*** At least one from: **art**, **biology**, **chemistry**, design and technology, drama (theatre studies), **English**, French, **geography**, German, **history**, ICT, Italian, **maths**, **music**, **physics**, **physical education**, **religious studies (theology)**, Spanish (subjects in **bold** are those most suitable for primary teaching). Some general primary courses may still accept applicants without one of the above A levels – check prospectuses. CACHE meets the entry requirements for early-years primary teaching and some primary teaching degrees ***N.B.*** For secondary teaching, students should have English language and maths at GCSE grade C or above. For primary teaching, they should have English language, maths and a science at GCSE grade C or above. ***Websites:*** Visit www.tda.gov.uk
Television, film and radio	***Helpful information:*** • Students must be very clear about the sort of course they are applying for. Some are more theoretical, others more practical. If they have chosen one of the more practical courses, do they know exactly what it will train them to do? Also, these courses by themselves will not guarantee a job in the media. So, do their reasons for applying *correspond with* the content of the course? • It shouldn't be presumed that traditional university courses are always best. Small colleges such as Ravensbourne can be centres of excellence. • Admissions tutors will expect to see some sort of work experience. Also, it is good to give examples of taking an initiative (for example, writing a sixth-form newsletter or contributing to a website) and of working in a team (teamwork is very important in media industries).

	• Students should be aware that there are also postgraduate courses, for example at the National Film and Television School (www.nftsfilm-tv.ac.uk) • Whatever degree you do, work experience will be crucial when it comes to actually applying for jobs. ***Essential AS levels:*** None. ***Websites:*** • For general information, there is Skillset, www.skillset.org • Also look at www.ft2.org.uk • And www.bbc.co.uk/jobs
Travel and tourism	***Helpful information:*** • Many travel and tourism courses are similar to business studies courses in that they cover economics, marketing, finance and human resources. However, case studies will relate to the travel and tourism industry and students will also study travel and tourism operations. • Courses can be a springboard to many leisure-related industries. ***Essential AS levels:*** None. ***Websites:*** • Travel Training Company, www.ttctraining.co.uk • People 1st, the sector skills council for the hospitality, leisure, travel and tourism industries. People 1st covers: contract food service providers, events, gambling, holiday parks, hospitality services, hostels, hotels, membership clubs, pubs, bars and nightclubs, restaurants, self-catering accommodation, tourist services, travel services and visitor attractions. www.people1st.co.uk
Veterinary science	***Helpful information:*** • It is only possible to apply for four veterinary science degrees through UCAS (there are seven in all). Competition is intense. Have these would-be vets got a fallback plan? For example, there are now some veterinary nursing degrees that have lower entry requirements. • Applicants will need to explain fully why they want to become a vet and provide evidence to back up their claims. What qualities do vets need? Do they possess these qualities? • It is essential for students to have done some relevant work experience and to be able to explain what they learned from it. To play safe, they should have done two weeks in a veterinary practice, two weeks with large domestic animals or livestock (farm) and two weeks with others animals (kennels, stables, zoo, etc.). • It is a good idea to be aware of some current issues or difficulties facing vets. Is there one that they could talk about in more depth? • Perhaps they could say what diseases/health problems in animals interest them. Why? • Students should remember that an interest in humans is also

	essential (they own the animals, after all). ***Essential AS levels:*** Chemistry and biology, plus either maths or physics. This would allow the student to consider all seven veterinary science courses. ***Websites:*** • The Royal College of Veterinary Surgeons, www.rcvs.org.uk

Appendix B: The Moral Maze: Universities, what and who are they for?

Listening to this edition of the BBC Radio 4 programme The Moral Maze brought to mind the story of the blind men and an elephant, which originated in India. In various versions of the tale, a group of blind men (or men in the dark) touch an elephant to learn what it is like. Each one feels a different part, but only one part, such as an ear, a leg or a tusk. They then compare notes and learn that they are in complete disagreement.

The same applies, in my experience, when different people are asked to answer the question: universities, what and who are they for? Each will provide their own unique answer based around the themes emphasised below, and they are normally in disagreement. Just like the blind men and an elephant!

Each student has unique reasons for the course they study and the university they go to. Our only role is to give them informed, non-directive guidance.

I transcribed what follows from the edition of The Moral Maze broadcast on 24 October 2009. Michael Buerk chairs. The panel are Melanie Phillips, Clifford Longley, Claire Fox and Matthew Taylor.

Introduction
Michael Buerk quotes the oft-spouted opinion that:

"Hundreds of thousands of first-year students are now sobering up from Freshers' Week, possibly wondering what their three years or more at university are going to do for them. According to many academic whistle blowers and several scathing reports, precious little. Many, perhaps most, will be leaving a second rate institution with an inflated third-rate degree in a pointless subject, with £30-£40,000 of debt which they will never have to repay because in difficult economic times they are virtually unemployable!"

Michael Buerk – That view, hotly contested both inside and outside the university system, doesn't seem to have stopped people going to university: they are packed, with the [Labour] Government's target of 50% of people going to university.

All of this raises the question of what universities should be for and who they should be for. Are universities essentially about scholarship and the pursuit of knowledge for its own sake? Or are they vocational, training people for specific roles in a competitive and efficient economy? Or perhaps more subjectively, is their purpose to turn out well-stocked minds who can think critically – and can you do that if universities turn out students on courses such as surf science and creative knitwear, as well as Hegelian philosophy? Are they only for the bright or should the stupid have a right to go too? Or at any rate, the no-more-than-average. Would this lead to a widening of opportunity or an erosion of purpose and standards?

Universities, what and who are they for?
Panel:
Melanie Phillips – Daily Mail
Claire Fox – Institute of Ideas
Clifford Longley – Catholic Writer
Matthew Taylor – Chief Executive of the RSA (the Royal Society for the encouragement of Arts, Manufactures and Commerce)

Opening statements
Melanie Phillips – University taught me how to think. I was very clear at the time that that was what the role of university was. I think we have a hang up in this country about social class and we think that academic education is superior. We have collapsed the idea of knowledge, training and skills into each other so that academic education has been devalued and vocational training has been devalued too.

Claire Fox – I went to university and was introduced to the idea of the "life of the mind". There weren't many people who went to university in those days and I was one of those people who wanted to storm the ivory towers and let more people have access to that knowledge for its own sake. Unfortunately we have allowed a lot more people to go to institutions with the name university on the front, but they are not being introduced to the life of the mind and they are being sold a con, effectively, and not being introduced to knowledge. I would like to have more people looking at knowledge for its own sake and for the university system to go back to as it was.

Matthew Taylor – I spent three years as a political activist at Southampton University but shared a room with an engineering student who went home every weekend – people have different approaches to university; they always have and they always will do.

Clifford Longley – I did an engineering degree at Southampton University. It taught me how to think. Yet people were very sniffy about doing engineering, it wasn't a proper academic subject and that atmosphere seems to somehow still be around. There still seems to be a lot of snobbishness about the notion of using university for anything other than ivory-tower activity. The idea that a course should have its feet on the ground and somehow have a practical use is somehow an anathema, and I think it's something that needs to be got rid of.

Discussion
(From the audience) Andrew Long, Ten Ltd – Always wanted to be an entrepreneur – told his careers adviser this, but careers adviser encouraged him to go to university – did a classics degree at Exeter and ended up dropping out, as he didn't see the point of it. His company does not ask for graduates and he thinks blue chip companies have got it wrong by only recruiting graduates.

Claire Fox – Andrew, how do you feel that youngsters are sold the idea that going to university will improve employability – more money, better job etc?

Andrew Long – If you are clear what your objectives are and university can help you fulfil those objectives, then vocational degrees can be fantastic. However for some students they are not learning to think, they are learning to drink and we should be honest about that.

Melanie Phillips – Other countries have much higher participation rates in higher education and this has been used as a main basis for bumping up the numbers. Do you not think that we will miss out unless we encourage as many people as possible to go to university?

Andrew Long – No, if people want to be entrepreneurs rather than go to university they should be encouraged. But some vocational degrees should be valued, though not all.

Matthew Taylor – Universities are well-run businesses.

Greg James – medical student – Universities should be allowed to answer questions outside of business.

John Coyne – Vice-Chancellor, Derby – Are all university subjects equally valid? Are all young people equally appropriate to learning? I think any university system must be broad and wide ranging and we should have a spirit that gives students the opportunity to develop themselves. Each generation has always had its own debates about the validity of certain subjects and many of the earliest courses were vocational.

Melanie Phillips – Do you think there is a difference between teaching people to think and teaching people to do?

John Coyne – Some of the distinction between academic and vocational is false.

Melanie Phillips – In Switzerland institutions are either academic or vocational. Why are we hung up on this debate on the teaching of ideas?

John Coyne – I do not recognise this debate, and courses that are considered vocational now may be the academic courses of the future.

Michael Buerk – Such as Culinary Arts, Pop Music and Computer Games as done at Derby?

John Coyne – They are frameworks to which students can apply analytical skills, such as advanced chemistry in culinary arts.

Claire Fox to John Coyne – Do you think it's a coincidence that the social inclusion (Aimhigher) policies happened at the same time as the growth of all these newer vocational courses?

John Coyne – I think the breadth is much to be applauded: extending more opportunities for more students to enter university has to be the right thing. If you have more, the audience you are drawing upon packages their skills and qualifications very differently. But you are still looking for the same access to learning and analytical skills.

Claire Fox – It is interesting that the desire to bring more working-class youngsters into universities has not led to a rise in applications for classics or PPE. Does this not assume that the working classes are not up to it?

John Coyne – Every generation has to accept that its universities will have to be relevant to the challenges that their society faces.

Claire Fox – We need to spend more time studying the knowledge we already know, rather than being relevant and faddish.

Dennis Hayes – Professor of Education, Derby – Is it higher education or is it remedial secondary education passed off as something else [as suggested by Alan Ryan, warden of New College, Oxford]? A happy student and a degree may not be a higher education! A lot of the discussion we have had is prefixed on the assumption that a lot of the people in higher education are just not up to it in some way or another. Both the university sector and this debate itself reflect the view I call the therapeutic contempt: a kindly, considerate approach to students that doesn't stretch them. I gave a lecture the other day and the evaluation said, "He made my brain hurt!" Every university is capable of stretching their students and capable of excellence.

Clifford Longley – Why stop at 50%? Why not more?

Dennis Hayes – This is based on the assumption of correlating qualifications with a dynamic economy. Alison Wolf and others have shown that there is no correlation whatsoever. That universities drive the economy is an entirely false premise.

Clifford Longley – What then is an appropriate course for a university to offer?

Dennis Hayes – Any subject can be appropriate for a university, but it depends on the content of what is on offer.

Matthew Taylor – Is there any evidence that the education that students are receiving at Cambridge is being damaged by the education that students are receiving at Derby?

Dennis Hayes – No.

Matthew Taylor – This is what you are implying by your answers.

Matthew Taylor – I think the expansion of higher education from 1 in 10 people to nearly 1 in 2 people is a fantastic social experiment. There may be some bits of it that don't work, there may be some courses that aren't sensible, but shouldn't we be celebrating this?

Dennis Hayes – Yes and No. But they should be stretched.

Conclusion
Clifford Langley – More people should be encouraged to go.

Matthew Taylor – We are complicated people. They may do it for labour market reasons, or learning for learning's sake. Why do we think people only have one view?

The studying of English for its own sake is just as valuable – no more, no less – as studying media studies for its own sake.

Claire Fox – I think more people could be up to an academic higher education if they were taught better at school.

John Coyne – You are using an arbitrary definition of academic.

Claire Fox – Nobody in academia or government is arguing for education for education's sake.

Melanie Phillips – Vocational education doesn't always need a lot of abstract theorising but to say that culinary arts contains advanced chemistry is ridiculous. The aim behind the expansion of higher education is to get youngsters off the unemployment register. There is dumbing down: because so many of those young people cannot do thinking, standards have been lowered in order to shoehorn people into higher education and the whole concept of learning and knowledge through higher education has been eroded.

Michael Buerk – Education for education's sake? Or should we follow the utilitarian approach?

Claire Fox – Should universities have anything to do with employability?

Michael Buerk – But if we are charging £30,000?

Bibliography

The following books, articles, research papers and websites have been invaluable to me in the preparation of this handbook. These are in addition to the resources referred to throughout the handbook.

Bedford, T., *Vocational Guidance Interviews Explored* (Careers Service Branch, Department of Employment, 1982).

Brown and Hesketh, *The Mismanagement of Talent – Employability and Jobs in the Knowledge Economy* (OUP, 2004).

Gardner and Hamnett, *The University Interviews Guide* (JFS School, 2009).

Kubler and Forbes, *Student Employability Profiles, A Guide For Employers* (CIHE/Graduate Prospects, 2003).

Levitt and Dubner, *Freakonomics* (Allen Lane, 2005).

Mignot, P., "Working with Individuals" in *Careers Guidance in Context* (Gothard et al, Sage, 2001).

Peck, P, *Careers Services: History, policy and practice in the United Kingdom* (Routledge Falmer, 2004).

Warburton, N., *Thinking from A-Z* (Routledge, 2000).

Moving On – Graduate Careers Three Years after Graduation (DfEE-CSU-AGCAS-IER, 1999).

www.nottingham.ac.uk/sedu/recruitment/interview-q/qtypes.php

www.prospects.ac.uk/nicec/distance-learning-unit/DLUnit2/FIRST.html